Scarecrow Studies in Young Adult Literature
Series Editor: Patty Campbell

Scarecrow Studies in Young Adult Literature is intended to continue the body of critical writing established in Twayne's Young Adult Authors Series and to expand it beyond single-author studies to explorations of genres, multicultural writing, and controversial issues in young adult (YA) reading. Many of the contributing authors of the series are among the leading scholars and critics of adolescent literature, and some are YA novelists themselves.

The series is shaped by its editor, Patty Campbell, who is a renowned authority in the field, with a thirty-year background as critic, lecturer, librarian, and teacher of YA literature. Patty Campbell was the 2001 winner of the ALAN Award, given by the Assembly on Literature for Adolescents of the National Council of Teachers of English for distinguished contribution to YA literature. In 1989 she was the winner of the American Library Association's Grolier Award for distinguished service to young adults and reading.

Mixed Heritage in Young Adult Literature

Nancy Thalia Reynolds

Scarecrow Studies
in Young Adult Literature, No. 32

THE SCARECROW PRESS, INC.
Lanham, Maryland • Toronto • Plymouth, UK

SCARECROW PRESS, INC.

Published in the United States of America
by Scarecrow Press, Inc.
A wholly owned subsidary of
The Rowman & Littlefield Publishing Group, Inc.
4501 Forbes Boulevard, Suite 200, Lanham, Maryland 20706
www.scarecrowpress.com

Estover Road
Plymouth PL6 7PY
United Kingdom

British Library Cataloguing in Publication Information Available

Library of Congress Cataloging-in-Publication Data

Reynolds, Nancy Thalia.
  Mixed heritage in young adult literature / Nancy Thalia Reynolds.
    p. cm. — (Scarecrow studies in young adult literature ; no. 32)
  Includes bibliographical references and index.
  ISBN-13: 978-0-8108-5969-2 (cloth : alk. paper)
  ISBN-10: 0-8108-5969-6 (cloth : alk. paper)
  ISBN-13: 978-0-8108-6710-9 (ebook)
  ISBN-10: 0-8108-6710-9 (ebook)
  1. Young adult literature, American—History and criticism. 2. Young
adult literature, English—History and criticism. 3. Racially mixed people in
literature. 4. Racially mixed people—Race identity. 5. Ethnicity in
literature. 6. Race in literature. 7. Cultural fusion in literature. I.
Title.
  PS173.R33R49 2009
  810.9'9283—dc22   2008043257

⊚™   The paper used in this publication meets the minimum requirements of
American National Standard for Information Sciences—Permanence of Paper
for Printed Library Materials, ANSI/NISO Z39.48-1992.
Manufactured in the United States of America.

To my daughter, Emily Sarah Webb,
and mixed-heritage teens everywhere

Contents

Acknowledgments

*M*y heartfelt gratitude goes to:

- All the young adult librarians who shared their time, book picks, and enthusiasm for this project with me.
- The extraordinary faculty and students of the Vermont College of Fine Arts MFA program in writing for children and young adults. Their expertise, comments, questions, and feedback were invaluable. An extra helping of thanks goes to Tim Wynne-Jones.
- The Dedications: Mary Atkinson, Frances Lee Hall, Page Koehlert, Margaret Nevinski, Michele Regenold, Barbara Younger, and Lisa Doan, sisters on the long, hard road.
- Patty Campbell, a pearl among editors.
- My patient, ever-supportive family: my son and daughter, Nick and Emily Webb, and especially my husband, Mike Webb.

Introduction

To name oneself is to validate one's existence and declare
visibility.

—Maria P. P. Root

*W*hen I set out to research young adult literature with multiracial and
multiethnic characters, I quickly exhausted the handful of resource
guides on the subject. I scoured the Internet for more resources, visiting
every website that related in any way to multiracial people, following
links, and perusing school and library multicultural booklists. Gradually
I acquired books about characters with blended identities, but it wasn't
easy. There were plenty of YA titles with mixed-identity characters; the
hard part was finding them. They were hidden among novels set in many
countries, tales of immigrant journeys, historical fiction about American
Indians, and colorful ethnic folktales. To speed up the slow process, I sent
out pleas for reading suggestions.

As recommendations poured in, I realized that although I had asked
for books with "multiracial and multiethnic characters," many of my
contacts interpreted this as "monoracial and monoethnic nonwhite characters." Repeatedly, I was steered to books by Tanuja Desai Hidier, Gary
Soto, Kyoko Mori, and others that focused on characters whose family
members shared the same race and ethnicity. Even after I learned to
phrase my requests more precisely ("a character whose parents are of different races"), some still heard only "nonwhite." This semantic disconnect came to symbolize for me the challenge of writing about people of
mixed heritage: the slipperiness of language, how we use code words like
"multiracial" not only to convey meaning but also to avoid doing so.

This disconnect became a metaphor for the status of being "mixed" itself, illustrating how people of mixed heritage remain collectively invisible in a world that, scientific consensus to the contrary, persists in viewing races as discrete, impermeable categories. *Merriam-Webster's Collegiate Dictionary* defines "multiracial" as "composed of, involving, or representing various races." Nothing in the definition suggests an *individual* whose parents are of different races. We say "we live in a multiracial society," meaning "we live in a diverse society." We attend conferences on "multiracial education" whose subject is teaching a group of children each drawn from different monoracial groups. The multiracial individual is hidden within the group definition. To overcome this semantic invisibility, multiracial individuals often prefer "mixed" or "mixed-race" as descriptors—crude and simple but straightforward, clearly conveying "two or more elements combined into one."

Race remains an anxious and vexing topic in twenty-first-century America. Our need to know and apply the "right" racial label to those whose appearance is ambiguous to us persists even in the absence of any general consensus about what race is, or precisely how and where it differs from ethnicity and culture, whose definitions are also vague.[1] The obsession continues, although genetic science tells us that the phenotypical traits we use to distinguish races, such as hair and skin color, are less significant than genetic variations among individuals of the same phenotype. We depend on the race label to convey essential data—information we use to interpret, to decode one another. When the label is hard to read, when we are unable to find and decode the message race carries for us, we are uneasy. So we also use words like "multiracial" and "multiethnic" to mask our unease; they have become a polite way to avoid specifying a particular race by name and the accompanying worry about whether one has used the "right" word. (Is it better to say "African American" or "black"? "Native American" or "American Indian"?)

In the end, I found what I was looking for. Mixed-heritage characters have a long literary pedigree, both distinguished and painful. In teen fiction from edgy YA titles to mass-market series, authors—many of them multiracial—have begun to explore the topic of teens grappling with mixed identity. The catch is that these books are seldom labeled, shelved, or honored as mixed-identity narratives. When they win identity-based awards, it is under the rubric of monoracial categories: works by black or Latino authors or about black or Latino characters. The mixed-heritage novel, like the mixed-heritage person, has a visibility problem.

MULTIRACIAL AMERICA TODAY

Millions of Americans consider themselves multiracial, but no official effort was made to enumerate them until 2000. Then, for the first time, the U.S. census allowed respondents to identify themselves as belonging to two or more races, and 7,270,926 (2.6 percent of the total U.S. population) did so.[2] Of American children under age eighteen, 2.85 million were identified as belonging to two or more races (4 percent of all American children). Thirty-nine percent of mixed-race individuals enumerated were under age eighteen, as opposed to 26 percent of the total population, indicating that the mixed population is growing much faster than the monoracial equivalent. Between 1970 and 2000, racial intermarriages increased from less than 1 to 5 percent of all U.S. marriages, while the number of children living in interracial families grew from 900,000 to more than three million.

Interracial families are also formed by adoption. Like most intercountry adoptions, many domestic adoptions are transracial and transethnic, creating interracial families. Between 1989 and 2004, Americans adopted 211,648 children from other countries. In 2000, 1.6 million adopted children under eighteen were living in American families. More than 20,000 children from other countries are adopted into American families annually, most from Asia, Latin America, and Eastern Europe. Today, more than one in six adopted children are of a race different from their parents. An additional 560,000 children under eighteen are in foster care in any given year, placements that are often transracial and transcultural.

The U.S. census does not track religion, but the Pew Forum on Religion and Public Life does. A study released in February 2008 found that 37 percent of marriages in the United States are interfaith, formed by partners raised in different religions or denominations.[3] In 1970, 17 percent of Jews were in interfaith marriages—the figure today is closer to 40 percent.[4] Roman Catholic intermarriage rates vary among communities, from 17 to more than 50 percent.[5]

So the question becomes: When mixed-heritage people are one of the largest and fastest-growing demographics in the United States, why do they remain culturally hidden? The answers are rooted in our nation's history of conquest and settlement, colonialism and slavery, and immigration. Above all, the invisibility of multiracial people stems from the idea of race itself.

THE BINARY CASTE SYSTEM

The concept of race and the source of racial categories in use today date from the late fifteenth century, but "whereas the idea that the human species might be divided up into distinct subspecies marked by skin color or other superficial features had occurred before, it was not until the scientific revolution that accompanied the Industrial Revolution in Europe and North American that such divisions were elevated to the status of 'science.'"[6] Thereafter, biological determinists created elaborate race theories to justify slavery and the dominance of the white caste in the nineteenth century and to justify Nazi racialism and extermination camps in the twentieth century. The belief that racial categories are biologically based persists, despite ample scientific consensus that our concepts of "race" are socially, not biologically, determined. The language we use to discuss these concepts, frustratingly, reinforces the very illusion we are trying to dispel. More recently, the concept of race has been used to bolster a positive identity among previously marginalized people seeking social and political change.

With European conquest and settlement, a three-caste race system—white, nonwhite, and mixed-race—evolved in most of the New World. The middle caste went by various names: *Mestizo, Métis, Creole.* The United States, however, evolved a two-caste system: a dominant white caste and subordinate nonwhite caste.[7] Early patterns of settlement and the institution of slavery led to and reinforced this binary system. To keep the white caste "pure," no one with any degree of nonwhite heritage, however small, could be admitted into it. As in the rest of the New World, interracial unions occurred in colonial America, beginning with the marriage of Pocahontas and John Rolfe in 1614. But colonial America, unlike Latin America, soon passed laws banning interracial marriage. The first such ban was enacted in 1661; the last were not repealed until the Supreme Court ruled them unconstitutional in *Loving v. Virginia* (1967).[8] Lacking a third option, mixed-race Americans were slotted into the nonwhite caste, but never fully assimilated by it. The binary caste system evolved into the practice of *hypodescent,* which continues to work against the recognition and validation of multiracial identity. This so-called one-drop rule provides that any individual of mixed white and nonwhite descent is automatically assigned to the nonwhite caste. Long embedded in U.S. law and affirmed by the Supreme Court in *Plessy v. Ferguson* (1896), hypodescent was used primarily to identify people of any African descent as black, but has also been applied to other races. During World War II, the definition of who was Japanese for the purpose of internment in concentration camps included those with as little as one-sixteenth (one great-great-grandparent) Japanese ancestry.[9] Although up to 90 percent of African Americans may have some white heritage, most choose to identify themselves simply as black, affirming for very different reasons the principle of hypodescent once used against them. Descendants of slaves whose ancestors include white slave owners see no reason to honor that heritage by calling themselves multiracial, feeling that "it is not something we like to talk about or want to celebrate. For us it is a painful history of rape, rejection, and exploitation."[10]

The evolution of identity politics in the 1950s and 1960s, in which individuals banded together to achieve social and political goals based on a shared identity, bolstered hypodescent further when that identity was based on race: black, Latino, Asian, and so forth. A group that uses hypodescent to determine who is entitled to membership will, by definition, be larger than a group that does not. Thus, when the government announced that individuals for the first time could declare two or more races, "many minority advocacy groups advised their members to report only one race (the minority race) in the 2000 census because these groups feared a loss of political clout if their population total was eroded by people choosing more than one race."[11]

Racial categories differ among countries and cultures and change over time, as do ethnicities. American Indians, first presumed to be of the same race as European Americans,[12] were not enumerated in early censuses. This policy changed in the mid-nineteenth century.[13] Today, American Indian and Alaska Natives apply criteria based on ancestry to define who is entitled to tribal membership. The criteria usually specify a minimum "blood quantum," a degree of Indian ancestry expressed as a fraction. This has led to a precise parsing of racial heritage.

Boundaries between race and ethnicity are porous and confusing enough; religion adds another wrinkle. Judaism is both an ethnicity and a religion. Some sects define Jewish identity as transmitted only by matrilineal descent and do not recognize as Jews the children of a Jewish father and non-Jewish mother, or adopted persons whose mothers were not Jewish.

Many Latinos identify themselves as *mestizo:* of mixed indigenous, Spanish, and/or African descent. In the United States, which does not recognize a mixed-race caste, they share the "Hispanic" label with monoracial Latinos.[14] Now the surging Latino population may be changing how Americans view race.[15] Even today, race and ethnic categories remain as volatile as ever.

To acknowledge a multiracial individual as such is to acknowledge that the boundaries separating races are permeable. And this is a problem, says ethnic studies scholar Cynthia Nakashima: "The U.S. system has depended on very clear racial categories for its political, social, economic, and psychological organization." To keep these racial categories separate means denying the reality of mixed-identity people. "By insisting that they exist and that they are what they are, multiracial and multiethnic people have blurred the boundaries between groups." Those who rely on these boundaries "for privilege or political or economic interest or sense of self" have a vested interest in preserving them, Nakashima says, and consequently are troubled by the prospect that the categories might be dismantled and changed. "It worries those who have static, undynamic ways of defining cultural and group pride and preservation. But in the end, less 'us versus them' thinking—in this country and in this world—will be good for us all."[16]

YOUNG ADULTS WITH MIXED HERITAGE

Regardless of intent or the races involved, the effect of hypodescent rules on mixed-heritage individuals is to invalidate part of their identity. For adolescents engaged in the process of figuring out who they are and where they belong, constructing a functional multiracial identity poses special challenges. Identity is not limited to race and ethnicity, of course.

It includes many elements: gender, race and ethnicity, family status, socioeconomic class, sexual orientation, age, physical ability or disability, and so forth. Not all identities are equal. "Ethnic identity, the identification of an individual or group of individuals with a particular ethnic group or groups, is particularly important to the self because it is a master status, an identity that overrides all others in others' judgments of the self. As such, it is also basic to the establishment of self-meaning."[17] Despite the fluidity and subjectivity of racial and cultural identity over time and among peoples, "ethnic identities do not seem to involve conscious selection. One does not experience electing to be Hispanic, for instance, but instead experiences being Hispanic."[18]

Since the mid-twentieth century, considerable child-development research on young adults of mixed heritage has been carried out by social scientists. Early studies warned that they were more likely than their peers to suffer from low self-esteem and unlikely to find social acceptance. Recent studies have revisited and tested long-held beliefs about the effects of multiraciality on human development, finding instead that multiracial youth are at no greater risk for serious psychosocial problems than other young adults.[19] Nonetheless, teens experience plenty of challenges arising from their "mixed" status.

Pearl Fuyo Gaskins, whose interviews with multiracial young adults are collected in *What Are You? Voices of Mixed-Race Young People*, recalls growing up as a mixed-race teen in Vallejo, California, in the 1970s: "For myself and many of my peers, racial identification determined the music we listened to, the clothes and hairstyles we wore, the slang we used, who our friends were, and whom we dated. As teenagers trying to carve out identities for ourselves, we found in race and ethnicity instant self-definition and a sense of group belonging." But for mixed-race kids, instant self-definition was not possible. "It was a tough time and place to be biracial. Racial purity was cool, being mixed was not. I wasn't white enough and I wasn't nonwhite enough. There were no positive words to describe what I was or what group I belonged to."[20]

Given the right support, mixed-heritage young adults not only weather problems, but develop superior coping skills and increased resilience. And these skills in turn can build confidence. "Indeed, some studies have suggested that biracial adolescents may have as high or higher self-esteem than monoracial adolescents."[21] Support from family, peers, and community helps teens reach that well-adjusted pinnacle.

Intact families, integrated schools and neighborhoods, and a multicultural social life are associated with positive psychosocial adjustment. Even more helpful are parents who encourage their children to explore their full heritage and provide them with opportunities and role models to do so.[22] Appearance is a major component of mixed-race identity, as well as a perennial concern of adolescents. Being stared at is a common experience for multiracial people. It can be uncomfortable and offensive at any age; for teens it is often excruciating. "So many people who are white, black, Asian, or what have you, take for granted that they're going to see people like themselves on the streets, and on television, and in books and newspapers," says Sara Busdiecker, who is multiracial, adopted by white parents. "Whereas if you're mixed, that never happens. You could be in the presence of somebody who is mixed and you'd never know it. So you can feel very isolated."[23] Studies suggest that one factor that influences teens in deciding how to identify themselves is which slot others are likely to sort them into.[24]

Young adults whose mixed identity extends to religion, as with children of one Jewish and one Gentile parent, may not have to endure stares but can encounter rejection and hostility from those who refuse to acknowledge half their identity. "Sometimes I'm considered 'not Jewish enough' by hardcore Jews, and then I turn around and I'm considered 'not Armenian enough' by hardcore Armenians. It's one of those things I talk about with my other 'halfie' friends," says Jesse Soursourian.[25]

Transracially adopted young adults can experience all of the above, plus bias based on their adoptive status. Adoption across races remains controversial in the United States. Even in the most successful placements, adoptees must come to terms with having lost their birthfamilies and cultural heritage. Those whose birthparents were of different races have an extra identity issue to sort out. Again, intelligent support is key to working through these issues. Parents who "take seriously the identity needs of their adopted children of color and try to provide for them increase the likelihood that their adopted children of color will grow to adulthood feeling good about themselves and their adoptive parents."[26]

Every day, answering the question "who are you?" gets more complicated, and the complexity is reflected at all levels of youth experience: at home, at school, in the workplace, and in the culture at large. Yet teens are still expected to fit a "multi" identity into a world of binary choices. In homage to the ideal of diversity, we have replaced the old "melting pot" ideal with the "salad bowl." But this still excludes those of mixed heritage (unless we visualize adding a vegetable that is half-tomato and half-celery). Meanwhile, as figures on interfaith and interracial marriage and families make clear, Americans, like much of the rest of the world, are joining our lives with people from different races and ethnicities and cultures more than ever before and at an accelerating rate. Yet with all the lip service paid to valuing diversity and multiculturalism, there is still no place set at the table for the mixed-heritage individual.

YA FICTION ABOUT CHARACTERS WITH BLENDED IDENTITIES—GOOD AND BAD NEWS

From the time of slavery and the abolitionist movement, fiction has been an important voice in the American cultural conversation about race. Early negative caricatures such as the tragic mulatto and degenerate half-breed have mostly disappeared from fiction, but continue to lead a half-life in popular culture. (Their unquiet ghosts linger on in old films like *Show Boat* and TV reruns of old Westerns.) Counteracting them, first-rate writers, from Zora Neale Hurston through Leslie Marmon Silko and Danzy Senna, have created powerful, vivid mixed-heritage characters to set alongside the stereotypes in *Last of the Mohicans* and *Uncle Tom's Cabin*.

Since 1990, more than one hundred young adult novels with mixed-race protagonists or significant secondary characters have been published in the United States. At their best, these books offer "multiculti" readers the validation of seeing their images reflected in fiction in realistic and positive ways. The bad news is that in recent years being "multi" has become chic, and this multiculti visibility has inspired some very bad writing indeed, with characters who resurrect old racial (and racist) stereotypes in works that reveal a stunning ignorance of mixed-heritage identity and experience, including the long history of racist tropes such as the tragic mulatto.

Fictional treatments of social issues unfolding in the larger society often follow a fairly linear and predictable timeline.[27] Early narratives, timid and schematic, are succeeded by better ones that integrate the "problem" into the story, with more nuanced characterization. This sequential evolution has yet to occur with YA fiction about mixed-heritage characters. Too many books continue to be published, often to blandly approving reviews, that treat mixed identity superficially or inauthentically. (When characters of color announce that race is irrelevant, we can be certain their author was white.) Adoption myths—such as the feelings, or lack of feelings, adoptees have for their family and culture of birth—have been slow to die. The learning curve has proven anything but linear, so date of publication gives few if any clues to the book's quality or treatment of the subject matter. However, regardless of how well they do it, that authors continue to explore the world outside their own racial and cultural boundaries and comfort zones is a good thing. It takes courage to do this and even failed attempts can contribute in a meaningful way to the evolving cultural dialogue that fiction has always been a part of and that influences its own evolution.

EMERGING TRENDS

From 2000 on, novels have started to appear that present characters from blended ethnicities and backgrounds previously underrepresented in YA fiction. Marie Lamba, Anjali Banerjee, and Mitali Perkins have protagonists who share South Asian and white parentage. Sharon G. Flake's characters of black and Korean heritage and Nancy Osa's Polish Cuban protagonist add to the diversity. Novels by Dana Reinhardt and Marie Lee explore the experience of transracial and transcultural adoption with new depth and understanding.

A growing number of authors who are multiracial, among them Sundee Tucker Frazier, Mitali Perkins, Carrie Rosten, Danzy Senna, and Cynthia Leitich Smith, present complex issues of blended heritage through vivid characters and compelling narratives. Their themes—establishing identity, seeking wholeness, negotiating two or more worlds, being forced to favor one side of one's heritage at the expense of another, learning to construct a cohesive identity out of disparate, sometimes warring elements—speak directly to the mixed-identity experience.

Some authors are addressing hot-button issues of race, ethnicity, family status, and religion through the genres of fantasy and science fiction. This allows them to free topics from their cultural context to arrive at a new understanding. By creating a world in which dark-skinned people rule and light-skinned people serve, Malorie Blackman shows readers of each caste what it might feel like if these tables were turned. Tales of being "mixed" have too often been dreary or tragic, leavened, if at all, by a twist of grim irony. The marked lightening of what has been a deadly serious tone is most welcome. Mental health benefits aside, humor offers unique possibilities for exploring cultural collisions and misunderstandings. Authors adding a dash, sometimes generous helpings, of humor to stories of blended identities include Sherri L. Smith, Carrie Rosten, and Sundee Tucker Frazier writing on "multiculti" themes; Rose Kent and Greg Leitich Smith addressing transracial adoption; and Ilene Cooper on the "December dilemma" in a Jewish-Christian family.

ABOUT NAMES

One of the frustrating challenges in talking about interracial and multiracial matters is that there are no universally accepted definitions for "race" and "ethnicity." To avoid driving readers and myself mad by repeating the same terms for "mixed identity" over and over, I have used several terms more or less interchangeably: mixed heritage, mixed identity, mixed roots, the trendy "multiculti," and, where warranted, multiracial and multiethnic. For naming offspring of interfaith unions, I have come to accept that the only term in circulation is "half," as in "half-Jewish." For some categories, no name exists at all, as in the monoracial adult in an interracial union or the monoracial parent of a multiracial child. Often, the choices boil down to which of several inaccurate designations is least unacceptable.

In this book, in addition to honoring the name preferred by who is being named, I have tried to use descriptors that are the most precise and least ambiguous without being cumbersome. American Indian is preferred to Native American, Kiowa or Cherokee preferred over American Indian. Neither black nor white is capitalized.[28] Names have power: they establish and define identity; they stake out territory. Because of that, who gets to bestow them matters. Most descriptors in this book were chosen first and foremost because they are currently preferred by those described. The right to define ourselves is important for everyone, but most of all for those prohibited from doing so in the past. This right includes the right to redefine and rename. Names can change for many reasons; one reason is that the group named has lost control of how the name is used. The previously neutral term "mental retardation" acquired a pejorative connotation after "retard" became a schoolyard epithet; thereafter, "developmentally disabled" took its place. Accusations of "political correctness" are heard when a group tries to regain control over its descriptors. Such complaints are valid only if we assume groups do not have the right to name themselves.

SELECTION CRITERIA

Most of the books discussed here were written for young adults and are shelved in the YA sections of libraries and bookstores. There are several significant exceptions:

- English and American literary classics that were written for adults but are shelved with children's and YA fiction, taught in schools, and/or form part of our literary lingua franca.
- Adult fiction with crossover YA appeal.
- Middle-grade fiction for older readers with significant mixed-heritage content.
- Adult memoirs of growing up as a mixed-heritage person.

NOTES

1. No universally accepted definition for "race" exists, although broad consensus exists that it is a socially constructed concept, without scientific meaning. At a minimum it refers to a collection of physical traits and characteristics, transmissible by descent. "Ethnicity" and "culture" can include language, religion, traditions, the arts, dress, and customs that characterize a group. "Ethnicity" implies geographical and/or tribal roots, although sometimes only historically. "Culture" does not imply a geographical origin and also may be used to describe generational trends or behaviors of groups ("corporate culture") whose commonality is limited. For resources on race, ethnicity, and culture, see the bibliography.

2. This number reflects census participants' self-identification *only*. There is reason to believe that the number of mixed-race people is far higher. The decision to allow census participants to identify themselves as of more than one race was a compromise reached after an intense, heated, multiyear lobbying effort by multiracial advocacy groups such as Project RACE (in favor of a multiracial category) and monoracial groups such as the NAACP, Urban League, and National Council of LaRaza (opposed any change to the race categories). Some groups and individuals advocated for eliminating racial categories altogether.

3. Pew Forum on Religion & Public Life, "The U.S. Religious Landscape Survey Reveals a Fluid and Diverse Pattern of Faith," 25 Feb. 2008, pewresearch .org/pubs/743/united-states-religion (27 March 2008).

4. The 1990 Jewish Population Survey found 28 percent of Jews reported being married to non-Jews. Since then, most sources believe the number has risen by at least 10 percent. Jewish Outreach Institute, www.joi.org/qa/stats .shtml (21 March 2008).

5. Barbara Hughes, "Double Belonging Families Affirmed at Virginia Beach," *The Catholic Virginian* 81, no. 21 (14 Aug. 2006), www.aifusa.org/ Catholic_Virginian_article_081406.html (22 July 2008); also, "Interfaith Marriage—Prevalence," *US Catholic Study of Catholics in the United States* (Official Catholic Directory 1997), family.jrank.org/pages/897/Interfaith-Marriage-Prevalence.html (27 March 2008).

6. Carlos A. Fernández, "La Raza and the Melting Pot: A Comparative Look at Multiethnicity," in *Racially Mixed People in America,* ed. Maria P. P. Root (Newbury Park, Calif.: Sage, 1992), 138.

7. Regional exceptions existed, especially in New Orleans and southern Louisiana and Hawaii.

8. Even after this ruling, South Carolina and Alabama retained antimiscegenation laws on their books until they were repealed in statewide referendums in 1998 and 2000, respectively. In South Carolina 62 percent voted to overturn the ban; in Alabama, 59 percent.

9. Tetsuden Kashima, *Judgment without Trial: Japanese American Imprisonment during World War II* (Seattle: University of Washington Press, 2003), 135.

10. Heather Dalmage, *Tripping on the Color Line* (New Brunswick, N.J.: Rutgers University Press, 2000), 5.

11. Sharon M. Lee and Barry Edmonston, "New Marriages, New Families: U.S. Racial and Hispanic Intermarriage," *Population Bulletin* 60, no. 2 (June 2005), 4.

12. Terry P. Wilson, "Blood Quantum: Native American Mixed Bloods," in *Racially Mixed People in America,* ed. Maria P. P. Root (Newbury Park, Calif.: Sage, 1992), 117. See also Gary B. Nash, *Forbidden Love: The Secret History of Mixed-Race America* (New York: Henry Holt, 1999), 8.

13. Nineteenth-century assimilationist governmental policies aimed to close reservations in future and absorb tribes into the general population. The "blood

quantum" rules used to define who is eligible for tribal enrollment were originally intended as a countdown to such assimilation. Now most tribes reject cultural absorption as a goal and seek ways to preserve their distinct cultures in per-
petuity. Blood quantum rules work against this goal because each time
outmarriage occurs, the blood quantum of the next generation is diluted until
it eventually disappears. This has led U.S. tribes to search for alternative means
of establishing identity.

14. Hispanics are the only ethnicity tracked by the U.S. census. Those who
so identify are then asked to identify their race as well, using the same racial categories as everyone else. Before the 2000 census, many people of mixed race
checked "other" under the race category; studies later determined that 90 percent of them were Hispanic.

15. Fernández, "La Raza and the Melting Pot," 140.

16. Cynthia L. Nakashima, "An Invisible Monster: The Creation and Denial
of Mixed-Race People in America," in *Racially Mixed People in America,* ed.
Maria P. P. Root (Newbury Park, Calif.: Sage, 1992), 177–78.

17. Cookie White Stephan, "Mixed-Heritage Individuals: Ethnic Identity
and Trait Characteristics," in *Racially Mixed People in America,* ed. Maria P. P.
Root (Newbury Park, Calif.: Sage, 1992), 51.

18. Stephan, "Mixed-Heritage Individuals," 62.

19. Maria P. P. Root, ed., *Racially Mixed People in America* (Newbury Park,
Calif.: Sage, 1992). This groundbreaking anthology by social scientists and historians offered solid science to refute beliefs about negative traits and problems
stemming from multiracial status. Later and larger studies have supported the
findings. All contributors were themselves multiracial and/or in interracial families. Heritage information and photographs of each contributor were included,
putting a professional "face" on multiracial identity, an important step in demar-
ginalization.

20. Pearl Fuyo Gaskins, *What Are You? Voices of Mixed-Race Young People* (New
York: Henry Holt, 1999), 7.

21. Ana Marie Cauce, Yumi Hiraga, Craig Mason, Tanya Aguilar, Nydia Ordonez, and Nancy Gonzales, "Between a Rock and a Hard Place: Social Adjustment of Biracial Youth," in *Racially Mixed People in America,* ed. Maria P. P.
Root (Newbury Park, Calif: Sage, 1992), 217.

22. Beverly Daniel Tatum, "Identity Development in Multiracial Families," in
*"Why Are All the Black Kids Sitting Together in the Cafeteria?" And Other Conversa-
tions About Race,* rev. ed. (New York: Basic, 2003), 167–90.

23. Gaskins, *What Are You?* 194. See also Angela Nissel, *Mixed: My Life in
Black and White* (New York: Villard, 2006), 44.

24. David L. Brunsma, "The New Color Complex: Appearances and Biracial Identity," *Identity: An International Journal of Theory and Research* 1, no. 3
(2001) 225–46.

25. Daniel Klein and Freke Vuijst, *The Half-Jewish Book: A Celebration* (New York: Villard, 2000), 5.
26. Tatum, *"Why Are All the Black Kids Sitting Together in the Cafeteria?"* 187.
27. For an example of such a publishing timeline, see Michael Cart and Christine A. Jenkins, *The Heart Has Its Reasons: Young Adult Literature with Gay/Lesbian/Queer Content* (Lanham, Md.: Scarecrow Press, 2006).
28. In quotations, the authors' capitalization choices with respect to race have been retained.

Mulatto Heiress to Tragic Mulatto

The Evolution of an Archetype

𝓜ost mixed-heritage characters in contemporary literature are of recent vintage, with one significant exception. Debuting in the eighteenth century, the mulatto character of European and African ancestry was and remains a key fictional trope. This chapter analyses literary mulattos in two centuries of English and American novels and films, paradigms that continue to inform contemporary YA fiction and shape the mindset readers bring to it. The discussion of contemporary YA presented in subsequent chapters refers to tropes first presented here.

Few literary stereotypes have had such a long run as the fictional mulatto,[1] who thrilled, titillated, angered, and moved readers of all races for 150 years. Beginning with the eighteenth-century novel, this enduring character first figured in classic works by white authors: Tobias Smollett, Jane Austen, James Fenimore Cooper, Charlotte Brontë, William Makepeace Thackeray, Mark Twain, and William Faulkner, among others. Most of the critical attention directed at the literary mulatto, however, has gone to works by black Harlem Renaissance authors, especially Jean Toomer, Nella Larsen, and Zora Neale Hurston. A product of its society, like other cultural institutions, literary criticism has followed the dictates of the binary caste system and consigned the study of multiracial characters to black or ethnic studies. Consequently, mulatto stereotypes by white authors of the "great books" canon are seldom analyzed except in the context of black literature. Apart from scholarly studies aimed at academics, little if any analysis of mulatto characters in the work of these authors has been offered for younger readers. Young adults who encounter these stereotypes in their high school reading, if not earlier, may be "imprinted" with negative images of multiracial people that go unnoticed and unchallenged. Harriet Beecher Stowe's *Uncle Tom's Cabin* is a partial exception, but its mulatto characters represent only one branch of a large and complicated family tree.

"The mulatto, even more than the full-blooded Negro, is 'America's Metaphor,'" says Judith Berzon in *Neither White nor Black: The Mulatto Character in American Fiction*.[2] Mulatto characters have always reflected societal fears, longings, desperation, anger, lust, and racism. Perhaps most importantly, they have reassured readers that the color line is, if not impassable, close to it, and that efforts to cross or eradicate it are bound to end badly. Like their authors, mulatto characters have been male and female, black and white. Abolitionists used mulattos to epitomize the horrors of slavery; racists used them to illustrate the horrors of desegregation; black writers used them to assuage white fears. Leslie Fiedler might well have been describing the tragic mulatto when he offered this definition of the literary archetype:

> A coherent pattern of beliefs and feelings so widely shared at a level beneath consciousness that there exists no abstract vocabulary for representing it, and so "sacred" that unexamined, irrational restraints inhibit any explicit analysis. Such a complex finds a formula or pattern story, which serves both to embody it, and, at first at least, to conceal its full implications. Later, the secret may be revealed, the archetype "analyzed" or "allegorically" interpreted according to the language of the day.[3]

THE MULATTO HEIRESS

The first literary mulattos were minor characters, literary grace notes in eighteenth-century English fiction. "In Britain, the only people of mixed parentage with whom novelists were concerned, and then rarely, were West Indian heiresses, whose role, far from being tragic, was to throw a comic sidelight on the cupidity of society."[4] Of vaguely multiracial parentage, she was less a character in her own right than a clue planted to tell readers something about other characters. In Tobias Smollett's novel *The Expedition of Humphrey Clinker* (1771), Jeremy Melford's description of a ball in Bath, then a fashionable spa—"a monstrous jumble of heterogeneous principles: a vile mob of noise and impertinence, without decency or subordination"—ends with the observation, "the ball was opened by a Scotch lord, with a mulatto heiress from St. Christopher's" (53). The mulatto heiress is a mirror, reflecting the avarice of those around her; we never see through her eyes. She is always object, never subject. Miss Lambe, the heiress in Jane Austen's unfinished novel *Sanditon*, set in an English seaside town under development as a fashionable spa, is a case in point. She is one of three young women brought to Sanditon by a paid companion, Mrs. Griffiths. "Of these three, and indeed of all, Miss Lambe was beyond comparison the most important and precious, as she paid in proportion to her fortune. She was about seventeen, half mulatto, chilly and tender, had a maid of her own, was to have the best room in the lodgings, and was also of the first consequence in every plan of Mrs. Griffiths" (206). In search of a wealthy wife for her impecunious nephew, Lady Denham zeroes in on her prey: "In Miss Lambe, here was the very young lady, sickly and rich, whom she had been asking for" (207). Austen completed only twelve chapters of *Sanditon*, so it is unwise and unfair to read too much into the depiction, but what exists conforms to stereotype.

The suggestion of ill health, associated with mental illness, instability, or retardation, became a hallmark of the nineteenth-century mulatto heiress. To decode Miss Swartz, the memorable mulatto heiress in *Vanity Fair,* we have Thackeray's art as well as his words: The Osborne family, hoping to acquire her fortune by marriage, fawns over Miss Swartz, whom Thackeray has drawn as a pop-eyed idiot. The caption reads: "Swartz in her favorite amber-colored satin, with turquoise bracelets, countless rings, flowers, feathers, and all sorts of tags and gimcracks, about as elegantly decorated as a she chimney-sweep on May-day" (190). In case this reference isn't clear enough—the faces of chimney sweeps on the job were blackened by fireplace soot—the name "Swartz" suggests "swarthy."

"Insofar as these heiresses were given 'racial' characteristics, they were the contemporary stereotypical characteristics attributed to black people, rather than any specific to those of mixed parentage."[5] But while the mulatto heiress may not have resembled a true multiracial person, her depiction suggests common beliefs held about individuals born of racial mixing: that they were sickly, physically inferior, mentally feeble,[6] and thus easy prey for fortune hunters.

THE MISSING LINK: BERTHA MASON
AND ANTOINETTE COSWAY

In *Jane Eyre,* Charlotte Brontë transforms the silly heiress into a mysterious, terrifying presence: Bertha Mason, first wife to the novel's romantic hero, Mr. Rochester. Bertha displays the familiar mulatto heiress attributes, but here they are anything but funny. Bertha Mason shadows *Jane Eyre* with a gothic intensity worthy of Poe.

As she makes the journey from governess to Mr. Rochester's fiancée, Jane's nights at Thornfield Hall are disturbed by disquieting noises and laughter from another part of the house. She accepts the explanation that a servant, Grace Poole, is responsible. But shortly before she is to be married, Jane wakes up in the night to find a woman in her room, handling her bridal outfit and trying on her veil. Later, Jane describes the woman to Mr. Rochester: "'Fearful and ghastly to me—oh, sir, I never saw a face like it! It was a discoloured face—it was a savage face. I wish I could forget the roll of the red eyes and the fearful blackened inflation of the lineaments!'" Jane adds that "'the lips were swelled and dark; the brow furrowed: the black eyebrows widely raised over the bloodshot eyes.'" It reminds Jane of a vampire as, tearing off the veil "'from its gaunt head, [it] rent it in two parts, and flinging both on the floor, trampled on them'" (311). F. H. Townsend's illustration, published with the book's second edition, shows a dark, shadowed figure stamping on the veil in the foreground while Jane cowers in her bed.

After the wedding is called off by the revelation that the "creature" is Rochester's first wife, he describes how he was manipulated into marrying a beautiful, orphaned Jamaican heiress. In an early use of the "passing for white" motif that would later become the hallmark of the tragic mulatto, he tells Jane how he discovered Bertha's true ancestry. "'Bertha Mason is mad; and she came of a mad family; idiots and maniacs through three generations! Her mother, the Creole, was both a madwoman and a drunkard!'" (320). He describes Bertha's heritage as inferior and tainted: "'Her family wished to secure me because I was of a good race; and so did she'" (332). Bertha Mason's attributes add up to a checklist of traits for what would become the tragic mulatto: "tainted" ancestry, mental instability to the point of madness, physical beauty, a passionate but "intemperate and unchaste" nature, and violent, coarse, and animalistic behavior.

In her celebrated 1966 postcolonial novel *Wide Sargasso Sea,* winner of the 1967 W. H. Smith Award, Jean Rhys turns *Jane Eyre* upside down, retelling the story from Rochester's and Bertha's points of view. Bertha, we learn, is actually Antoinette Cosway. Rochester has forced the family name "Bertha" on her, a symbolic erasure of her identity. Their marriage is a crass grab at her fortune, but a strong attraction grows between them, especially on Antoinette's part. But Rochester notices that her eyes "are too large and can be disconcerting. She never blinks at all it seems to me. Long, sad, dark, alien eyes. Creole of pure English descent she may be, but they are not English or European either" (67). Rochester is first frightened, then disgusted by Antoinette's sensuality and family history. His treatment of her drives her insane.

From the book's first sentence, Rhys shows us that, neither white nor black, Antoinette fits nowhere: "They say when trouble comes close ranks, and so the white people did. But we were not in their ranks" (17). Early in their marriage, Antoinette translates a song for Rochester that her maid is singing: "'It's a song about a white cockroach. That's me. That's what they call all of us who were here before their own people in Africa sold them to the slave traders. And I've heard the English women call us white niggers. So between you and me, I often wonder who I am and where is my country and where do I belong and why was I ever born at all'" (103). The novel ends as Antoinette—imprisoned at Thornfield, robbed of fortune, home, and name—steals down the passage with a candle to set the house on fire.

A native of the West Indian island of Dominica, Rhys was a powerful writer and this novel is considered her masterpiece. Her heroines—like Rhys herself—were intelligent victims of unrequited love, alcoholism and poverty, and their own stubborn self-destructiveness. These traits match those of the tragic mulatto, along with a sense of cultural displacement that may help to explain why her portrait of the doomed Antoinette Cosway is so compelling.

THE MULATTO CHARACTER IN AMERICA

Although we see the events from opposing vantage points in *Jane Eyre* and *Wide Sargasso Sea,* Bertha/Antoinette plays the same roles in each: mulatto heiress and tragic mulatto. The mulatto heiress never made it to

America,[7] probably because she was a hick colonial, taken advantage of by unethical but cultured Englishmen and -women. Americans, only decades past colonial status themselves, probably found the joke less than amusing. Instead, the first major fictional representation of a mulatto in American literature comes in James Fenimore Cooper's historical novel *The Last of the Mohicans* (1826), set in 1757. The beautiful Munro sisters, Cora and Alice, are caught up in the French and Indian War, repeatedly kidnapped and rescued. Cora, of part-African descent, is dark, courageous, mature, and tainted. Her half-sister, Alice, is blonde, helpless, childlike, and pure. Cora is far more engaging; her independence and strength resonate better today than Alice's shrinking, incompetent femininity. At first attracted to both women, the dashing Major Heyward soon settles on Alice and approaches their father, Munro, for permission to marry her. Munro mistakenly believes Heyward is asking for Cora, and so tells him about her mother, his first wife: "'She was the daughter of a gentleman of those isles, by a lady, whose misfortune it was, if you will,' said the old man, proudly, 'to be descended, remotely, from that unfortunate class, who are so basely enslaved to administer to the wants of a luxurious people!'" In even more stilted language, Munro rails against slavery and those who support it: "'Ha! Major Heyward, you are yourself born at the south, where these unfortunate beings are considered of a race inferior to your own'" (159).

Cora is desired by the noble Uncas, whose love she seems to return. Yet Cooper kills them off because, Fiedler says, "though Cooper's own contemporaries urged him to let Cora and Uncas be joined in marriage, his horror of miscegenation led him to forbid even the not-quite white offspring of one unnatural marriage to enter into another alliance that crossed race lines."[8] Cooper presents Cora as passionate, sensual, and vital. "The tresses of this lady were shining and black, like the plumage of the raven. Her complexion was not brown, but it rather appeared charged with the colour of the rich blood, that seemed ready to burst its bounds" (19). Such hints of burgeoning sexuality are echoed in later fictional mulattos, tragic and otherwise, as well as in fiction, film, and popular culture. "Perhaps the most common and most constant offshoot of the biological-psychological profile of people of mixed race is the stereotype that they are sexually immoral and out of control," says Cynthia L. Nakashima, noting such attacks are made by those invested in preventing outmarriage. "The mixed-race person is seen as the product of an immoral union between immoral people, and is thus expected to be immoral him- or herself."⁹

RACISTS AND ABOLITIONISTS

By the mid-nineteenth century, whites' belief in black inferiority had crystallized into a full-blown racist ideology, flimsily supported by pseudoscience. Racists managed to adapt Darwin's theories on the origin of species to argue that black and white races had separate origins. From this argument, many tried to assert that unions between blacks and whites would be barren or biologically flawed.¹⁰ For their part, abolitionists used mulatto characters to make their case for putting an end to slavery while countering the racist biological argument. Their heroes were usually sons of a slave-owning white father and black slave mother, and invariably intelligent, noble, sensitive, and proud. Although bitter over the injustices of slavery, they were nonviolent, taking the high road, and never scaring the white readers whom the story hoped to persuade.

When the mulatto character was female, her vulnerability and beauty were emphasized, which yielded a vicarious thrill, as in "The Quadroons" (1842) by Lydia Maria Child. This short story combines melodrama and a titillating forbidden romance. Rosalie, a quadroon, falls in love with Edward, who is white. Legally barred from marrying, they live in unwedded bliss with their daughter, Xarifa. Like Cooper's, Child's references to race and slavery are arch, almost coy, and superficially abolitionist; yet they carry an undercurrent of eroticism. Here is Xarifa: "The iris of her large, dark eye had the melting, mezzotinto outline, which remains the last vestige of African ancestry, and gives that plaintive expression, so often observed, and so appropriate to that docile and injured race" (2). The family's bucolic idyll ends when Edward, who has political ambitions, courts and marries the white daughter of a wealthy, influential man. When she learns about Rosalie, Edward's blonde wife, Charlotte, withdraws emotionally from him. Edward compares "the wintry chill of her polite propriety" to Rosalie's "gushing love" (4). The evolving stereotype of the mulatto woman defined her as more passionate, emotionally out of control, and more fragile than white women. When Rosalie dies brokenhearted, Edward is filled with remorse.

Edward has educated Xarifa, but dies without providing for her future. Xarifa finds true love with George, her harp teacher, but both are unaware that her grandmother's owner never had freed her legally. George is away when Xarifa is seized and sold along with the rest of the owner's property by the creditors of his estate.

> The gentle girl, happy as the birds in spring-time, accustomed to the fondest indulgence, surrounded by all the refinements of life, timid as a young fawn, and with a soul full of romance, was ruthlessly seized by a sheriff, and placed on the public auction-stand in Savannah. There she stood, trembling, blushing, and weeping; compelled to listen to the grossest language, and shrinking from the rude hands that examined the graceful proportions of her beautiful frame. (6)

George returns, but his plans to rescue Xarifa go awry and he is killed. Xarifa's master, "about forty years of age, with handsome features, but a fierce and proud expression," who is in love with her, grows angry when she ignores his lavish gifts. Xarifa ends a "raving maniac," and the reader is warned that "scenes like these are of no unfrequent occurrence at the South" (6). Ostensibly about the evils of slavery, the story offers readers the titillating pleasures of picturing a beautiful girl manhandled on the auction block, forced to submit to the lascivious slave owner's desires.

Abolitionist writers assumed white readers would identify better with the sufferings of slaves who were part white themselves. With little if any interest in the experience of being multiracial, they created mulatto characters solely to advance the argument against slavery, pushing lifeless characters across their stories like chess pieces. However, there were exceptions. In George Harris, Eliza's husband in *Uncle Tom's Cabin* (1852), Harriet Beecher Stowe created more than an emblem. Son of a Southern aristocrat and a beautiful slave, George is strong, handsome, brave, loving, and resourceful. Stowe bases her argument against slavery on his exceptional goodness, abilities, and accomplishments, but she does not make him meek, passive, or tragic. When he and his family are tracked down as runaway slaves on their way to Canada, George is armed and prepared to fight to the death for his family's freedom. The book's wholly African slaves are invariably docile. In his review of *Uncle Tom's Cabin* in *The Liberator* (1852), William Lloyd Garrison pointed out the double standard: "We are curious to know whether Mrs. Stowe is a believer in the duty of non-resistance for the white man, under all possible outrage and peril as well as for the black man."[11]

A fair question. But to be fair in turn to Stowe, she makes it clear that George does not see himself as "part white." He sees himself and wants to be seen as black. "'I have no wish to pass for an American, or to identify myself with them,'" he writes to a friend at the end of the book. "'It is with the oppressed, enslaved African race that I cast in my lot; and if I wished anything, I would wish myself two shades darker, rather than one lighter'" (460). From Canada, George moves his family to France, where he gets a college education, then on to Liberia.

William Wells Brown's novel *Clotel* (1853) was the first mulatto fiction published by an African American author. Clotel and her sister are the children of a slave mother and Thomas Jefferson. As in "The Quadroons," Clotel has a daughter with a white father who later rejects Clotel, marrying a woman whose family can advance his career. The wife persuades her husband to sell Clotel "down the river" (to the Deep South), away from her child. Clotel escapes and, disguised as a white man, searches for her daughter, Mary. Clotel, discovered before she can free Mary, kills herself. Mary survives and moves to Europe.

THE MULATTO CHARACTER IN THE NOVEL OF IDEAS

Mark Twain's *Pudd'nhead Wilson* (1894) is a significant exception to the largely forgettable post–Civil War mulatto novels. It is set in Dawson's Landing, a small, idyllic (except for slavery) town in antebellum Missouri. Roxana, the main character, is a beautiful, intelligent mulatto slave who can pass for white. When she gives birth to a son who also looks white, Roxy switches him with her master's son to prevent him from ever being "sold down the river."

There is no protagonist, per se. Wilson is an outsider, a young lawyer trying to establish himself, although not very hard. His nickname derives from the townsfolks' belief that he is softheaded, a belief that, until the end, he does little to counter. He is not deeply engaged personally with the story's events; he watches and putters around with his hobby of taking fingerprints. Roxy is the closest we get to an emotional center. Part mystery, part polemic, *Pudd'nhead Wilson* doesn't quite hang together as a novel. Like most mulatto stories of the era, it is first and foremost a novel of ideas. What sets it apart is that those ideas are original and complex, examining in microcosm how the institution of slavery enslaves whites and blacks alike. Twain is anything but an essentialist—he demonstrates that slave owner and slave are learned roles. Roxy's biological son, Tom, grows up into a violent, oppressive horror, and the master's son a groveling, dehumanized wretch. After Tom kills her master in a robbery gone wrong, Roxy tries and fails to save him. Wilson identifies the culprit using his fingerprints in a dramatic courtroom denouement. In an especially ironic twist, Tom—who as a slave is too valuable to be hung—is sold down the river. Although Tom's white counterpart is theoretically free to take his place in white society, "his gait, his attitudes, his gestures, his bearing, his laugh—all were vulgar and uncouth; his manners were the manners of a slave. Money and fine clothes could not mend these defects or cover them up; they only made them the more glaring and the more pathetic." He is illiterate and speaks a slave dialect. "The poor fellow could not endure the terrors of the white man's parlor and felt at home and at peace nowhere but in the kitchen" (144).

At the turn of the twentieth century, amid resegregation and proliferating Jim Crow legislation, novels by white racists depicted mulattos atavistically "reverting to type," committing terrifying acts of brutality and mayhem. Robert Lee Durham's *The Call of the South* (1908) tells the story of a biracial Harvard man who succumbs to his true nature. *The Clansman*, by Thomas Dixon, was adapted as the silent film epic *Birth of a Nation* (1915) by D. W. Griffith. Glorifying the Ku Klux Klan, it was criticized for its overt racism, but was hugely popular.

In the hands of black authors, the mulatto paradigm evolved further. "The Negro novelists answered the white racists with political arguments and with a succession of characters of spotless virtue and outstanding intelligence," Berzon notes. Black authors produced literate novels of ideas that "argued the merits of the different means of achieving political, social, and economic rights for the Negro. In these novels, the political programs of Booker T. Washington, W.E.B. DuBois, and various separatist platforms were discussed. The mixed-blood characters in [Sutton] Griggs's novels are almost all political leaders. There are female as well as male race leaders among them."[12]

However, the most widely circulated and remembered iteration of the tragic mulatto was the twentieth-century version, whose appeal to readers was melodramatically emotional rather than reasoned. A woman raised as white discovers, to her horror, that she carries the "taint" of black blood. She agonizes over whether to try to pass, titillating readers. Berzon notes that "not only does the romance of the lonely passer—cut off from all others by her 'desperate' secret—appeal to many white readers, but the latter can turn their speculation to those around them. Who can tell the passer?" The lonely passer, unmasked and outcast, shunned by white and black society alike, has had the longest shelf life of any version of the tragic mulatto. "[S]he is the fictional symbol of marginality," says Berzon. "Rejected out of fear and hatred by the dominant group, [s]he is often rejected out of envy and hatred by the lower caste as well."[13]

Distinguished writers, both white and black, including leading figures of the Harlem Renaissance, spun tales of tragic mulattos who chose to pass, to deny their true identity, at a high personal cost. Jean Toomer's *Cane* (1923) and Nella Larsen's *Passing* (1929) are still read today. The same cannot be said for the efforts of their white peers; Gertrude Stein's *Melanctha: Each One as She May* (1909) and Willa Cather's *Sapphira and the Slave Girl* (1940) are among their weakest works.[14]

BREAKING THE MOLD:
THEIR EYES WERE WATCHING GOD

The most influential novel by a Harlem Renaissance writer with a mulatto protagonist, and a staple of the U.S. high school syllabus, is Zora Neale Hurston's *Their Eyes Were Watching God* (1937). Hurston died in poverty and obscurity in 1960, but received new attention and critical acclaim after her grave was famously rediscovered in 1973 by Alice Walker, whose account "In Search of Zora Neale Hurston" appeared in *Ms.* in March 1975.

Although she bears an impeccable tragic mulatto pedigree, Janie Starks, Hurston's heroine, is no victim. The novel opens as Janie, a wealthy widow last seen leaving town with a younger man, Tea Cake, returns alone, in overalls, ignoring the speculation and disapproval of onlookers: "'What dat ole forty year ole 'oman doin' wid her hair swingin' down her back lak some young gal?'" (2). The novel that follows is Janie's account of her adventures to her friend Pheoby.

Janie's mulatto heritage derives from the rape of her grandmother, Nanny, by a white master late in the Civil War. Their child, Janie's mother, is out of the picture. Nanny, who has raised Janie and recognizes that Janie's racial status leaves her vulnerable, arranges her marriage to a well-to-do man: "'Ah don't want yo' feathers always crumpled by folks throwin' up things in yo' face. And Ah can't die easy thinkin' maybe de menfolks white or black is makin' a spit cup outa you: Have some sympathy fuh me. Put me down easy, Janie, Ah'm a cracked plate'" (20). Janie complies, but her heart isn't in it. After Nanny dies, she abandons her safe, loveless marriage to run off with Joe Starks, an ambitious man who, with Janie's help, ends up the mayor and leading citizen of Eatonville, Florida. Joe holds the reins of power in the community and in the marriage; he lets her know when she falls short. "So when the bread didn't rise, and the fish wasn't quite done at the bone, and the rice was scorched, he slapped Janie until she had a ringing sound in her ears." Joe's violence prompts Janie to stop and think. "She stood there until something fell off the shelf inside her. Then she went inside there to see what it was. It was her image of Jody tumbled down and shattered" (72).

After Joe's illness and death leaves her an affluent widow, Janie is pestered by suitors, but no man has the slightest appeal for her until Tea Cake arrives. Together, they leave for the Everglades. Tea Cake is never utterly reliable or the patriarchal provider Joe was, but Janie does not want to be provided for. She wants to be happy and, by and large, she is—willing to make her own choices and live with the consequences, joyous or sorrowful. It's the value that Janie places on freedom and self-sustained independence that makes this novel truly contemporary. Repeatedly, Janie weighs what her heart longs for against safety and security. Her heart always wins, but Hurston never downplays the costs of the road Janie chooses to follow.

Janie's multiracial status has consequences, but they flow from how others see her, not how she sees herself. Janie refuses to read anything into color distinctions among blacks (Tea Cake himself is dark-skinned). Mrs. Turner, a neighbor with colorist social pretensions, seeks out Janie for her light skin, but Janie rebuffs her efforts to draw her into a light-skinned alliance. When Mrs. Turner says she "can't stand black niggers," Janie replies, "'We'se uh mingled people and all of us got black kinfolks as well as yaller kinfolks. How come you so against black?'" (141). In one of the book's few didactic passages, Hurston steps back and compares this colorism to worship of a false god. "Mrs. Turner, like all other believers, had built an altar to the unattainable—Caucasian characteristics for all. Her god would smite her, would hurl her from pinnacles and lose her in deserts, but she would not forsake his altars" (145).

After a disastrous hurricane and flood drives them from home, Tea Cake is bitten by a rabid dog and, when the white doctor is unable to obtain a rabies vaccine in time, succumbs to madness, attacking Janie, who kills him in self-defense. When she is tried for murder before a white judge and jury, jealous black neighbors show up to testify against her, but the doctor confirms her story. The white women who attend her trial ally themselves with Janie; when she is acquitted "the white women cried and stood around her like a protecting wall and the Negroes, with heads hung down, shuffled out and away." Later, Janie overhears the men talking about her: "'Aw you know dem white mens wuzn't gointuh do nothin' tuh no woman dat look lak her.'" Janie ignores the talk and, wearing overalls, puts on a splendid funeral for Tea Cake ("she was too busy feeling grief to dress like grief" [188–89]) and makes her way home.

Hurston, a Floridian, was educated at Howard University and Barnard College, where she studied with the anthropologist Franz Boas. A folklorist and gifted playwright, she collaborated on projects with Langston Hughes and other Harlem Renaissance figures. Hurston is the quintessential anti–tract-writing, anti-didactic novelist. Her eclipse for three decades, suggests scholar Henry Louis Gates, is connected to her refusal to center her writing on racial oppression and its toxic effects on black people. "Hurston thought this idea degrading, its propagation a trap, and railed against it."[15] In other words, Hurston was not interested in the novel of ideas as such. Janie's mixed-race status is an attribute, but never a defining one.

Hurston's writing celebrates a people that, having survived the cultural genocide of slavery, represent vibrant, creative humanity at its best and worst. Her characters feel grown organically from the soil of their world. Her lyrical style—especially her skillful hand with dialect and her sumptuous imagery—make the book at once light as a feather and richly satisfying. Janie's refusal to base her self-esteem on what others think of her or to place her happiness in untrustworthy hands, is the antithesis of the tragic mulatto. Although her light skin is the target of so much lust and resentment that men are willing to lie about her to see her convicted of Tea Cake's death, Janie does not let them define her and never internalizes their opinions. Janie's liberation does not come from triumphing over racism or colorism, which she treats as facts of life like the hurricane and floods, like the rabid dog that bites Tea Cake. Her strength is playing the hand she's dealt with her eyes open and without losing heart. Hurston led a complicated, difficult, ultimately lonely life. Like her creator, Janie Starks is sui generis and decades ahead of her time—the antidote to the classic tragic mulatto, forever marginalized, peeking timidly from the pages of our literary canon.

THE TRAGIC MULATTO IN FILM AND TELEVISION

With the advent of motion pictures, the tragic mulatto gained a new lease on life. In her memoir *Bulletproof Diva: Tales of Race, Sex, and Hair,* Lisa Jones, daughter of the black author Amiri Baraka and white Jewish author Hettie Jones, takes on the tragic mulatto: "Vessel of desire and pity, martyr or redeemed heroine, the tragic mulatto has been a Hollywood standard since the silent era." Not all film mulattos were women of black-and-white parentage—some were the American Indian "half-breeds" and "exotic Orientals" discussed in later chapters. "Each decade she resurfaces with a new wardrobe," says Jones, "the postwar 'moral mulattos' (seen in *Pinky* and *Lost Boundaries*), who taught white America compassion for the Negro Problem, gave way to the island half-breeds of the 1950s. Dorothy Dandridge carried the weight of this imagery in movies like *Island in the Sun*."[16]

Perhaps the best-known tragic mulatto in film is Julie, a character in Edna Ferber's novel *Show Boat* (1926), which was made into a hugely successful Broadway musical by Jerome Kern. When Julie discovers she has "negro blood" that renders her marriage to a white man illegal, her husband cuts her hand and sucks her blood to invoke—literally—the one-drop rule. Now he, too, is black. Despite this gallant gesture, their relationship sours, and Julie ends up a lonely alcoholic. Along with multiple New York revivals, *Show Boat* has been produced and reproduced in theaters around the country. Three film versions were made; the most famous, in 1951, featured the white Ava Gardner as Julie.

The white actress Natalie Wood played a French mulatto passer in *Kings Go Forth* (1958) set in World War II. Two soldiers pursue her, but reject her when they learn her father is black. "At the movie's end, one of the soldiers is dead; the other, missing an arm, returns to the mulatto woman. They are comparable, both damaged, and it is implied that they will marry."[17]

More recently, tragic mulattos appeared in *Angel Heart, Mona Lisa,* and *The Crying Game.* "Though now front and center to the narrative," says Jones, "the character remains true to blueprint—a lost child. She no longer seeks to pass, yet she still hasn't found a home."[18]

On television, Most Famous Tragic Mulatto honors go to Mr. Spock of the first *Star Trek* series, in nonstop reruns since the 1960s. The son of a Vulcan father and human mother, Spock is forever trying to negate his human side and gain recognition and acceptance, to pass as purely Vulcan. While his human shipmates repeatedly try to catch him out in acting "human," he repeatedly fends off emotion—including the pain caused by his mixed status.

An endangered species, the tragic mulatto archetype is far from extinct. Although white authors created the stereotype, contemporary white authors of multiracial characters often seem oblivious to the gloomy cultural ghost hovering cloudlike above them, dripping sorrowful subtext onto their pages. Black and multiracial authors tolerate the tragic mulatto with humorous exasperation, an annoying relative who can't be sent packing because—after all—she *is* family.

NOTES

1. The word "mulatto" is properly used, as here, in a historical context only.

2. Judith Berzon, *Neither White nor Black: The Mulatto Character in American Fiction* (New York: New York University Press, 1978), 52.

3. Leslie A. Fiedler, "Come Back to the Raft Ag'in, Huck Honey," in *The Collected Essays of Leslie Fiedler,* Vol. 1 (New York: Stein and Day, 1971), 142–51.

4. Ann Phoenix and Barbara Tizard, *Black, White or Mixed Race? Race and Racism in the Lives of Young People of Mixed Parentage* (London: Routledge, 2002), 27.

5. Phoenix and Tizard, *Black, White or Mixed Race?* 27–28.

6. Berzon, *Neither White nor Black,* 23–24.

7. The mulatto heiress may not have crossed the pond, but she could still be discerned in Britain as late as the 1960s, as shown in Francis Wyndham's comment in his introduction to the first U.S. edition of *Wide Sargasso Sea:* "Miss Rhys knew about the mad Creole heiresses in the early nineteenth century, whose dowries were only an additional burden to them: products of an inbred,

decadent, expatriate society, resented by the recently freed slaves whose super-
stitions they shared, they languished uneasily in the oppressive beauty of their
tropic surroundings, ripe for exploitation" (12).

    8. Leslie A. Fiedler, *Love and Death in the American Novel* (New York: Dell,
1966), 198.

    9. Cynthia L. Nakashima, "An Invisible Monster: The Creation and Denial
of Mixed-Race People in America," in *Racially Mixed People in America,* ed.
Maria P. P. Root (Newbury Park, Calif.: Sage, 1992), 168.

    10. Berzon, *Neither White nor Black*, 24. Berzon credits George M. Fredrick-
son for the research behind these findings, as presented in *The Black Image in the
White Mind: The Debate on Afro-American Character and Destiny, 1817–1914* (New
York: Harper & Row, 1971).

    11. Berzon, *Neither White nor Black,* 56–57. Berzon credits Fredrickson, *The
Black Image*, 118.

    12. Berzon, *Neither White nor Black,* 61.

    13. Berzon, *Neither White nor Black,* 100.

    14. It is tempting to read something into the fact that these two writers, who
themselves occupied a socially marginalized niche, chose that theme.

    15. Henry Louis Gates, afterword to *Their Eyes Were Watching God,* by Zora
Neale Hurston (1937; reprint, New York: HarperCollins, 1998), 199.

    16. Lisa Jones, *Bulletproof Diva: Tales of Race, Sex, and Hair* (New York: Dou-
bleday, 1994), 50–51.

    17. David Pilgrim, "The Tragic Mulatto Myth," Jim Crow Museum of
Racist Memorabilia, Ferris State University, www.ferris.edu/news/jimcrow/
mulatto/ (13 Sep. 2007).

    18. Jones, *Bulletproof Diva*, 51.

FICTIONAL WORKS CITED OR CRITIQUED

Note: An asterisk denotes a work critiqued as well as cited in the chapter.

Jane Austen, *Lady Susan, The Watsons, Sanditon* (1817; reprint, London, U.K.:
Penguin, 1974).*
Charlotte Brontë, *Jane Eyre* (1847; reprint, London, U.K.: Penguin, 1971).*
William Wells Brown, *Clotel, or the President's Daughter* (1853; reprint, New York:
Penguin Classics, 2003).
Willa Cather, *Sapphira and the Slave Girl* (1940; reprint, New York: Vintage,
1975).
Lydia Maria Child, "The Quadroons," in *The Online Archive of Nineteenth-
Century U.S. Women's Writings,* ed. Glynis Carr, www.facstaff.bucknell.edu/gcarr/
19cUSWW/LB/Q.html (14 May 2007).*

James Fenimore Cooper, *The Last of the Mohicans* (1826; reprint, New York: Penguin, 1986).*

Thomas Dixon, *The Clansman: An Historical Romance of the Ku Klux Klan* (1905; reprint, Lexington: University Press of Kentucky, 1970).

Robert Lee Durham, *The Call of the South* (1908; reprint, Whitefish, Mont.: Kessinger, 2007).

Edna Ferber, *Show Boat* (1926; reprint, New York: Grosset & Dunlap, 2007).

Zora Neale Hurston, *Their Eyes Were Watching God* (1937; reprint, New York: HarperCollins, 1998).*

Nella Larsen, *Passing* (1929; reprint, New York: Norton, 2007).

Jean Rhys, *Wide Sargasso Sea* (New York: Popular Library, 1966).*

Tobias Smollett, *The Expedition of Humphrey Clinker* (1771; reprint, New York: Holt, Rinehart & Winston, 1964).*

Gertrude Stein, *Melanctha: Each One as She May* (New York: Grafton, 1909).

Harriet Beecher Stowe, *Uncle Tom's Cabin* (1852; reprint, New York: Signet, 1966).*

William Makepeace Thackeray, *Vanity Fair* (1854; reprint, Ware, Hertfordshire: Wordsworth, 1992).*

Jean Toomer, *Cane* (1923; reprint, New York: Boni & Liveright, 1993).

Mark Twain, *Pudd'nhead Wilson* (1894; reprint, Oxford, U.K.: Oxford University Press, 1992).*

Contemporary YA Fiction
in Black and White

*A*lthough black-white unions are the smallest category of interracial marriages in the United States, more young adult novels, usually by white authors,[1] have been published about characters with one black and one white parent than any other combination. In 1967, the year that saw publication of the first YA novel, S. E. Hinton's *The Outsiders,* the U.S. Supreme Court, in *Loving v. Virginia,* ruled unconstitutional all antimiscegenation laws (most of which were directed at black-white intermarriage). Two decades later, the first YA novel with a multiracial protagonist of black-and-white descent was published.[2] Out of twenty novels discussed in this chapter, in fourteen the protagonist has one white and one black parent.[3] Of these, nine are by white authors, two by mixed-race authors, and three by black authors (that number increases to seven if novels by black authors with minor mixed-race characters are included).

Few black YA authors have built fiction around characters with interracially married parents, especially one white and one black parent. Although black-white interracial unions are growing fast,[4] they are controversial among many American blacks and not much celebrated.[5] The reluctance of black writers to tackle the subject has left a vacuum that has been filled mostly by white authors. In recent years, several multiracial novelists have created authentic multiracial protagonists, but for a full, balanced representation of black-white interracial families and multiracial children in YA fiction, more black writers need to step up to the plate.

WE DON'T KNOW WHAT WE DON'T KNOW

Confronting issues of race in fiction takes courage. But courage alone is not enough; writers must also be culturally competent[6] to succeed in this challenging task. The corpses of books that failed to get it right are littered across the critical landscape. Many are by well-known and highly respected white authors, so why do their efforts often fail?

White writers may reason that "even if I don't know what it is to be black, I *do* know what it is to be white; therefore, at least half of my character's identity and experience will be authentic." Such thinking is fallacious. Many whites *do not know* what it means to be white.

Just as only the wealthy can afford the luxury of not having to think about money, only those in the dominant caste—white—have the luxury of being oblivious to race. A cursory look through any memoir by a person of color confirms that nonwhite people are more aware of race at all times and in all places than white people are—and never more so than in the presence of whites. Even as our society becomes less white overall, whites are still omnipresent. "Thing about white people," a black father tells his son in Jacqueline Woodson's novel *If You Come Softly*, "they know what everybody else is, but they don't know they're white" (134). Black psychologist Beverly Daniel Tatum would agree. "There is a lot of silence about race in White communities, and as a consequence Whites tend to think of racial identity as something that other people have, not something that is salient for them."[7] To create authentic nonwhite characters, white authors must find a way to overcome their racial oblivion. Failure to understand how the caste system operates for those who are not in the dominant caste will render an otherwise well-constructed plot and characters less than credible.

Many white authors also fail to recognize that a person who is defined as part black or part Asian or part American Indian is no longer white. (Observers do not say: "Look at that part-white boy.") Although significant differences exist, multiracial teens have more in common with monoracial nonwhite teens than with monoracial whites.[8] To get a multiracial character right requires *more* work, not less, for monoracial authors, and there are fewer legitimate literary models to follow. We lack a societal consensus on what multiraciality is, what it means. Racial essentialists, many of whom are black, deny that multiraciality exists at all.[9] In the absence of that consensus, how authors portray being mixed rests on

their personal knowledge, experience, and interpretations of racial identity. The impulse to write mixed-race characters may be admirable, but
unless the author is prepared to invest considerable time and attention to
learn about the experience and implications of being multiracial, the effort will fail. Because multiraciality is about crossing lines, blurring caste
boundaries and the consequences of doing so, the author needs to understand how the color line works for all of us. For such insight, writers
can turn to a respectable and growing body of studies by social scientists
and recent memoirs by "multiculti" authors describing in detail what it
is like to grow up with mixed heritage. The hardest step for the author
may be the first: recognizing her own ignorance.

IN SEARCH OF MY MISSING HALF:
A NEW MULTIRACIAL PARADIGM

Since her last hurrah in the early twentieth century, the literary tragic
mulatto has largely retired. When she does make an appearance, she is
usually an ironic presence, commenting from the sidelines on the passing racial scene. Unfortunately, a new stereotype has taken her place,
here titled "In Search of My Missing Half." In this paradigm, the multiracial protagonist is plucked from daily life and sent on a journey to discover the half of his racial and ethnic heritage that, for reasons seldom
satisfactorily explained, has been withheld from him. The story begins at
home where the protagonist—often an only child—lives a happy, or at
least placid, life. Unlike the tragic mulatto, he isn't much affected by his
mixed status. He enjoys good relationships with his parents. They may
be happily married or, if they have split up, the custodial parent may
have remarried, often monoracially. One parent (always representing the
missing heritage) may be deceased. Whatever the nuclear family config-
uration, one parent is estranged from his or her family, so the hero is being raised without access to half his racial/ethnic heritage. The estrangement is total; there is no contact with the parent's siblings, aunts,
cousins. The parents have kept the cause of the rift to themselves, so it
does not disturb the family equilibrium.

Early on, through some plot device, contact is reestablished with
the missing half of the family. Soon, our hero is packed off, usually
alone, to connect with his newly discovered relations and fill in the

"empty half" of his identity. "Missing Half" relatives usually live in the South. We follow the hero to Texas to experience life with his long-lost black relatives or to Appalachia to discover his white relatives. Few if any obstacles stand in the way of this reunion. The grandparents are over-joyed to see the long-lost grandchild. There may be a jealous cousin or two, but problems are soon ironed out. Great-grandma feeds him hearty doses of history and culture while she fills in the blanks in the family tree. When our hero has shaded in the missing part of his heritage, he is ready to go home, where the author leaves him, whole at last.

The stories rarely offer convincing reasons why half the hero's her-itage has been kept secret. The likeliest explanation—opposition to the interracial union—if invoked at all, is easily overcome and, apart from a few nervous references, rarely confronted head on. The complete sever-ance of family ties is treated as normal, not exceptional. After contact is restored, the years of estrangement leave no scars and are forgotten as if they never happened. In Missing Half stories, no one pays much of a price for the long-standing severing of ties.

These stories depict multiraciality as an identity crisis. The mixed-heritage hero can't know who he is until he uncovers his roots. The "problem," the narrative engine that moves the story along, is all about the past—searching for ancestral heritage, mending familial fences. Res-olution equals restoration of family ties. Leaving aside the fact that no evidence exists to suggest that mixed-race youth are deprived of their heritage more than monoracial youth, multiracial identity is not an in-ternal "who am I?" crisis. It is socially and culturally based, originating outside the individual. Being multiracial means having to straddle, to in-tegrate in oneself, what are still seen by society at large as mutually ex-clusive categories of identity. It means being a walking refutation of cherished myths and beliefs about race. Problems mixed-race people ex-perience do not arise from ignorance of their heritage or from the con-dition of being multiracial. Their problems arise from the *social conse-quences of being multiracial*. Missing Half stories end precisely where they ought to begin.

There is something powerfully appealing in the image of the long-sundered family reunited at last. When those sundered sides are black and white, the paradigm may answer a deep desire (on the part of whites, anyway) for racial healing and the unconditional forgiveness that, if it ex-ists anywhere, is most likely to be found within the bosom of the family. The power of this healing archetype may help explain why so many Missing Half narratives are published and often generate more critical praise than they deserve. Add to this the fact that editors and publishers, whose life experience is probably closer to the authors' than to their characters', are unlikely to question the authenticity of work from established, well-respected writers whose previous books have won awards and sold well. The net result is that books continue to be published that present inauthentic mixed-heritage characters in inauthentic situations.

Black, White, Green—What Does It Matter?

Kiara, thirteen, the first-person protagonist of Colby Rodowsky's novel *That Fernhill Summer* (2006), is the only child of Joyce, a white picture book writer and artist who was disowned by her wealthy Baltimore family when she married Warren, a black professor at Columbia University. Rodowsky, white, a well-published author of books for young readers, is a competent writer, but the book is flawed by her inability to tackle the issues of race she has taken on. When Joyce's mother, Zenobia, falls ill, Joyce and Kiara dash to the family estate, where they enjoy a reunion with Joyce's sisters and their families. No hard feelings linger from the years of estrangement. Kiara and her cousins spend the summer as companions to Zenobia who, though difficult, is not, we are told repeatedly, a racist.

After a breezy introduction, the topic of race is abandoned except when the author points out how irrelevant it is to her characters. Not only does Kiara not experience racism, she doesn't anticipate or worry about it. For a mixed-race adolescent whose white mother was permanently disowned for marrying her black father and who is still too traumatized to talk about it fourteen years later, this doesn't wash. In a flashback, Kiara recalls the first and only time she asked why they never visited her mother's home or met anyone in her family: "My mother turned a spooky greenish-white that day. . . . Her eyes were slits and her hands shook as she said, 'Don't ask that, Kiara. Please, don't ask that ever again'" (6). The idea that racism might be responsible for the family rupture first occurs to Kiara on the way to Baltimore, while noticing the difference in skin color between her hand and her mother's. "An idea began to take shape in my head. 'Is it because of me? Because of Dad and me? Why your mother didn't talk to you?'" she asks. "'Maybe—I don't know. I've been back and forth on this for years,'" Joyce answers. "'But it wasn't just that. There was always—something else.'" Kiara persists, "'What kind of something else? . . . why didn't you just stop whatever it was?'" But here Joyce stonewalls her. "'Not now, Kiara,' Mom said, sighing. 'Not now'" (18).

When the issue of racism comes up in connection with the family rift, Rodowsky offers an alternative explanation: Joyce dropped out of art school to marry, angering and disappointing her famous artist father. Midway through the book, Kiara finally comes out and asks Joyce if the family disowned her because she married a black man. Joyce hedges: "'Black, white, green—I told you it wasn't completely to do with that. Black? White? I've never been sure. Maybe. Maybe not. The fact that your father was a black man didn't help, but the real, deep-down reason my parents reacted the way they did was because of the art thing'" (68). This explanation needs an explanation. The author's squeamish discomfort with the topic of race is almost palpable.

Kiara's experience of her racial identity is raised in order to be dismissed. Apart from brief expository flashbacks, we don't see Kiara negotiate her way through daily life, among her peers, at school. If Rodowsky had envisioned such scenes, she might have produced a more authentic character. Her cousin Maddie asks if Kiara likes being half black. "'I don't know—I never think about it,' I said" (161). Stacks of memoirs and studies by social scientists confirm that a thirteen-year-old, brown-skinned girl with a white mother will be noticed. ("Our family vacation photo album actually has a section called Staring White Women," Angela Nissel says.[10]) Kiara tells her cousins the only instance of racial bias she experienced was in second grade when "'a black kid called me an Oreo and a white kid called me a zebra all on the same day.'" Kiara's parents' advice to her was terse: "'They said I am who I am and that's the only thing that matters.'" Kiara asks her cousins, "'Do you like being all white?'" Maddie answers, "'I never think about it.' And for some reason that struck us as incredibly funny" (160). Since Maddie is white, not thinking about race makes sense for her. For Kiara, it conflicts with a world of evidence.

Race is literary kryptonite. Something so fundamental to individual identity has weight—even if we acknowledge that race is a cultural construct only, a deplorable myth. *That Fernhill Summer* is an object lesson in how not to write multiracial characters. The book-jacket illustration reflects the peculiar schizophrenia that often strikes artists tasked with depicting multiracial youth. Against a mustard-colored background, disembodied heads grow straight up from stems positioned along the boughs of a family tree. Some heads wear jolly smiles. Zenobia's head frowns up at Kiara's, perched at the top, wearing a blandly surprised expression.

Like *That Fernhill Summer,* Jane Louise Curry's *The Black Canary* (2005) features a thirteen-year-old, black-white multiracial American protagonist. Curry, who is white, has authored an impressive array of middle-grade and YA fiction, but this work is hampered by its unconvincing hero, James, whose black mother, white father, and grandparents are all musicians. A variation on the Missing Half theme, here James travels back in time to find his missing heritage, a musical ancestry. James is discontented. "You could say, he lived in three different countries— Black, White, and a mixed-up In-Between—even if they were all on the same planet and overlapped at the borders." James's discontent is not race-related; he is resisting his parents' efforts to develop his musical gifts: "He had resented music from the day at age four when he realized that it was music that took his parents away so often and for so long" (21–22).

His family is spending the summer in London while his mother, an opera singer, is on a European tour. In their London flat, James discovers a hole in time that takes him back to Elizabethan England in 1600 when boys were sometimes sold, kidnapped, or otherwise acquired and trained in music and theater arts to perform for high society. This happens to James who, thanks to his good voice, is groomed as a soloist— the Black Canary—for the Children of the Chapel Royal, to perform for the monarch at Whitehall Palace. Through his adventures in 1600, James realizes that music is his true vocation.

Race is part of James's identity only intermittently. Although he is warned that with his dark skin he could be sold into slavery, the prospect doesn't worry him much or remind him of his own enslaved ancestors. The story of a boy of African heritage, kidnapped and forced into work—even if the work is singing for the queen of England—has disquieting overtones of slavery that the author doesn't seem to have heard.

Like Rodowsky, Curry brings race into her story in order to dismiss it. James is grappling with the conundrum of who he is and wants to be, but the problem has nothing to do with race:

> At home he seemed to swing from visible to invisible like a pendulum. On the street, in school, all he wanted to be was invisible, and

usually he was. At home he never was. Everyone in his family, black and white, both sets of grandparents, and all the aunts and uncles and thirteen cousins crowded in on him, seeing themselves in him, expecting him to be like them, think like them, enjoy the same things, do the same things, pulling him one way and then the other. Even Reenie and Phil [his parents]. The truth was, that was just another way of being invisible. *And he didn't want to be.* What he wanted was for them to see *him.* Him himself. More than just a part of themselves. (147–48)

This passage suffers from the schizophrenic waffling that also mars *That Fernhill Summer.* Although multiracial status itself can often be invisible, the mixed-race individual is anything but. "Being a mixed child, you get used to people staring," says Angela Nissel.[11] The experience of being looked at, of standing out, is seminal, the reason Pearl Fuyo Gaskins titled her book of interviews with mixed-race young adults *What Are You?*

Racial Amnesia

Something Terrible Happened (1994), by the white author and storyteller Barbara Ann Porte, covers six years in the life of a girl whose black mother is dying of AIDS. Gillian's white Vietnam-veteran father died of a drug overdose when she was three. The novel is narrated by a friend of Gillian's grandmother, whom we never get to know in her own right (she gives new meaning to "psychic distance") and who addresses the reader directly, speculating on what characters might have thought or intended. Sorrowful multicultural folktales are tucked into the narrative, presumably to demonstrate that tragedy is a kind of lingua franca. By interweaving horrifically tragic tales with Gillian's story, the author seems to suggest that Gillian's troubles are a walk in the park by comparison.

When her mother can no longer look after her, Gillian, ten, is sent to live with her father's brother Henry; Corinne, his wife; and daughter, DeeDee, in Tennessee. Home for Gillian is New York. Even after her mother dies, she hopes to return there, but never does. Uncle Henry's family does not truly become home, either. Gillian locates, but never integrates, her missing half.

Being multiracial is not a problem for Gillian. Her white relatives are free not only of racial bias, but of any concerns about taking in a strange niece whose father was an addict and whose mother is dying of AIDS. As the novel unfolds over about six years, Gillian writes to the narrator about her new life. "'February was definitely not the best time of year for me to start school here. It is Black History Month. Any other time, I might have gone unnoticed. As it is, I'm asked a lot, "What are you?" Can you believe such rudeness?"' (70). The suggestion that her race would go unnoticed at any other time of year is odd. Her response that she is part Gypsy—not true—is also strange. The author seems unconscious of the weight carried by choosing, even as a put-on, to "pass for white."

Although Gillian doesn't seem to worry about bias from any other source, she expects it from Aunt Corinne and behaves coolly toward her. Yet, our narrator makes clear, Aunt Corinne always treats her fairly. Porte describes an exceptionally mild racial incident at DeeDee's summer day camp. When she passes around a snapshot of her cousin Gillian, DeeDee's fellow campers don't believe they are related because Gillian is not white. The counselor agrees with them. Gillian writes to the narrator about what happened: "'The next day, Aunt Corinne went to camp with DeeDee. When she came home, she was still angry. "Next time some child brings a picture of a relative to show, I think the counselor will know enough simply to say 'how nice,'" Aunt Corinne told Uncle Henry.'" Gillian gives her aunt's intervention a negative interpretation. "'I was surprised at first, but then I thought, well sure—Aunt Corinne was only sticking up for DeeDee'" (86). This incident signals readers that Gillian has been wrong about Aunt Corinne—if anyone is biased, it is Gillian herself. The implication that someone in Gillian's circumstances is unreasonable to anticipate being the victim of bias is itself unreasonable. By portraying Gillian as seeing racism where none exists, Porte seems to support the view, popular among some whites, that charges of racism are likely to be overblown.

Carolyn Meyer, a well-regarded and experienced white author, has written outside her culture frequently. Two of her YA novels are Missing Half narratives. Each has a multiracial, black-white protagonist who leaves home on a journey to reunite with long-estranged families and fill in the missing pieces of their heritage. *Denny's Tapes* (1987) is among the first YA novels with a multiracial protagonist. A decade later Meyer published *Jubilee Journey* (1997). Meyer's strength is creating strong and engaging characters.

Denny's Tapes is presented as a journal on cassette tape that Denny, who has just graduated from high school, records on his road trip west. Denny's mother, a white teacher, and his father, a black musician, split up when he was an infant. His mother soon remarried a divorced white doctor, Grant. Stephanie, Grant's daughter from an earlier marriage, moves in with the family, and she and Denny fall in love.[12] When Grant discovers them making out, he tells Denny, "'Get out of here, you black bastard, and don't ever show your face around here again'" (2). This sends Denny off on a road trip to find his father in California and discover his Midwestern roots along the way. Denny has never met anyone from either side of his extended family. His poor-white Nebraska grandparents disowned their daughter for marrying a black man; his black Chicago grandparents, cultured and well-educated, felt their talented musician son married beneath him.

The book chronicles Denny's restoration of ties to both sides of his family. Denny is a convincing seventeen-year-old and good company. He is searching for his dad because "I have to find out who *he* is if I'm ever going to figure out who *I* am, and who I am going to be" (28). Denny is deeply attached to his 1974 Plymouth Duster, Mary, "one of the last of her breed" (87). Much of the novel's minimal suspense hinges on whether Mary, high-maintenance and in need of repair, will make it to California.

Dropping in unannounced on his grandmother in Chicago, Denny receives a warm welcome. Denny's black identity has never been affirmed until now, and it feels empowering. "I had never in my memory been in a place where everybody was black" (48). In a long "eat your Black History vegetables" passage, Denny's snobbish grandmother tells him about Marian Anderson, Paul Robeson (a relative), and great figures of the Harlem Renaissance she has known. She disparages Denny's white relatives. "Your mother's family is, to put it bluntly, redneck. Everyone in our family, every single one, has a college education. . . . That's quite different from a dirt farmer in Nebraska who thinks all niggers should have been kept in slavery" (64). Put off by her snobbery, Denny sticks up for his mother, who is just a dissertation short of a PhD. Staying long enough in Chicago for readers to learn about African American contributions to arts and letters, Denny hits the road again to visit his white grandmother, camping out at night through Iowa and Nebraska. Although the only father he has ever known has just kicked him out of his home, calling him a "black bastard"; and although Denny is a lone, apparently black teenager with an iffy car and little money in a very white, very conservative part of the United States, race seldom crosses his mind. Here is where being a white writer becomes a handicap. Meyer keeps forgetting Denny is black. He makes no choices or decisions based on an awareness of his vulnerability—he doesn't worry about the cops until one stops him for speeding; he doesn't worry about whether his reception by his mom's estranged family will be racist (and boy, is it). He knows he stands out, but he doesn't anticipate or prepare for the consequences.

Arriving at her farm, he finds his grandmother, Grace, nearly bedridden and living with her son Tom, his wife Loreen, and their two kids, all of whom fulfill every white-trash stereotype. They live on junk food in the midst of squalor; Loreen has plastic curlers in her hair. The children pester Denny with racist questions: "'If you're a nigger, how come you're our cousin?'" (142). The message is fairly crammed down the reader's throat. Denny's other grandmother had the mot juste. In Grandma Sutherland, Meyer gives us a more rounded character. Although racist, she is genuinely touched that Denny has come. Denny sets up his tent and stays for a few days, taking Grandma to church and reading the Bible to her. When he leaves, she tells him, "'I've been wrong about a lot of things, Dennis. I'm real sorry'" (179).

Denny has an experience in Colorado apparently inserted in the novel to show that Meyer "gets it," that she knows racism is still a problem in some parts of the country. After Denny meets a white girl named Texas, their plans to camp out on a lake together are interrupted by a couple of drunken white racists. After Texas fends them off with her rifle and blows out their tires, she and Denny go their separate ways. Denny arrives at his father's San Francisco apartment where his roommate invites Denny to stay. He asks if Denny is a musician, too. "I didn't even have to think about it. 'Yes,' I said. 'I'm planning to be.' Suddenly everything clicked into place" (207).

Denny's mother has not equipped him to handle racism. "When I was six years old and ready to start school, I didn't know about being black. She never talked about it" (20). She fails to protect or defend him when his stepfather calls him a "black bastard" and orders him out. When Denny calls home, she is oddly passive. She asks when he is coming home and he reminds her he was kicked out. "'Well, Denny, he was upset, of course, but he's much calmer now. Believe me. He was upset about Stephanie. He says things he doesn't mean when he's upset'" (40). The fear or suspicion that white parents will fail to stand up for their children of color when they are targeted by racism has long been expressed by those who oppose transracial parenting. Whites, the argument runs, lack the experience and skills—acquired by blacks over long years of dealing with white oppression—to protect these children. Denny does not seem to feel betrayed by his mother. Readers may not feel so forgiving.

A sequel to Meyer's historical novel *White Lilacs* (1993), *Jubilee Journey* reflects some of what Meyer learned—and failed to learn—in the decade after *Denny's Tapes* was published. It takes place seventy-five years after *White Lilacs* and is narrated by Emily Rose, thirteen, great-granddaughter of Rose Lee, the earlier novel's protagonist. Emily Rose is one of three children of a European American father and African American mother, Susan, who owns a French restaurant (Café au Lait) in Connecticut. Susan has been estranged from her family in Texas since before her marriage. Her rationale for the rift is that she was embarrassed about getting pregnant before getting married and that later she could not afford to travel to Texas (although the family owns a French restaurant and the children attend private schools). Although her husband's white relatives reacted to the marriage by cutting their son and his family off financially, connections with them have been restored. Why Susan has never introduced her children to their black relatives is murky; but Emily Rose accepts this at face value and in the absence of other text or subtext, so must we, other than to note that this estrangement is essential for the Missing Half narrative to unfold as designed.

Invited to visit their great-grandmother Rose Lee in Texas for Juneteenth, Emily Rose and her brothers, Steven and Robby, are perplexed. What is Juneteenth? Their ignorance allows their mother and the author to educate readers, but at the cost of Susan's character. A woman who has raised her biracial children in total ignorance of her family and culture is not a good role model for celebrating diversity.[13] Susan takes all three kids to Texas by bus for the Juneteenth celebration, leaving dad to hold the fort in Connecticut.

At a rest-stop café, Emily Rose notices that their family is served last. "'How come she's so slow?' I asked, wondering if this was what Dad meant about things being different in the South. 'Because she's a bad waitress,'" is Mom's terse reply. "I wondered if that was the real reason, but Mom seemed so annoyed I decided not to say anything" (17).

Other red flags signal that Emily Rose has not received the grounding needed to survive racism. Steven is dark-skinned, Robby is fair, and she falls in between the two. A white girl who sits next to Emily Rose on the bus is horrified to learn that Steven is her brother: "'You're black,' she said accusingly. 'You didn't say nothing about that. You don't look black. But you don't look white, neither, come to think of it.'" Emily Rose reflects on how her parents have instructed them to answer questions about their racial status: "'*Just tell them you're not half anything, you're double. Tell them you've got twice as much history, twice as much culture, twice as much of everything that counts.*'" When Emily Rose tells the girl she's a "double," Bonnie asks, "'Double what?'" Emily Rose reflects, "Bonnie's attitude kind of shocked me" (20).

Well-informed on some aspects of racism, the characters seem wholly ignorant of others. Steven warns Emily Rose about the prejudice she will encounter in high school. "'You're not black enough for the blacks—I'm not even black enough for some of them. Remember when those guys at Northdale High School beat me up because they said I was acting white? And no matter what, you'll never be white enough for the whites'" (23). Yet later, in a Texas community deeply divided on race lines, Steven ignores warnings from his black relatives, who have lived there all their lives, about the consequences of dating a white girl. He is badly beaten up.

Over the summer, Emily Rose connects with Mother Rose and Brandy, a girl cousin who ridicules her proclaimed "double" identity. "'Maybe up in Connecticut you can say you're double—whatever that means—and you can get away with telling that to those Yankees who believe just about anything. But around here you are black, Emily Rose. *Black* just like everybody else'" (106). Emily Rose and her brothers get an education on the history of the black struggle for civil rights before returning to Connecticut. But Brandy, the novel's most vivid character, says, "'Y'all come down here for what?—a week, ten days? And then you get on the bus and go home, and what have you learned about being a black person here today? Zip! Exactly nothin'! Am I right?'" (251–52). Emily talks her mother into letting her stay on in Dillon for the entire summer. "'Mom,' I said, 'I have to learn what it means to be black. Or I'll never really understand what it means to be me!'" (262). The reader is left wondering why her black mother didn't teach her this years earlier.

The intergenerational bonding in Missing Half stories is mostly emotional padding. Being multiracial is not about searching for your roots; it's about living with those roots in the here and now. And for young adults, it is these peer relationships in the here and now that count most. The novel's strongest scenes, from the bus trip to Emily Rose's arguments with Brandy, are about being multiracial in practice: fighting for the right to define yourself in a world that asserts the right to do it for you. What's next for Emily Rose, after she spends time with her black relatives and learns what it means to be black? Will she be accepted as black by black folks? Will her decision to call herself black, should she make that decision, mean that those in Dillon, Texas, who have two black parents will accept her as black? And if they do accept her as black, will she wonder about the part of herself that is white? Will she feel disloyal to her white father, conveniently offstage in Connecticut? Will this acceptance exact a price?

The Omniracial Mosaic

Although the protagonist of Michael Dorris's *The Window* (1997) is half American Indian, the novel—a prequel to *Yellow Raft in Blue Water* and *Cloud Chamber*—is really a Missing Half story about white-black heritage. (Dorris, who committed suicide in 1997, was of European and mixed-blood Modoc heritage.) Rayona's alcoholic mother, Christine, here serves mainly as a device to move Rayona, eleven, into her father's black-and-white world. Before landing in a detox center, Christine has left Rayona alone for days. They are reunited at the end of the novel. In between, Rayona's black father, an unreliable presence in their lives, takes charge intermittently. He arranges Rayona's informal, unsuccessful foster placement with a well-intentioned, but clueless white family, the Potters. When it fails, she asks for another placement, and this time lands in the home of an elderly black woman, Mrs. Jackson, a retired school teacher. After a prickly start, they get along well until Mrs. Jackson's daughter, who lives out of town, asks for help. Rayona tells Mrs. Jackson to go to her. (An emotionally and physically abandoned eleven-year-old who cheerfully tells the only stable adult in her life, "'Never mind me, go to your daughter; she needs you'" requires a fairly substantial suspension of disbelief.) Out of options, Rayona's father flies her across the country to stay with his mother in Kentucky. On the way, he tells Rayona that although his father, now deceased, was black, his mother and her family are white, of Irish extraction.

As soon as he delivers her, Rayona's father leaves. Again, Rayona proves to be the world's pluckiest foster child: "Okay, I'm not exactly a stranger to being a stranger. All my life I've been the new kid in school, the new tenant in the apartment house, and lately the illegal foster child in two under-the-counter placements. What's weird to me is being a stranger in a place that everybody insists is home" (54).

Nonetheless, Rayona takes to her brand new extended family in a big way. "Suddenly, after being so alone—just Mom and me—it seems as though I'm getting a new relative every five minutes. As far as I'm concerned, there can't be too many." Rayona remembers the social worker asking what color foster family she wanted. "'Black or white?' she had asked me. Little did she suspect I was so rich that the only right answer was 'Both!'" (59). Her grandmother, free of racial bias herself, shields Rayona from racism directed at her in Kentucky. "If she notices the looks we get from some of the salesladies and waitresses, looks that ask what a normal-looking white lady like my grandmother is doing with a different colored kid like me, she never once lets on" (62). Her great-grandmother, the family matriarch, presents Rayona's missing heritage to her, sharing family stories about colorful ancestors, teaching her to make sweet potato pie and pineapple upside-down cake. "'It's your legacy,' she tells me. 'You're my only great-grandchild and this knowledge must not be lost to the world'" (63).

Her family's sterling qualities extend far beyond racial tolerance; they refrain from judging Rayona's troubled mother. Rayona basks in their unconditional love. When they all tell Rayona she is beautiful, "I can't help it, I blush. I know compliments are like gusts of air in Kentucky—one waiting behind every tree—but I'm still not used to receiving them. When I look up, they're all smiling at me" (74).

Rayona knows she would be welcome to stay but she chooses to go back to her mother. Her grandmother and aunt drive her on a road trip to Washington state. At Mount Rushmore, Rayona's bond with her new family is tested by an American Indian, in elaborate regalia, who invites tourists to take his picture for a dollar. He approaches Rayona: "'You're a breed, right? I can spot one a mile away.'" She explains that her mom is Indian. "'I knew it. I've been trying to figure you out, you and the two old white women.'" This does not sit well with Rayona. "'My grandmother and my great-aunt,' I inform him." He thinks he understands. "'Right. Adopted?' 'No. They really are.'" The Indian dismisses this.

"'And you believe them,' he says. 'They've got you fooled.'" Rayona is not even tempted to side with him in the race battle. "He doesn't know anything, this jerk, but he thinks he does" (91).

Early in the novel, Rayona left the Potters and begged her social worker to find her a black family instead. The episode at Mount Rushmore signals that Rayona has embraced her white heritage, through a nonwhite person who tests her by asking her to identify with the race she appears to be instead of as the complex, multiracial person she is. He will accept her if she will reject her white identity. Refusing to do so means she passes the test. With her grandmother and aunt, Rayona drives on to Yellowstone where they watch "Old Faithful" erupt. "Standing between them, I slip one of my hands into one of each of theirs" (94). This classic Missing Half tale is emotionally satisfying, a romance. Rayona is the daughter every parent longs for. She weathers grim family upheavals—alcoholism, poverty, despair, and irresponsible adults—thrives, forgives, and moves on. She holds no grudges, and when abruptly surprised by a new racial and family heritage, quickly and easily embraces it. Though it sounds churlish and Scrooge-like to say so, Rayona is too good to be true.

In *Zane's Trace* (2007), by white author Allan Wolf, the novel in verse meets the coming-of-age road trip with a multiracial twist. Our protagonist is Zane Guesswind and, in a supporting role, the 1969 Barracuda he absconds with. Zane's troubles read like a caricature of the "problem" YA novel—a family history of suicide, substance abuse, mental illness, and epilepsy. He copes by writing obsessively on his bedroom walls with permanent markers and later on the dashboard of the car he is driving to his mother's graveside in Zanesville, Ohio, where he intends to shoot himself with the same heirloom pistol she used to kill herself. Along the way he picks up a hitchhiker, the intriguing Libba, and others, each of whom proves to be a forebear holding a piece of Zane's identity. Collectively, they add up to an American racial mosaic. In an archaeological dig through his genealogy, much of what Zane learns first reveals his ancestors to be an unsavory bunch. But as more family stories are added, their choices appear in a more sympathetic light. His Grandma Katie, black, left her family during the Depression and reinvented herself by passing for white. When her abusive, racist husband discovered she was black, Grandma Katie walked out, leaving him to raise Zane's mother alone. Zane's estranged, alcoholic dad, Stanley, appears to tell the complicated story of his ancestor Bear Breaks the Branch, a Wyandot Indian. Other ancestors pick up the narrative threads until the story is finally told and Zane realizes the gun he is carrying with him is a relic of his complicated family history.

A slave ancestor describes why he passed for white: "'Ha. In the first place, no black man was ever hired to drive a stagecoach. Freight wagons, yes. But not the coaches. Not ever. In the second place, I was hiding out from a white man in Virginia who thought he owned me. And in the third place, there was a little law called the Fugitive Slave Act'" (95). It is rare and refreshing to hear a character defend passing as nothing more nor less than a legitimate survival strategy.

Each character disappears when Zane has made the connection required except for Libba, who proves to be his schizophrenic mother as a teenager. Her companionship helps Zane come to terms with his grief and unsettled feelings about her and to see his ancestry whole rather than in fragments. The novel's simple theme is that racial and generational conflict and pain are resolved in the individual who inherits them. If the one who inherits this legacy can forgive the past, he can achieve harmony and peace retroactively. When Zane arrives at his mother's grave, he finds her tending it. She says: "'You are the seventh generation. The one where all three bloodlines meet. Daddy Sam, Bear Breaks the Branch, and Betty Zane have all reunited in you. . . . The pistol in your hand. Two hundred years ago it failed. But it's still trying. Pull that trigger today, son, and they all die. Three souls claimed by a single bullet'" (165–66). Zane returns home, healed. He envisions his family, including grandparents and parents, in harmonious death: "all of us there—living or dead, crazy or sane, friend or foe, black or white, family or stranger—we all crowd around and add our own names to the twisted, crazy-beautiful family branches" (177).

The appealing image of a warring family brought together in the person of their descendant offers one way to approach racial healing. Once again, however, our multiracial protagonist finds wholeness not by negotiating his way through the here and now, but by reaching into the past. What we do not know at the end of *Zane's Trace* is how the neatly tied-up threads of his ancestry will help Zane move through the world he has decided to live in.

Getting It Right

The multiracial novelist Sundee Tucker Frazier won the John Steptoe Award division of the 2008 Coretta Scott King Award with her first novel, *Brendan Buckley's Universe and Everything In It* (2007). Her first-person protagonist, Brendan, is ten. This middle-grade novel probably won't reach many YA readers. However, within an age-appropriate context, Frazier provides a more nuanced and insightful examination of interracial dynamics than is offered in many YA novels. As a bonus, Frazier is a gifted comic writer. It is worth investigating its exemplary presentation of an interracial family to see what works and why. Brendan is an only child whose white mother, an only child herself, was disowned by her parents for marrying his black father. She won't talk about her family to Brendan, and his father supports her. Thanks to his close relationship with his paternal grandparents, Brendan has not felt a need to fill in the branches of his family tree; but after his grandfather dies, he wonders about his other grandfather. Curious and interested in everything, he keeps a journal: *Brendan Buckley's Book of Big Questions.* His quest to learn about his family leads to bigger questions about race and bias. Refreshingly, his parents are not high-powered professionals, creative geniuses, hugely wealthy, or desperately poor. His father is a police officer; his mother works in a social welfare agency. When Brendan's bike is stolen, the family cannot afford to replace it. But they can more than provide for everyone's needs.

When he's at the mall with his grandmother, Gladys, Brendan comes face to face with his grandfather, Ed DeBose, manning an exhibit for a rock collectors' club. Gladys hustles Brendan away and won't tell him why, but Brendan figures it out and enlists his friend Khalfani's help in tracking down Grandpa Ed. Through their shared passion for rocks and minerals, they become friends, but keep this a secret from the family.

With Tae Kwon Do lessons and talks about racism, his father has tried to prepare him for what to expect as a young black man. When Brendan and Khalfani are bullied by racist white boys, he tells his parents and grandmother about the incident over dinner. "'One of the boys made monkey sounds at me,' I said." They all offer opinions. "Dad sat back with his fist on his hip. His jaw bulged on one side. 'Some white people like to think we're more closely related to monkeys and gorillas than they are.'" Grandma has her own take on it. "'*Humph.*' Gladys crossed her arms. 'Last time I saw an ape, it had thin lips and straight hair.

Looked more like a Caucasian to me.' She looked at Mom. 'No offense.'
'None taken,' Mom said." As a scientist, Brendan tries to make sense of
what happened: "My most recent Big Question came into my mind.
'Why are white people so mean to black people?'" Mom, the only white
person present, speaks up: "'Some white people, honey.'" Brendan's dad
weighs in: "'It starts with the parents. They pass on their attitudes to their
kids—'" Mom can't let this generalization go unchallenged: "'Not all
kids,' she said." Dad is a peacemaker: "'I know, I know. You turned out
all right.' He smiled, but Mom had gotten as straight and stiff as the
toothbrush I didn't use for a week when I wanted to see if I could grow
algae on my teeth" (77).

With humor and insight, Frazier shows how hard it is to manage
dicey questions of race, even among family, and interweaves these lessons with the discoveries made by her young scientist, motivated by the
pure and energetic curiosity of childhood. When his mother catches
Brendan with her father, she forbids Brendan to see him anymore and
tells him that his grandfather opposed her marriage. Brendan has already
noticed that when Ed introduced him at a rock collectors' club meeting, he failed to acknowledge Brendan as his grandson, but he is determined not to lose his grandpa, and they plan a clandestine rock-col-
lecting trip together.

On their trip, Brendan asks, "'Why didn't you want them to get
married?'" After a pause, Ed says, "'I guess I didn't much like the idea.'"
Prompted by Brendan pushing for details, he adds, "'Well, I guess it just
didn't seem right . . . at the time. Races mixing like that.'" Brendan
points out that Grandpa plays chess with a black neighbor every week.
Grandpa says that's different: "'You're too young . . . for all the details. I
just think families should look alike. White people belong with other
white people and black belong with black.'" When Brendan asks if that
is the reason Grandpa wouldn't acknowledge him, "his eyes narrowed. 'I
tried to tell Kate, the children are the ones who suffer.'" Brendan doesn't
buy that. "I leaned against the door with my chin in my hand. I thought
of kids I'd seen suffering on TV—ads that showed children with dirty
faces and their bones poking through their skin, kids who always had
their fingers in their mouths and flies around their eyes. That wasn't me.
'I'm not suffering,' I said. We were silent the rest of the way home"
(165–66).

Brendan comes to understand that while he can explain race scien-
tifically, he can't use science to explain bias. After their outing nearly

ends in Grandpa's death, averted by Brendan's act of heroism, they part. But Grandpa shows up for Brendan's birthday with a gift and apologizes to Mom and Dad. The first step toward healing has been taken.

Although Frazier explores healing a family rift and restoring Brendan's white heritage, this novel differs in important ways from Missing Half narratives. The rift was caused by racism, and Grandpa continues to hold racist views throughout the novel. He has traveled partway to overcoming them, but has a long way to go. Brendan's story takes place at home, while he is interacting with his black relatives, his friends, engaging in normal activities of daily life. Brendan's mother, because of the estrangement from her family, is a bit isolated and defensive. She's the only white person in a family of strong-willed people.

In the tradition of nineteenth-century writers, black and white, who made their mulatto characters intimidating paragons of perfection, many current YA authors portray the parents of their mixed white-and-black protagonists as extremely high achievers. A few authors veer to the other extreme, portraying the parents as social and economic basket cases. Historical and fantasy fiction aside, of the contemporary novels analyzed in this chapter, *only* Frazier's depicts an ordinary working-class family. Eight of the novels feature parents who are successful musicians, filmmakers, novelists, academics, and visual artists; in one, the parents are restaurateurs. In the remaining four novels, the parents are destitute, criminals, alcoholics, and/or drug addicts.

MIXED-RACE CHARACTERS ON THEIR HOME TURF

Madge, seventeen, protagonist of Helen Benedict's *The Opposite of Love* (2007), is the only child of a long-gone black father and white mother, Brandy, an aging delinquent, illegal English immigrant, and petty criminal. (Brandy appears in Benedict's earlier novel *A World Like This* [1990]). Brandy and Madge live a hand-to-mouth existence from which Brandy wanders off at whim. At such times, Madge moves in with her mother's sister, Liz, a legal immigrant. Refreshingly, this is not in any way a Missing Half story.

Irresponsible Brandy is roguishly appealing, and Madge, the narrator, is reasonably persuasive as a multiracial character. Benedict, a white English expat herself, is at her best in depicting Madge's dysfunctional home life and how she copes with living in a community where there are few people of color. During spring break, Aunt Liz sends Madge off to visit her son Bob, a journalist in New York. He is investigating abuses in the city's child welfare system, writing about how the city won't allow decent foster parents to adopt children, preferring to send them "from one horrible home to another" (14).

The account of Madge's home life, school, friends, and romance adds up to an interesting, well-told YA narrative. She is romanced by Gavin, a popular jock at school who tries to push her into sex and is surprised to hear she is a virgin. When he asks probing questions about what it's like "being different," Madge senses something unsavory at work. "'You're saying you think I'm a different species from you. You're saying I'm so different from you that you can't even imagine what it's like to be me'" (105). Gavin first protests, then leaves in a huff. A few days later, a friend of Gavin's approaches Madge and tells her, "'I hear Gavin's been getting a taste of hot chocolate. You gonna gimme some, too?'" (109). Madge hits him, but when Gavin walks by and raises an eyebrow at her, she flees, mortified. Her best friend, Krishna, the only other brown-skinned kid at her school, comforts her and their own romance takes off.

However, the child-welfare story is the intended thematic core (the title is a quote from Elie Wiesel: "The opposite of love is not hate, it's indifference"). This story edges out Madge's personal story halfway through the book. Caught up in Bob's investigations and horrific stories about children returned repeatedly to abusive biological and foster parents, Madge is deeply stirred. She persuades Krishna to help her rescue Timmy, a neglected child she has befriended, and, against Krishna's advice, brings him home with her. Here the story loses its footing.

The overburdened, underfunded child-welfare labyrinth is a big topic for an already busy novel, but having introduced it, Benedict needs to follow through. Instead she disposes of the topic in a remarkably simplistic way. Everyone, including the investigative reporter, buys the explanation that social workers make a practice of snatching children from loving foster homes and placing them in abusive ones for no reason other than irrational cruelty. Even if willing to swallow this analysis, readers may question the suitability of a hard-living, petty-criminal mom who lacks legal status in the United States and is prone to abandon her own child for months at a time, and Madge, an undersupervised high school student, as caregivers for a five-year-old. As a solution for child neglect, this leaves a lot to be desired, too. Eventually Timmy's aunt, an immigrant from the Dominican Republic, tracks Madge down. His mother is dead and she wants him back. Madge brings Timmy to her, but in the end, the aunt decides Timmy is better off with Madge.

Madge is engaging and convincing, but when Brandy's around, it is she who steals the show. Brandy is outraged on learning Madge has kidnapped Timmy: "'You, Madge, the kid—all of you, driving carefully, no accidents, no stopping for a piss, right back to his house. Put him on the doorstep, don't even ring the sodding bell, and skedaddle. And, Madge, if any of your mates spread one word about this, you'll be done for kidnapping and I'll be booted out of the States right on me arse'" (148). Had her advice been followed, this would have been a better book.

Before his renowned fantasy trilogy *His Dark Materials* was published, Philip Pullman wrote a YA novel about a teenager of English and Haitian descent, *The Broken Bridge* (1992). Pullman had already authored a series of acclaimed YA mysteries set in Victorian England. This novel, too, contains mystery elements, but is fundamentally a realistic, and moralistic, exploration of family and identity. The plot is odd, sometimes awkward and disjointed, but the characterization is strong enough to sustain reader interest. It is a Missing Half story turned on its head. The protagonist, Ginny, sixteen, discovers that her heritage, her "missing half" is not what she expected or wanted, but with this comes the realization that her ancestry does not hold the secret to her identity. *That* she finds within herself.

Ginny and her handsome white father live in coastal Wales. Ginny has been told that her mother, who was a black Haitian artist, is dead. She has confused early memories of living somewhere else without her father when she was little. She is already a gifted artist and knows this will be her career. Her world is shaken when her father's son from a prior marriage Ginny knew nothing about, Robert, comes to live with them. This alone would be deeply unsettling, but she also learns that her father has served time in jail, that her parents were never married, and that her mother may be alive. The infrastructure of Ginny's world collapses. Throughout the novel, Ginny's assumptions and beliefs are shaken repeatedly, forcing her to reevaluate everything and everyone she thought she knew. She learns that appearances deceive, that we are accountable only for our own actions, and that the only sane and ethical path through life is to avoid judging others.

Ginny's mixed race is a defining attribute for her, but her primary identity is as an artist, and this never changes. Pullman has a gift for creating strong female characters and a fairly sophisticated understanding of racial identity. Ginny's friend Andy, black, adopted by a white family, is an ally. Each has grown up looking black, but feeling white. Andy describes taking a catering course in Bristol: "'I felt a bloody idiot because these other guys, black guys, they came up to me first day and started talking dialect, patois, you know? Rasta kind a ting, maan? Well, *Duw*, I never felt such a fool in all me life. I couldn't understand a word.'" This is the other side of his experience in the white world. "'Okay, I sound Welsh, but I'm not Welsh. . . . Not African either. I'm just a white kid with a black face, that's what I am. Don't belong anywhere'" (40–41). But he also recognizes an upside to not belonging anywhere. When Ginny tells him she doesn't know where she belongs either, he points out that this can be liberating, that she is "'free to do anything. Like me. I don't know where I belong, so I'm free. No one's got a hold on me'" (41).

When Robert and Ginny, who don't immediately hit it off, take a bus to Chester at their father's suggestion to visit his parents, Ginny asks questions about her early childhood, hoping to add more pieces to her heritage mosaic. One of those questions prompts an agitated, abusive, racist tirade from their grandmother. She calls Ginny's mother a "black whore" and "colored filth" and blames her for the breakup of her son's marriage to Robert's mother.

Desperate, Ginny tracks down her mother at an art gallery opening of works by contemporary Haitian painters. Her mother does not acknowledge her, however. When Ginny asks point blank, "'Is it true or not? Are you my mother?'" her mother's response is, "'You're interested in painting?'" Ginny replies, "'It's the only thing.'" But her mother disagrees: "'Painting isn't the most important thing, but it'll have to do till we find out what is'" (184–85). And those are the last words she speaks to Ginny. The only point on which she is willing, or able, to connect with her daughter is through the gift they share.

The one certainty through all Ginny's life upheavals is her art. Instead of relying on her ancestry to interpret and fill in her missing identity, Ginny uses her identity as an artist to help her interpret her heritage. "'I've seen African sculptures, you know, ritual masks, that kind of thing. They're really strong, really powerful, but I can't . . . relate to them. I

don't know what they mean,'" she tells a friend. "'All that ancestor stuff.
. . . I mean I've got English ancestors too, haven't I? It's no good saying
like my ancestors were African, so I've got to go back to my roots. . . .
It was my English ancestors who sold my African ancestors into slavery.
Where does that leave me? Am I innocent or guilty or what?'" Her
friend tells her she has to learn to live with ambiguity and duality, and
that this heritage is there for her to put in her work: "'You can't go back.
. . . You can only go forward. You can't forget, either. You have to use
everything you know'" (81). And that is what Ginny does.

The novel's title refers to a bridge that Ginny finds intriguing, but
it also suggests the broken human connections that have influenced her
life. Ginny, like so many fictional multiracial protagonists, is searching
for her missing half. But the answers she had hoped to find in her missing ancestry are denied her. To find personal completion, Ginny will
have to do without her family history. Her mother has rejected her; her
grandparents are pathetic racists. Ginny learns that she can't trust her
own assumptions about people, and she can't trust other people's assumptions either—the truth is more nuanced, contradictory, and excul-
patory than she wanted to believe. In the end, who she becomes is in
her own artist's hands.

HISTORICAL FICTION: MULTIRACIAL
HEROES ON THE CUSP OF EMANCIPATION

The experience of black-white multiraciality during slavery is a tough,
bitter subject to fictionalize. The three YA novels discussed here take
place shortly before or after emancipation.

Valuing Whiteness

Send One Angel Down (2000), by white, Canadian-born writer Virginia
Frances Schwartz, was an American Library Association Best Book for
young adults, but also received sharply negative reviews, including one
from *Publishers Weekly,* which found the narrative "unconvincing" and
the dialogue lacking in credibility.[14] Set in the final years of slavery, the
novel, narrated by an orphaned slave named Abram, tells the story of
Eliza, fathered by the slave owner and born to Abram's Aunt Charity.

(Schwartz based her plot on an account of a former slave, Doc Daniel Dowdy, recorded as part of a Works Progress Administration project transcribing oral histories of individuals born into slavery.) The book's name and chapter titles are drawn from traditional slave spirituals.

Under Granny's supervision, Aunt Charity and other young slave women, "breeders," are assigned to bear children destined to add to the owner's pool of slaves. Most are sold away shortly after birth. Abram helps Granny look after the pregnant women and maintain the breeders' cabins. Aunt Charity, a light-skinned mulatto who is eighteen at the start of the novel, is allowed to keep her firstborn child, a blonde and blue-eyed daughter she names Eliza.

Having selected a difficult subject, Schwartz doesn't shy away from it or create special circumstances to cushion her characters from harsh realities. She brings her characters and slavery itself alive, with a fine instinct for what to leave unsaid. The story is moving and powerful, but two elements are troubling. One problem—which Schwartz had nothing to do with—is the book-jacket illustration of Eliza. The plot centers on the clash between Eliza's white appearance and slave reality. The girl in the illustration has African American facial features, hair, and skin color. This kind of snafu is emblematic of a strange inattention by publishers to getting issues of racial identity right. The second problem is that Schwartz does not always make it clear why Eliza attracts more love and admiration from the plantation's slave community than that accorded to other young slaves. It sometimes seems she is suggesting that Eliza's white appearance is what makes her special. Other rationales are offered, but questions remain.

The breeders are relatively well fed, but the other slaves are always hungry. Between running errands for Granny, Abram looks after Eliza, and takes her to the big house where a young nanny, Miss Layotte, cares for the master's two daughters. She admires Eliza. "'Like a promise. Looks as sweet inside as she is outside'" (18). She puts aside food for Eliza, as Abram hoped she would. On Eliza's visits to the big house, her half-sisters play with her. Eliza asks Abram why Abigail can do whatever she wants. "'She's Master's daughter,'" he snarls. Eliza compares her skin color to Abram's and wonders. Her looks are an increasingly dangerous burden. Abigail has questions, too, about Eliza's fair skin and blue eyes that resemble her own. As Abigail begins to suspect the truth, she first bullies Eliza, then rejects her completely.

At age eleven, Abram is sent to pick cotton. Some field hands are nursing mothers who place their babies under nearby trees, so they can nurse and attend to them in their few breaks. During a storm in which the overseers have forbidden the women to go to their babies, the children are drowned in a flash flood. Thereafter, Eliza is ordered to accompany the field hands with babies and look after them while their mothers pick cotton. Eliza is a loving and much-loved nanny. Aunt Charity becomes more attached to Eliza as she loses her other children. One day Abram discovers Charity dressing Eliza in an old dress of Abigail's. "'You dressin' her like a white girl!'" Abram shouts. "'Look at that pale skin of hers,' she pleaded. 'Not dark like ours. She's gonna fry out there if I don't cover her up. Not enough shade for miles around.'" Aunt Charity knows what is in store for Eliza: "'She's gonna have a hard life ahead. We got to make it easy for her, long as we can'" (93).

When Eliza is finally told who her father is, she is horrified and blames her mother. "'Why did you have his babies?'" Charity explains she had no choice. Eliza asks why her mother didn't fight back. "'Cause Master gave me something I wished for—you! . . . He promised I could keep my firstborn. That morning you were born, I laughed and cried for hours, I was so happy. For that one thing he gave me, I obey him'" (115).

When Eliza is grown, her resemblance to her half-sisters is noticed by the young men courting Abigail. "'That's why your daddy is so uncommon rich! . . . He fathers his own slaves!'" (119). The story gets back to the master and Eliza is punished, made to pick cotton instead of looking after the babies in the shade. Her fair skin blisters, and her young charges call to her in vain. When Abram sees a white man looking at her working in the field, "I knew right away he wanted something precious from us. And the only precious thing we had was Eliza" (128).

Soon, the news goes out that Eliza is to be sold. To prevent this, Abram approaches a white abolitionist who buys slaves their freedom. He tells Abram to collect all the money he can; with contributions from slaves and abolitionists they raise $400. Although the original plan goes awry, an abolitionist visiting from New York succeeds in buying her at the auction.

Her purchaser gives Eliza her manumission papers and prepares to leave. She asks, "'But sir . . . what will I do now? Where will I go?'" He isn't much interested: "'There must be some freed slaves living in town.'" He heads off. "'Go there. Get a job'" (150). Aunt Charity runs after him and tells him Eliza is a trained nanny; she begs him to take Eliza with him to New York because she will be killed or enslaved again if she stays. Reluctantly, he is talked into employing her. The novel ends as Eliza, now fifteen, leaves her family and goes to New York.

The abolitionist's indifference to Eliza's future seems harsh. Schwartz may have made him unsympathetic so that instead of owing her freedom to a white stranger's philanthropy, Eliza owes it to Abram's efforts to raise money, the sacrifices made by the slaves to buy her freedom, and Aunt Charity's powers of persuasion.[15]

Eliza is beloved for reasons beyond her white appearance. She is like a sister to Abram; she is the only child her mother is allowed to raise; the babies are attached to her and their mothers are grateful for her care of them. Miss Layotte is attracted to Abram, who returns her feelings; she takes pleasure in helping Eliza for his sake. Nonetheless, Eliza looks white, and it's not entirely clear if her part-white status affects how other slaves see her.

Abram's statement that "the only precious thing we had was Eliza" is poorly chosen. It is possible to read into this book that Eliza is just a tragic mulatto served up for young readers. One factor contributing to this impression is the decision to have Abram narrate the story. We see Eliza only from outside, as an object of Abram's and others' attention. Yet while this decision may weaken the portrait of Eliza, centering the story in Abram also keeps the focus on slavery itself and his experience of it. While Eliza is the thematic focus, most of the incidents, the descriptions of daily life, don't concern her at all. The bulk of the novel is Abram's life as a slave. We know he is freed only because the epilogue tells us. For this element, the clear and powerful vision of a life lived in slavery, we might want to give Schwartz a pass on Eliza, and the benefit of the doubt.

Refusing to Pass: A Test of Character

The mixed-race Wescott family struggles to keep up with a wagon train bound for California in Diane Lee Wilson's *Black Storm Comin'* (2005), set in 1860. When his father abandons the family, taking their only horse, Colton, our first-person protagonist, must lead them to Sacramento. The legal status of Colton's mother, daughter of a slave and a white man, is unclear, and therefore so is that of her children. (In her afterword, the author notes that in California territory in 1860 one could legally claim a black person as a runaway slave.) They have chosen to go to Sacramento because Mrs. Wescott's sister lives there; they are bringing manumission papers to her. The early chapters, in which a terrified Colton rises to the challenge, making mistakes and learning from them, are masterfully written. Colton's voice is pitch perfect and his story compelling. Wilson, who is white, vividly portrays the hardships of wagon-train life and the brutal, grinding racism the family must swallow in order to survive. When Colton catches sight of a Pony Express rider on the trail, he vows to become one himself. Here, the story wobbles on its realistic axis. Simply getting his family to Sacramento would be heroic enough, the challenges more than adequate for an exciting story. But through an overelaborate plot twist, Colton becomes a Pony Express rider, which requires him to pass for white, and helps to ensure Union victory in the imminent Civil War by thwarting a scheme to aid the Confederacy.

With his mother recovering from childbirth, the only help Colton gets is from his two little sisters. He accepts the status quo stoically, observing that "the dipper was never extended when our bucket mysteriously turned to salt water overnight, and some mornings when the other wagons were headed toward the horizon, we were still tugging on our oxen, trying to get 'em hitched" (13–14). Colton's understated account of the family's treatment as they move away from human settlements into the Utah desert is chilling. When the baby dies, Colton digs a grave and buries him. The only person who has shown kindness to the family brings them steaks, saying someone on the train had butchered a sickly ox. The next morning, Colton realizes the oxen slaughtered were his family's own. The two that are left can't pull their heavy wagon.

Abandoned by the wagon train, the family struggles on to a town where a kindly woman doctor nurses his mother back to health. Along the way Colton learns lessons about racism and skin color. "'That your own slave? You're kinda young, ain't ya?'" a man at a relay station asks. Colton says it's his sister Althea. The man takes a closer look and warns Colton, "'You better not be tryin' to pass yourself off as a white boy, or you're gonna find yourself strung up one of these days. Not everyone's as tolerable as I am'" (54).

Colton's mother has told him that he could pass for white. "'People are gonna look at you and they're gonna look at your sisters and they're gonna treat you different from one another. Different from me, too. . . . They're gonna look at your light skin, Colton, and welcome you into their houses, and they're gonna look at your sisters and their dark faces and tell 'em to wait outside'" (62). His skin color will give him opportunities. "'I'm telling you now, Colton, it's all right with me, whichever you choose. Even if it's your pa's world'" (63).

Knowing he has her blessing if he chooses to renounce his ancestry by becoming a Pony Express rider torments Colton. The melodramatic events of the last third of the book pivot on the issue of whether Colton will choose the easier, "safe" route of passing for white or own up to being colored. Contemporary ideas of race, in which choosing to "pass as white" is seen as contemptible, dictate that Colton resist the temptation to accept his mother's offer. After initially choosing to pass, he reveals himself as colored, risking death to do so.

Colton finds passing a heavy, dangerous burden as he carries the mail between posts. Wilson turns Colton's passing into a morality play—does he have the guts, is he manly enough, to declare himself colored? Hiding out from possible exposure by someone who has seen through his white "disguise," he agonizes over his decision: "I took my meals in the kitchen along with the other hands so no one in the dining hall would have excuse to take notice of me. The food looked the same, but my cowardice sure made it taste different" (176). This lament over his "cowardice" is more than slightly absurd. After all, slavery is legal, Colton has no papers stating that he is free, there is a slave catcher in the vicinity, and he is alone in a town in which he has reason to believe more than one white person would happily see him sold or strung up.

When Colton returns to his family, Ma accepts his choice to pass, but Colton is not satisfied. "I waited for her to say she was proud of me just the way I was, no matter what I did or didn't tell people, no matter where I slept. . . . Trouble was, I wasn't proud of me" (209–10). Braving a horrific mountain snowstorm, Colton foils a plot to blow up forts and assassinate Lincoln, and delivers his aunt's manumission papers to her. But only by saving the life of a man who had threatened to expose him as colored does Colton regain his self-respect. As the novel ends, he reviews lessons learned. "There was one thing I believed in, though. And that was, looking at just the outside of a man is no way to measure his inside. Oh, and one other thing. You can't run from who you are" (291). *Black Storm Comin'* presents the choice of whether to pass as white as a "be true to yourself" test of character.

"Passing" is among the most emotionally weighted terms in the black-white vocabulary of race, embodying the idea that individuals are trying to acquire race privilege to which they are not entitled, or equally, that individuals are renouncing their true heritage instead of taking pride in it. This view places a burden on the mixed-race person whose race is not instantly obvious to observers to declare it, says Maria P. P. Root, noting that the term "passing" is premised on the idea that racial categories are real, impermeable, and objectively determinable. She suggests that such terms "should be reexamined for their connotations and bias against multiracial persons and assignment of ethnic identity."[16]

Blood Is Thicker than Water, but Race Is Thicker than Blood

The Land (2001), the only winner of the Coretta Scott King Award with a multiracial protagonist and a prequel to *Roll of Thunder, Hear My Cry* (1976), is the linchpin of Mildred Taylor's fictional exploration of her family history. Its hero, Paul-Edward, is based on Taylor's great-grandfather, son of a white plantation owner and a black woman who was his slave until emancipation and thereafter his servant and life companion. The novel chronicles Paul's journey from a protected childhood to adult independence and maturity. *The Land* is a mythic tale, a moral fable. Taylor's gift is storytelling that transcends incident to capture a greater truth. Her characters and plots, although factually based, are larger than life. The book's flaws are those belonging to big stories. Good and evil are not nuanced. Some critics have complained that Paul is too good to be true. There is certainly a Dickensian dimension to many of the characters. The plucky Perry family belongs next door to the Cratchits.

The book has two main sections. "Childhood" presents what Paul has inherited from his parents. Here he learns the lessons that will shape him as an adult. Paul develops his gift for training and racing horses, indulges his intellectual curiosity, and learns a trade. Harsh experience teaches him that he must control his hot temper and rebellious streak. He forms his life goal of acquiring land of his own. The second section, "Manhood," is shaped like a fairy tale: by carrying out a series of formidable tasks, the hero earns the hand of the princess and the keys to the kingdom. Paul's is a hero's journey, but with a difference. His trials derive from slavery and its legacy, where the brutality of the lesson overwhelms any benefit or victory achieved. Slavery is never a blessing in disguise. Consequently, a tragic sense of loss and waste hovers over the events of the story.

Parallel to Paul's transformation from child to man is his evolution from white to black. At the outset, Paul is dependent on the connection to whiteness. As he matures, he realizes that this is an illusion; he will never be white. To reach his goals he must embrace his black identity; by placing his trust in it, he succeeds. Although Paul's goal is to divest himself of the whiteness that stands in the way of achieving his full human potential, there is nothing essentialist in Taylor's presentation of race. There doesn't need to be—she knows that culture can be just as powerful and destructive as any inherent vice or virtue ascribed to a biological racial identity.

The opening words state the theme: "I loved my daddy. I loved my brothers, too. But in the end it was Mitchell Thomas and I who were most like brothers, with a bond that couldn't be broken" (3). Paul's white father and brothers stand on one side, his black companion Mitchell Thomas—first adversary, then defender and supporter—on the other. In this world, blood may be thicker than water, but race is thicker than blood.

Paul and his sister, Cassie, live with their mother in a house on the plantation. Their father acknowledges them as his and raises them with his three white sons; he teaches them to read. Loving and affectionate, he treats Paul "almost as if I were white" (12). Mitchell Thomas, whose father serves Paul's father, is resentful of Paul's status and scornful of his naïveté. Although they come to a wary understanding, Mitchell does not trust him until Paul takes the blame, in front of both their fathers, for something Mitchell did. Paul knows any punishment he receives will be less severe than that meted out to Mitchell. By protecting Mitchell at his own expense, Paul takes the first steps toward discarding the mantle of white privilege that has protected him.

As he matures, Paul begins to see where the color line is drawn; his father can openly acknowledge him up to that line, but not cross it. And it hurts. His brother Hammond tells Paul it isn't easy having a brother who is black, either. It helps Paul to see Hammond's side, but their situations are not equivalent. "'When I go places with our daddy, he doesn't say, 'This is my son Paul.' He doesn't own up to me outside of this place, even though everybody knows I'm his. He makes different rules for his white children and his colored children'" (56).

Cassie moves to Atlanta and marries. On a visit home, she tells Paul it has been difficult for her, too, venturing, for the first and only time in the novel, into classic tragic mulatto territory. The family she was sent to stay with found her too white. Colored people were rude; whites who misread her color were worse. "'It was like they had contaminated themselves by treating me the same as one of them. I was trapped there, Paul, between two worlds, a white one and a black one, and neither one accepting me. I even passed a few times—'" Paul is horrified. *"You what?"* he exclaims. "'Yes, that's right, I did it!'" she tells him. "'And you know why? Just so I could feel good about myself again! Just so somebody would be accepting of me. I'd walk into stores or in the white part of the city and folks would treat me with respect'" (63–64). This passage is jarring, included perhaps to appease modern readers. Cassie treats her decision to pass as a momentary, shameful—if understandable—impulse, a social solecism. That, along with Paul's scandalized reaction, is an anachronism. It's a rare misstep. Taylor usually makes clear that in the 1880s, regardless of intent, it was very dangerous for a colored person to allow a white person to believe he was white. That is why the first thing Paul does on meeting a white person is to make his own colored status known. The one time Paul passes for white, he does so because it is the only way to keep white men from assaulting, maybe killing, Mitchell. By passing, Cassie was risking reprisals by whites, at a time when she was living in a strange city without the protection of family or friends. The risk she was running wasn't ethical—that would imply she could derive some benefit or harm someone else by passing. The risk was to her personal safety. This passage suggests that Cassie's minor episode of passing was not dangerous, but a bit dishonorable. Paul's response "'*You what?*'" and her shamefaced excuses, shout "twentieth century." A cry of "What possessed you to take such a big a risk?" would have been a far more realistic reaction.

Paul's final lesson is delivered by his brother Robert, who betrays him when Paul needs his support. The aftermath of a confrontation between Paul and his brother's white friends from school leads to Paul's public humiliation. His father makes him strip naked, then whips him in front of the white boys and their angry father. Later, his father explains his actions to Paul as preemptive punishment, to prevent other whites from going after him. He warns Paul that the country belongs to white men and that forgetting this could cost him his life.

"Manhood" finds Paul and Mitchell supporting themselves by working in lumber camps under harsh conditions and white control. When Paul's white appearance brings dangerous attention from whites, they split up. Wherever he goes, Paul's first act is to identify himself to whites as colored. It is a calculation he cannot afford to forget. If he lets them treat him as an equal and they later discover he is not white, he will be made to pay for their embarrassment. The decision to pass or not has nothing to do with honor or rectitude, although sometimes Taylor shades it that way for modern sensibilities. In this world, multiraciality does not exist, but race infuses every human encounter. Paul approaches the white owner of land he hopes to buy and finds him with a colored workman. He introduces himself as a prospective purchaser and adds, "'Seeing that I'm a man of color, it might be difficult for me to get a bank loan to buy a parcel.'" When he has done this: "The workman looked at me now and met my eyes" (223).

Paul lays his plans to acquire land patiently, knowing they will take years to carry out. He finds an ally in Sam Perry, a strong black man of sterling integrity and wisdom, and his family. When Paul first visits the Perrys, Sam's wife, Rachel, snubs him because she sees him as white. Her daughter, Carolyn, explains that the cause is her mother's bitter experiences during slavery. Later, Rachel apologizes to Paul, who accepts Rachel's snubs, because "I saw her pride and felt her pain" (242). Her anti-white bias is pardonable because it derives from the abuses of slavery; whites' anti-black bias is unpardonable because it is the social and political infrastructure that keeps blacks subordinate.

While Paul's practical goal is to own land, his spiritual goal is to acquire freedom from white domination, to assert power over his own life and future. He achieves this with the help of loyal black friends, including the Perry family and Mitchell Thomas, who marries Carolyn Perry and becomes a partner in Paul's venture. After Mitchell is murdered by a white racist, Carolyn insists on taking his place, and in the end, she and Paul marry.

Like the town of Dawson's Landing in *Pudd'nhead Wilson,* everyone in Paul's world is dehumanized or victimized by slavery and its aftermath. To achieve full personhood, Paul must found his sense of self and community on his black identity and culture. Whites cheat him; bankers refuse to finance his purchase of land. To achieve his dream, he needs the money Cassie sends him, the proceeds from the sale of their mother's home. Cassie tells him their mother purchased it from their father with her own money. There is no interdependence between the races, no mutual understanding, no trust. There is no hope that things will improve—the gulf is impassable. Only one element in *The Land* points in another direction. The relationship between Paul's parents hovers over the novel—an unfathomable, poignant love story that feels as if it comes from some alternate universe. Taylor brings insight and empathy to her depiction of this mysterious relationship and how Paul makes sense of it. "What I know is that my daddy took care of my sister and me, and my mama stayed with him after her freedom came because she chose to stay with him. Now, some folks had looked down on them for being together, but I didn't live my daddy's and my mama's lives, and I've got no right to judge" (368).

MIXED RACE AS METAPHOR

Some writers have made multiraciality itself a lens through which to interpret other kinds of experience. No one does this better than the black author Jacqueline Woodson. Her works are spare; the sentences have a finely chiseled, yet limpid clarity. In *The House You Pass on the Way* (1997), Woodson relates the social marginalization attached to race to another kind of marginalized status: homosexual orientation. Staggerlee, twelve, is the daughter of a white mother and a black father whose own parents, musical celebrities and civil rights activists, died in a bombing in 1969. The family lives in a small town. They are affluent and happy, but owing to the rift caused by their interracial marriage, are estranged from their black relatives. After a death in the family causes a thaw in family relations, Tyler, an adopted cousin Staggerlee's age, is sent to spend the summer with her family.

Named Evangeline by her parents, Staggerlee has renamed herself after a song her grandparents used to perform: "It was about someone struggling to break out of all the gates life had built up around them. She was nine when the words started making sense. Nine when she changed her name." The Staggerlee of the song goes to Heaven, but is sent to Hell by St. Peter. When he gets there, "the Devil turned his back / Staggerlee said, 'There ain't no right or wrong. There ain't no white or black. . . .'" (33–34).

Staggerlee realizes that she is attracted to girls. She carries a bittersweet memory of kissing a girl in sixth grade who later disowned her and the experience. Tyler's arrival is the catalyst for Staggerlee's evolution into adulthood. She, too, has renamed herself—Trout—and is openly lesbian. Staggerlee falls in love with Trout and they have an enchanted summer.

"'Look at you—you could pass for white,'" Trout says. This upsets Staggerlee: "At school she had been called 'Light-bright.' She hated it, the way the word sounded so much like a swear, how girls' mouths curved so nastily when they screamed it. When she was younger, she hated how light she was, how people stared and called her beautiful or ugly just because of it." Trout picks up on Staggerlee's feelings and by her response suggests the connection between race and sexual orientation: "'Yeah,' Trout said. 'I hear that.' She turned away from Staggerlee and watched the passing land for a while, squinting against the dust. 'That's all anybody is—themselves. People all the time wanting to change that'" (58–59).

Along with a more established sexual identity, Trout has a firmer grasp of its social consequences. Trout tells her why she chose the name: "'Something about the way they fought. I guess, without even knowing it, I wanted to learn how to fight like that.'" But, Trout warns, "'You give yourself a name, you have to live up to it.'" Staggerlee asks Trout if she feels she has to fight. "'Yeah,'" she says. "'All the time'" (67).

After Trout goes home, she reverts to Tyler, once again allowing others to define her. She repudiates her lesbian orientation and acquires a boyfriend. Staggerlee feels hurt by this betrayal, but recognizes that Trout has helped her accept who she is and reach out socially to others. Unlike Trout, Staggerlee keeps her chosen name.

Woodson compares the no-man's-land of multiraciality, with its social and psychological costs and benefits, to homosexuality, and in doing so makes a subtle point. Because we view race as something we are born with, not a choice we make, the parallel reinforces the fact that sexual orientation is not a choice either, simply the biological hand we are dealt.

A major theme in Woodson's fiction is the contrast between those who have the courage to cross social boundaries and those who don't. Staggerlee's sympathetically drawn parents have crossed the color line and paid the price in ostracism. But they have gotten something in return: a loving family. The survival strategies her mixed-race family has acquired in part give Staggerlee the strength to affirm her sexual orientation. She has learned that labels prevent us from seeing what they are attached to: "Mama was more than 'white.' She was Mama, quiet and easygoing. She kept to herself. When she smiled, her whole face brightened, and tiny dimples showed at the edge of her lips. Why was *white* the word that hung on people's lips?" (6).

The analogy between multiraciality and sexual orientation goes only so far. Her family is more accepting in general than Trout's, but Staggerlee is uncertain about how far she can trust her parents to embrace her as she is. Perhaps they will accept her orientation, but will they celebrate it? She remembers the kiss in sixth grade: "Staggerlee had run home from that afternoon in the cornflowers with Hazel bursting to tell someone. But as she got closer to the house, she slowed down. Somehow she knew there was no one—no one who would say, 'That's wonderful that someone made you so happy'" (83).

A multiracial character plays a minor, but key role in Woodson's *If You Come Softly* (1998) and its sequel *Behind You* (2004). The first book chronicles a doomed romance. Jeremiah—known as Miah—black, and Ellie, white, both from affluent professional families, meet when Miah is sent to Ellie's elite prep school. They believe they can transcend the racial divide, but at the end of the first novel, after seeing Ellie home to her white neighborhood, Miah, absorbed in love and dreams, fails to register a call to stop as he runs through Central Park. Taken for a criminal, he is shot and killed.

Miah's best friend, Carlton, with a white mother and black father, supports Miah, who asks him what it is like to have one black and one white parent. "'My dad's a good man. My moms is a good woman. It's weird sometimes—you know—like when we go out west to visit her family. They're so . . . so stiff around us—they're not like my mama. You know how she is—she's cool. I don't feel like they're my people—I never really did even though I know they are. . . .'" Carlton has trouble putting it into words: "'Sometimes people stare when me and my moms and dad are together, like they're trying to figure it all out or something. Black people and white people. And sometimes they kind of look at us like, 'Oh, I get it—it's an interracial thing.' You know. Like that. I think Colette [Carlton's older sister] went to England to get away from it all'"

(86–87). Listening to Miah talk about Ellie, Carlton says, "'Sounds like love, man.'" Miah is not sure he is ready to go that far: "'But she's *white*.'" And Carlton reminds him, "'Hello, Miah. Look who you talking to, man. It happens. And you know what? It ain't the worst thing in the world'" (89). But for Miah, it is the worst thing in the world.

Without Carlton, this story would be wholly weighted against the possibility of an interracial future. Carlton's parents may not get along terribly well, but Miah's own monoracial parents are totally estranged. Yet Carlton's comments on his extended family make clear that in the long run a family does not stop at—and is always more complicated than—one young couple.

The sequel *Behind You* is less a novel than an elegant postscript. Miah drifts through the afterlife, watching those left behind take hesitant steps into life without him. We learn that Carlton is gay, his marginal sexual orientation intersecting with his interracial family's status. Through his own sense of isolation, Carlton intuits something of what his mother might be feeling. He stands outside, looking in the window of his home: "My mother was inside and she was probably reading on the couch. A romance novel. She was probably reading about a woman who fell in love with a man and lived happily ever after. The books with the shiny gold letters on them. Always white women. My mother's white and I wonder if she sees some part of herself in those books—wonder if she makes wishes" (31). Does his mother, too, feel marginal? Does she fantasize about living life in a monoracial, mainstream family?

Woodson draws clear parallels between multiraciality and homosexual orientation, but characters such as Ellie's racist lesbian sister convey her view that marginalized status itself does not lead to tolerance or understanding for other kinds of marginalization. In a 2006 interview, Woodson said, "People can have a consciousness about one thing, like queerness, but will not have a sense about race. I think you can be homophobic and fighting against racism. And I think you can be queer and completely racist. I think people have the sense that if you're marginalized in one way you're going to understand the margins of all people. Again and again I've seen that that is not true."[17] Woodson's work suggests that belonging to a victimized group does not in itself confer freedom from bias. And the only way to achieve that is to consciously choose tolerance.

INSIDE OUT AND UPSIDE DOWN

Naughts & Crosses, the first volume of the trilogy of that name by the black English author Malorie Blackman, picked up multiple awards and generated a lot of buzz in 2001. The first volume was published in Great Britain to critical acclaim and strong sales, but it took years for Blackman to find a publisher in the United States, where the first book was finally published in 2005.

Blackman's simple but brilliant concept reverses the world of binary racial categories: brown-skinned people ("Crosses") are the dominant caste, light-skinned people ("naughts") the underclass. Reviewers compared Blackman's world to South Africa during Apartheid,[18] but that comparison fails since, unlike South Africa, Blackman's world has no third "colored" caste. With just two castes, what her world truly resembles is the United States at the end of the Jim Crow era. Power still lies firmly in the hands of the crosses, but pressures for change are growing. Blackman is masterful at demonstrating how institutionalized racism corrodes and dehumanizes everyone. She attends to the big picture of laws and societal infrastructure and to the details of how they affect individuals. In this kind of world, the tragic mulatto is a given.

The first volume, *Naughts & Crosses,* tells the story of Callum, a naught, and Sephy, a cross. Callum's father struggles to support his wife and children. Sephy's father is a government minister; his wife, Jasmine, is a submissive, bitter alcoholic. Raised together—Callum's mother, Meggie, was Sephy's nanny—the two become close when her school is desegregated and Callum, bright and ambitious, is among the first naughts to be admitted. They fall in love, but the racial divide can be bridged only intermittently. Callum's father, brother, and eventually Callum himself, are drawn into the Liberation Militia (LM), a naught liberation movement determined to end the caste system by any means available. When she is kidnapped by the LM, Sephy and Callum have a brief tryst, and she becomes pregnant before escaping. Callum himself is caught, arrested, tried, and convicted as a terrorist. The book ends with his execution.

The second book, *Knife Edge* (2004), follows Sephy's life as the single mother of a mixed-race daughter. She has thrown in her lot with the naughts and lives with Meggie. A melodramatic plotline involves the delivery to Sephy of a phony letter written to her by Callum just before his execution. It says he hated her and saw their daughter's conception as a rape, payback for cross oppression. (Readers are aware that he was forced to write it under duress.) When she reads the letter, Sephy despairs, her hopes for racial healing dashed. Fearing that her mixed-race daughter faces an intolerable future, she tries to kill her, but is stopped by Meggie in time.

In the final installment, *Checkmate* (2006), Callie Rose is a teenager, estranged from her mother through the machinations of Callum's older brother, Jude, who grooms Callie Rose to carry out a major act of terrorism. Again the phony letter has surfaced. This time Jude has presented it to Callie Rose, and it has caused a deep rift between mother and daughter. Jasmine, dying of cancer, finds Jude, holds him hostage at gunpoint, and kills him and herself with the bomb that was intended to assassinate her ex-husband. Mother and daughter are reconciled when Sephy shows Callie Rose a genuine letter from Callum, expressing his love for them.

While the first book is taut and gripping, the other two suffer from wildly melodramatic plotlines. The subplot in which first Sephy and then Callie Rose are misled by Callum's phony letter makes the conflict between mother and daughter, and the choices each makes, the result of an artificial misunderstanding, rather than the mundane but deadly consequences of living under the racist caste system Blackman has so carefully, and believably, set in place.

The storyline may be unsubtle, but Blackman's portrayal of institutionalized racism is insightful, ironic, and detailed. She demonstrates how the worst effects of racism may not be the big injustices, but rather the daily, incremental instances of bias, individually insignificant but incessant and cumulative, that wear people down and waste lives. Blackman understands the power of naming. Early on, Callum muses on the name given to his race: "Even the word was negative. Nothing. Nil. Zero. Nonentities. It wasn't a name we'd chosen for ourselves. It was a name we'd been given" (66). In newspapers and some narration, "Cross" is capitalized, "naught" lowercased. But in Sephy's narration, both are capitalized. Jude refers to crosses as "daggers." Meggie, raised to defer to crosses, follows the official spellings.

Repeatedly, Blackman illustrates without comment how we use language, spoken and written, to dehumanize one another. The term "blanker," highly offensive to naughts, is hurled as an epithet of last resort. In *Knife Edge*, Sephy's sister takes her to lunch at an expensive, trendy London restaurant. "With a start, I noticed they had something called Blanker's Delight." This proves to be a dessert. "Charming! I looked around the restaurant. No Naughts eating and only one serving. I wondered how he felt when somebody ordered Blanker's Delight" (285).[19]

Blackman gives us very few mixed-race characters; those that exist are tragic mulattos. In the first volume, Mr. Jason, a teacher at the desegregated school Callum attends, singles him out for ridicule and abuse. Perplexed, he talks it over with a sympathetic teacher, Mrs. Paxton, who tells him that Mr. Jason can't be biased against naughts because his own mother was a naught. When Mr. Jason has pushed him once too often, Callum asks, "'Why d'you hate me so much?' My words tumbled out in angry frustration. 'If anything you should be on my side.'" Jason pretends not to understand: "'What're you talking about, boy?'" When Callum says, "'You're half-naught, so I don't understand—'" he is unprepared for the reaction he gets: "Mr. Jason's bag dropped to the floor, forgotten. He gripped my shoulders and started shaking me. 'Who told you that—that lie?'" Callum backs off, not wanting to implicate Mrs. Paxton. "Mr. Jason released me as suddenly as he'd grabbed me. 'How dare you? How dare you? Who else have you said this to?'" Callum swears he has told no one. Mr. Jason tells him: "'Every time I look at you, I thank God I'm not one of you. D'you hear me? I thank God.'" He leaves Callum deeply shaken: "'But at least that question was answered'" (133–34). Interestingly, Mrs. Paxton has misread Mr. Jason's feelings about Callum, assuming he would value their commonality. Instead, he sees Callum as a threat, someone who can expose him as "passing for Cross."

In the first book, Jude tells Callum that their ancestry includes cross blood, but Blackman does not make anything of it. There is no interracial underclass here. The few mixed-race characters tend to be clichés. After giving birth, Sephy sees her daughter as a harbinger of hope. "You're a trailblazer. Setting your own colour, your own look." She speculates that in the future, people will look like Callie Rose. "Something to live on whilst the rest of us die out, obsolete in our ignorance and hatred." But the immediate future is bleaker. "You have to live in a world divided into Naughts and Crosses. A world where you will be biologically both and socially neither. Mixed race. Dual heritage. Labels to be attached. Tags to be discarded" (37–38).

From across the racial divide, Meggie, too, looks on Callie Rose with hope and worry. "She's neither naught nor Cross. And in a world desperate to pigeon-hole and categorize and stereotype, she may feel forced to come down on one side or another." Meggie reflects on what this could mean. "Maybe that's what we all need—to be mixed and shaken and stirred as vigorously as possible until 'naught' and 'Cross' as labels become meaningless" (217–18).

The older Callie Rose is a disappointing construct, a fairly by-the-numbers tragic mulatto to the end. Blackman, so adept at painting her world, at piecing together the riveting racial jail that imprisons her characters, is less skilled at bringing those characters to life. Callie Rose mouths banalities about being caught between two worlds: "I was biologically in the middle. I had yet to work out my place socially. What did Naughts see when they looked at me—a light-skinned Cross? What did Crosses see when they looked at me—a dark-skinned Naught? I had to stop seeing myself through anyone's eyes but my own" (430).

Despite some deficiencies, Blackman's trilogy is required reading for white authors looking to discard their racial oblivion. *Naughts & Crosses* details how race is omnipresent, from the "skin" color of the bandages sold (cross-brown only) to the dessert on the restaurant menu.

THE SECOND COMING OF THE TRAGIC MULATTO

Danzy Senna's *Caucasia* (1998) presents multiracial reality through the eyes of mixed-race Birdie Lee. Arguably the most direct, detailed, and comprehensive literary exploration of black-white identity and racial categories in American literature, this Alex Award winner is seldom shelved with YA fiction. The novel spans roughly a decade, between the mid-1970s and early 1980s. Birdie and her sister, Cole, three years older, are the children of a black writer and intellectual and a white mother, estranged from her Boston Brahmin family. With their parents absorbed in radical Boston politics, the girls take refuge in their own world with its own language, "elemeno." Cole looks black. Birdie, not immediately identifiable as of any race, is taken for Puerto Rican, Jewish, or white. When Birdie is seven, her parents separate. The girls live with their mother and spend weekends with their father, who wants to send them to a new "Black Power" school in Roxbury. Birdie's mother says, "'I guess the school makes some sense with Cole. But Birdie? Look at her sometime, really look at her. Try to see beyond yourself and your goddamn history books. She looks like a little Sicilian.'" Confused, Birdie sees Cole study her, "struggling to see something on my face, something she had never seen before" (27).

At school the girls are teased. Birdie, with her light skin, is terrorized by older girls until Cole comes to her defense. Because of the way their appearance is read by others, a gulf is formed and widens between the two girls. Birdie sees that her father prefers Cole's company to hers, ignoring Birdie on their visits. On a rare outing alone together (Cole is sick), they are approached by police who ask her father "'Who's the little girl?'" (60). They are questioned repeatedly in a humiliating and public way. After this, Birdie's father withdraws further. His black girlfriend reaches out to Cole, but dismisses Birdie. When their mother takes the girls on a rare visit to her family, the situation is reversed; their grandmother favors Birdie and slights Cole. Increasingly, Cole spends time with their father away from Birdie and her mother.

After a political crisis occurs, never made clear to Birdie or readers, her father and his girlfriend, taking Cole with them, move to Brazil. Birdie and her mother go underground. As they move around New England, Birdie learns her mother is in some kind of trouble, pursued by the U.S. government. She crafts new identities for them; Birdie is reborn as "Jesse Goldman." For the next seven years, she will pass as white and have no contact with her father or sister. After four years on the move, her mother settles them in a small New Hampshire town, finding a job and a white partner. Birdie's sense of self is never very strong; here it almost floats away. She hovers over her body, looking down on it from above. "I would gaze down at the thin girl sitting by the fence, the one with her brown hair falling into her eyes, drawing patterns in the dirt, and watch this girl with the detachment of a stranger" (190).

At her school, one of the few other nonwhite kids is a biracial student, Samantha, who is shunned. Birdie, now fifteen, has allied herself with the white-racist clique as a kind of protection, but Samantha, who also has a white mother, fascinates her. At a party, when she and Samantha are alone outside, Birdie asks her, "'What color do you think I am?'" Birdie is desperate to be recognized. "She was silent, staring at me in a new light, it seemed, taking in my features, one by one. I tried to look different, more serious, and thought the word 'black' to myself, hoping through telepathy to transfer the correct word to her" (285).

Samantha shrugs it off and doesn't really answer. As the girls return to the house, Birdie pulls her to a stop and asks one more question: "'What color are you?'" And Samantha finally tells her, "'I'm black. Like you'" (286). This affirmation of Birdie's identity, suppressed for seven years, gives her the energy to search for her sister and her father and her lost black self. Birdie runs away from home and tracks down her father's sister, Dot, in Boston. Step by step, she gathers clues to her father's and Cole's whereabouts. With airfare coaxed from her white grandmother, she arrives at her father's apartment in Oakland, California, and he is there.

He tells her that after two years in Brazil, he and Cole returned to the United States. Birdie's deep sense of betrayal that her father and Cole never came to look for her is overwhelming. Yet at the same time, she understands it all too well.

Obsessed with a book on race he is writing, he shows her elaborate charts and tells her there is no such thing as race. She knows he is right. Except that there is. It has been controlling her life, every day. He explains his theory that the mulatto in America is like the canaries once lowered into coal mines to gauge whether the air was poisonous. If the canaries died, the miners knew it would be unsafe for human beings. "My father said that likewise, mulattos had historically been the gauge of how poisonous American race relations were. The fate of the mulatto in history and literature, he said, will manifest the symptoms that will eventually infect the rest of the nation." He smiles at Birdie, as if delivering good news, and tells her, "'My guess is that you're the first generation of canaries to survive, a little injured, perhaps, but alive'" (393).

Breaking in on this lofty theorizing, Birdie yells, "'Why did you take only Cole? Why didn't you take me? If race is so make-believe, why did I go with Mum? You gave me to Mum 'cause I looked white'" (393). He makes a few rambling excuses but never really answers. He drives her to Cole's house in Berkeley, where she is a college student, and the girls are reunited. Birdie is truly overjoyed, and yet still feels betrayed because Cole hadn't looked for her. "She had gone on with her life. I hadn't been able to" (406). Not until she watches Cole call their mother and hears her say, "'Mum, it's me,'" does she come to understand that when the family split up, Cole lost every bit as much as she did.

In *Caucasia,* Senna resurrects the tragic mulatto and sends her on a search for her missing half. What is missing is not family heritage, however. It is wholeness: that which is lost when one is forced to split a self and parcel it out in pieces. Birdie finds what is missing, but not through her ancestry and not with her father who has only his abstract intellectual banalities to offer. She finds it with the only other person who shares her loss: with Cole. Together, they might find their way home.

NOTES

1. I identify authors by race, where possible. It is usual to omit the designation "white" when referring to white people, which has the effect of making white the "gold standard" of normalcy. (For example, 2008 then–presidential aspirant Senator Barack Obama was referred to in the media as a "black man." His opponent for the Democratic nomination, Hillary Clinton, was identified as a "woman," not a "white woman.") If we must attach race labels to some, as this book requires, in fairness we need to attach them to everyone.

2. This was not the first YA novel with a multiracial protagonist to be published. That honor goes to *Arilla Sun Down,* first published in 1976, about an interracial family of American Indian and black heritage, by the late black writer Virginia Hamilton, discussed in chapter 3.

3. Although Rayona, protagonist of *The Window,* by Michael Dorris, has an American Indian mother, the novel concerns Rayona's discovery of her father's white family, and unfolds in the context of black and white. In *Zane's Trace,* by a white author, the hero's multiraciality is complex and multigenerational. In the other books, the protagonist is not multiracial, but other important characters are.

4. "In 1970, 1 percent of married blacks had a nonblack spouse. In 2000, 7 percent of marriages involving at least one black partner were interracial." Intermarriage rates for black men increased fivefold between 1970 and 2000, to nearly 10 percent. The intermarriage rate for black women increased from less than 1 to 4 percent. Sharon M. Lee and Barry Edmonston, "New Marriages, New Families: U.S. Racial and Hispanic Intermarriage," *Population Bulletin* 60, no. 2 (June 2005): 12.

5. Heather Dalmage, *Tripping on the Color Line: Black-White Multiracial Families in a Racially Divided World* (New Brunswick, N.J.: Rutgers University Press, 2000), 5. The author, a white, interracially married sociologist, explores the social consequences of black-white intermarriage and examines how the color line is policed by those invested in maintaining it.

6. "Cultural competence" means to understand a culture as it is understood by those who belong to it. Such competence is hard to achieve, especially when—as is the case with many white writers—the writer is unaware of his or her incompetence. Some literary critics insist that only insiders are capable of cultural competence, that writers are neither entitled to nor capable of writing

outside their own cultures. I disagree. Such moral censorship in the long run, if not sooner, results in bad literature and propagandistic cultural depictions.

7. Beverly Daniel Tatum, *"Why Are All the Black Kids Sitting Together in the Cafeteria?" And Other Conversations about Race* (New York: Basic, 1997), 94.

8. Individuals of mixed race are more likely to be recognized as such and accepted by nonwhite monoracial individuals and communities than by white ones. Acceptance may be conditional or partial depending on a variety of factors, such as physical appearance. For examples, see part III in Maria P. P. Root, ed., *Racially Mixed People in America* (Newbury Park, Calif.: Sage, 1992).

9. In a Zogby International poll, conducted November 1–2, 2006, 66 percent of black Americans identified Senator Barack Obama as black, 22 percent as biracial. Among whites and Hispanics, 8 and 9 percent respectively identified him as black, 55 and 61 percent as biracial. Similar results held for golfer Tiger Woods. Mark Williams and John Kenneth White, "Barack Obama and the Politics of Race," www.mindstorminteractive.net/clients/idonline/index.htm (9 April 2008). These findings are supported by other research on racial identity (see bibliography).

10. Angela Nissel, *Mixed: My Life in Black and White* (New York: Villard, 2006), 45.

11. Nissel, *Mixed*, 44.

12. Although they are not biologically related, Denny and Stephanie's brother-sister romance carries a queasy whiff of incest.

13. Authors with a didactic agenda often make characters ignorant of a subject so that they (and readers) can be educated on it. This tactic is common in mixed-heritage fiction where readers, presumed to be white, are educated about other cultures. Meyer wants readers to know about Juneteenth, a holiday familiar to blacks but less well known to whites. The children's ignorance of Juneteenth allows Susan to describe the holiday to them in dialogue. But a side effect of this authorial maneuver is to cast her in a bad light. Why has this black mother, raised in a Texas community where Juneteenth matters, kept her biracial children ignorant? Not only has she withheld her black family from her kids, but their cultural heritage as well.

14. *Publishers Weekly* 247, no. 18 (May 1, 2000), 71.

15. The harsh *Publishers Weekly* review cited this scene as proof that the dialogue lacks credibility. However, the scene has another agenda; it suggests a callous indifference on the part of abolitionists to the flesh-and-blood beneficiaries of their largesse, that their views on slavery may be more theoretical than real. In his 1843 novel *Martin Chuzzlewit* (London: Penguin Classics, 2002, 278–79), Charles Dickens made a similar point: the white abolitionists that Mark and Martin encounter in America are bigoted racists in their personal lives.

16. Maria P. P. Root, "Back to the Drawing Board: Methodological Issues in Research on Multiracial People," in *Racially Mixed People in America*, ed. Maria P. P. Root (Newbury Park, Calif.: Sage, 1992), 188.

17. Kathy Belge, "An Interview with Jacqueline Woodson: Author Jacqueline Woodson Talks to *Lesbian Life*," *About.com: Lesbian Life*, lesbianlife.about .com/od/artistswriterset1/a/JWoodson.htm (29 Aug. 2007).

18. Amanda Craig, "Black Is the New White," *TimesOnline*, 31 January 2004, entertainment.timesonline.co.uk/tol/arts_and_entertainment/books/article 1006827.ece (22 July 2008).

19. Blackman's details are firmly grounded in reality. For example, Lady Angkatell, a character in *Murder After Hours* (1946; reprint, New York: Dell, 1977), a bestseller by the late white mystery writer Agatha Christie, mentions that she is "'hoping Mrs. Medway would make a really *rich* nigger in his shirt,'" and describes the dish: "'Chocolate, you know, and eggs—and then covered with whipped cream. Just the sort of sweet a foreigner would like for lunch'" (185).

FICTIONAL WORKS CITED OR CRITIQUED

Note: An asterisk denotes a work critiqued as well as cited in the chapter.

Helen Benedict, *The Opposite of Love* (New York: Viking, 2007).*
———, *A World Like This* (New York: Dutton, 1990).
Malorie Blackman, *Naughts & Crosses* (New York: Simon & Schuster, 2005).*
———, *Knife Edge* (London: Corgi-Random House, 2004).*
———, *Checkmate* (London: Corgi-Random House, 2006).*
Jane Curry, *The Black Canary* (New York: Simon & Schuster, 2005).*
Michael Dorris, *Cloud Chamber* (New York: Scribner's, 1997).
———, *The Window* (New York: Hyperion, 1997).*
———, *Yellow Raft in Blue Water* (New York: Henry Holt, 1987).
Sundee Tucker Frazier, *Brendan Buckley's Universe and Everything in It* (New York: Delacorte, 2007).*
Carolyn Meyer, *Denny's Tapes* (New York: Margaret K. McElderry, 1987).*
———, *Jubilee Journey* (New York: Harcourt, 1997).*
———, *White Lilacs* (New York: Harcourt, 1993).
Barbara Ann Porte, *Something Terrible Happened* (New York: Orchard, 1994).*
Philip Pullman, *The Broken Bridge* (New York: Knopf-Random House, 1992).*
Colby Rodowsky, *That Fernhill Summer* (New York: Farrar, Straus and Giroux, 2006).*
Virginia Frances Schwartz, *Send One Angel Down* (New York: Holiday House, 2000).*
Danzy Senna, *Caucasia* (New York: Riverhead, 1998).*
Mildred Taylor, *The Land* (New York: Scholastic, 2001).*

Diane Lee Wilson, *Black Storm Comin'* (New York: Simon & Schuster, 2005).*

Allan Wolf, *Zane's Trace* (Cambridge: Candlewick, 2007).*

Jacqueline Woodson, *Behind You* (New York: Puffin, 2006).*

———, *If You Come Softly* (New York: Speak-Penguin, 1998).*

———, *The House You Pass on the Way* (New York: Speak-Penguin, 1997).*

· 3 ·

Natives and Newcomers

$\mathcal{I}$ndigenous Americans are the smallest racial minority in the United States, about 1 percent of the total population. Outmarriage is high, as much as 40 percent. For First Nations, the overwhelming catastrophe of genocide in situ—cultural and physical—continues to inform identity. Indigenous Americans are "from here," not "from there." The homeland, the source, the ancestors are here and the immigrants, the newcomers have built over their graves. There is no Ireland to mythologize on Saint Patrick's Day, no Mother Africa to honor with Kwanzaa celebrations, no Israel to return to. "Getting back to your roots" is a very different matter for First Nations than for anyone else.

WHO IS AN INDIAN? AMERICAN INDIAN MIXED RACE

Defining American Indian identity today is highly contentious and complicated. Yet this issue is usually ignored, glanced over, or misrepresented in YA fiction. "Official" Indian identity rests on legal definitions arrived at after centuries of territorial and cultural appropriation, governmental whim and manipulation, and attempts to fix problems that created new ones. To be entitled to the full legal benefits of American Indian status, one must be enrolled in a tribe. Each of the more than five hundred federally recognized tribes sets its own enrollment criteria. Important rights and privileges—to live and receive services on Indian reservations and to be eligible for college scholarships—are available only to the enrolled. Among factors used to determine eligibility, "blood quantum" is one of the most consistently applied; this is American Indian ancestry expressed as a fraction (one-eighth, one-sixteenth, and so forth).[1] Tribal enrollment is an official confirmation of one's status as a "real" Indian, a seal of ethnic authenticity. Without it, one's right to claim American Indian identity may be questioned, especially if one does not "look Indian." Many American Indian and some white literary critics hold the view that only those from the culture itself are entitled to write about it, which makes tribal enrollment an especially important issue for authors. "Mixed bloods," those of proven Indian heritage who don't qualify for tribal enrollment, live in an identity twilight zone. One of the many ironies of this limbo status is its contrast to black hypodescent.

The late novelist and critic Louis Owens—of Cherokee, Choctaw, Irish, and French ancestry—expresses the pain of being locked out from recognition as Indian in *Mixedblood Messages.* He points to Gregory Williams (author of the memoir *Life on the Color Line*) whose white mother left him to be raised by his black father, describing how Williams was harassed, even stoned, by whites for "passing," merely because he looked white. "Now if that man were claiming to be Indian, the very same white people might be ridiculing him for his claims and stoning him until he admitted his whiteness," was Owens's bitter comment. "Some essentialist Indian people, too, would probably be picking up rocks to force the man toward whiteness." Owens, who committed suicide in 2002, railed at the absurdity: "Clearly something is skewed here. If it takes only the most minute drop of 'black' blood to make a person black, why must it take a preponderance of 'Indian' blood—or a government number—to make a person a real Indian?"[2] Yet while Owens disparages essentialism, he is guilty of it himself. Longing for the rule of hypodescent to be extended to mixed bloods, he failed to grasp the commonality underlying these diametrically opposed ways of defining identity: both are attempts to turn culture into biology.

"There is great significance attached to being mixed blood or full-blood—or appearing the latter," observes the mixed-blood ethnic historian Terry P. Wilson. "In Montana many of my Native American acquaintances were 'card-carrying Indians,' having miniaturized and laminated their blood quantum certificates, which were drawn from purses or wallets at appropriate or, as it seemed to me, inappropriate times."[3] In other words, there is a hierarchy of indigenous identity based on and reinforced by documented biological ancestry and physical appearance.

This point is borne out by Tyonek Glee Ogemageshig, twenty-four. Living on the Quinault Reservation in Washington State, he is one of many multiracial young adults interviewed by Pearl Fuyo Gaskins in *What Are You? Voices of Mixed-Race Young People*. His mother is of European and Mexican descent, his father American Indian. "Being mixed has been a pretty big issue in my life—trying to figure out who I am as a person. I'm probably the lightest person in my family. When I was younger, I'd say, 'I don't look Indian, so I guess I'm not.' When I was growing up, I'd look at my sister and she'd be so much darker than I was, so I'd think, 'Who am I?'" His frustration is almost palpable. "To me, being Indian is about knowing the culture. But in so many ways, it's just how you look at a quick glance. Someone can't look at me and be able to tell I'm Indian. So I have to tell people. At this time in my life I practically shout it at people."[4]

"No more knotty issue preoccupies Indian America than that of identity," Terry P. Wilson says.[5] Tribal enrollment confers legitimacy, permanently removing one from the pool of potential imposters. For the mixed-race person who, despite known Indian ancestry, does not look Indian and can't meet the requirements for enrollment, the issue can become all-consuming.

THE REAL AND THE FAKE

Running through contemporary American Indian fiction is the tension between what is authentically Indian and what is fake. When the "full blood" becomes the gold standard of authenticity, the "mixed blood" is, by definition, less authentic. "Noble savage" and "degenerate half-breed" literary stereotypes have long played into this trope. The net result is that being mixed can carry a taint of fakery and may come with unearned and unfair baggage, consigning one to the category that includes idiotic Halloween dress-up regalia and bestselling memoirs of life on the rez that turn out to have been written by whites. Because of this conflation of authenticity with full-blood status, the conceptual distance between indigenous full-blood and mixed-blood identity—between "whole" and "mixed" race—is greater than for any other race. The full blood, the noble savage, carries associations of preconquest wholeness, unsullied "first-ness"—to borrow (and warp) a term from semiotics. The mixed blood, however, carries connotations of all that has been conquered, stolen, sullied, and extinguished in 500 years. At the same time, embracing mixed-blood identity, coming to terms with it, is what the future—like it or not—holds. No human race is getting any purer. The movement is irrevocably, irreversibly one way: toward integration.

The Noble Savage and the Degenerate Half-Breed

Fictional Indians past and present are mostly "pure bloods." The literary "noble savage"—Chateaubriand's Atala and René, Daniel Defoe's Friday, James Fenimore Cooper's Uncas—who lives in harmony with the pristine "wilderness," uncorrupted by "civilization," has had a three-centuries-long run that is not over yet.[6] Images in literature and popular culture that portray indigenous people as being close to nature with a mystical sensitivity that others lack borrow from the noble savage. (Any indigenous people on the planet may qualify.) The noble savage has the power of firstness that confers legitimacy, and the longer one has been first, the more legitimate one is.

In recent years, the noble savage trope has acquired new resonance. Rising environmental awareness, the sense that the planet is fragile and under threat from pollution, climate change, species extinction, and accelerating consumption of limited resources, has prompted nostalgia for an Edenic lost simplicity, a sense of wholeness long associated, through fiction and cultural mythology, with indigenous people. In this mythology, natives are the first to sense that things are "out of balance," prone to giving cryptic warnings to whites that go unheeded. Using their mystical woodcraft, they rescue "civilized" people who get into trouble because they have lost touch with their own native roots.[7] Underneath this tired stereotype is a respect and longing for firstness, a need to feel that we have sprung from generations who tilled the soil beneath our feet.

The glow from the noble savage image has never reached the "half-breed." Quite the contrary, according to multiracial author Pearl Fuyo Gaskins: "When I was growing up, the only mixed-race people I remember seeing on TV were the Indian 'half-breeds' who stole horses on Saturday afternoon Westerns. The good guys in the white hats despised them even more than they hated the full-blooded Indians."[8] Twentieth-century popular culture, including Western novels and films, portrayed mixed-blood Indians as dishonest, unreliable, disloyal, cruel—often with a pathological mean streak. Like other American Indian stereotypes, they "are deeply ingrained in American and Canadian culture and thought, due to a complex mixture of history, government policy, social attitudes, and the need for national identity."[9] Ludicrously biased portraits of most races and ethnicities lurk among children's literary classics, but for sheer toxicity, the degenerate half-breed is unmatched. The tragic mulatto has at least the dignity that unhappiness confers; the degenerate half-breed is merely repellent.

In Will James's 1927 Newbery Award winner, *Smoky the Cow Horse,* the eponymous horse is stolen and mistreated by a half-breed:

> All of him, from the toe of his gunny-sack covered boots to the dark face which showed under the wore out black hat, pointed out the man as being a half breed of Mexican and other blood that's darker; and noticing the cheap, wore out saddle, the ragged saddle-blanket on a horse that should of had some chance to feed instead of being tied up, showed that he was a half-breed from the *bad* side, not caring, and with no pride. (180)

The sentimental ballad "Half Breed," recorded by Cher in 1973, lamented the treatment accorded to mixed-blood people. Although the song's self-pitying tone still has the power to make mixed-race people cringe, it was wildly popular.[10]

Opportunists and Impersonators

Cigar store Indians, cheap reproductions of cultural artifacts, "autobiographies" of famous Indians by whites—for more than a century, fake versions of indigenous American cultures have made white people rich. Unauthorized and distorted versions of First Nations stories have been published, taught in schools and universities, and made the reputations of white scholars and artists. The irony of whites appropriating and purveying phony artifacts of cultures they have all but destroyed has not been lost on indigenous writers.

Some whites carry a longing for the legitimacy of "firstness," the unquestioned right to own the land and be owned by it—a kind of human *terroir*—so intense that they dress up as Indians, attempt to follow Indian traditions, pretend to be Indians. It is difficult to overstate how angry this can make those whose identity is being appropriated.

Impersonations of American Indians by non-Indians, including literary hoaxes, continue to this day. Fake memoirs and fiction based on fabricated personal histories remain on school curriculums, decades after the hoax has been disclosed. *The Education of Little Tree,* a memoir by Forrest Carter about his supposed Cherokee boyhood, was published in 1976; a later edition was named American Booksellers' Association book of the year. Across the United States, it remains a curriculum staple of middle and high school Native American history units, despite the long-proven fact that Forrest Carter was actually Asa Carter, a one-time Ku Klux Klan member and speechwriter for segregationist George Wallace.

Other heartbreaking accounts of growing up amid parental alcohol and drug abuse on the rez, by supposedly mixed-blood authors, have skyrocketed to bestseller status before being unmasked as the work of affluent suburban whites.[11] Not surprisingly, this has affected how American Indian readers and critics greet works by authors who claim, but cannot prove, mixed-blood status. Even when authors don't claim aboriginal heritage, books about Native Americans written for children and young adults receive unusually sharp scrutiny from influential bloggers, such as Debbie Reese.[12] While one can argue that some literary criticism is harsh, even brutal, the provocation is considerable.

DEMOGRAPHICS

Virginia Hamilton's *Arilla Sun Down,* the first YA novel about multiracial identity, published in 1976, was a groundbreaking portrait of an intact, contemporary black and American Indian family. Since then, writers like Canadians Sylvia Olsen and Margaret Robinson have produced vivid fiction about contemporary First Nations cultures and multiracial individuals. Yet too many books are still published that recycle mixed-heritage stereotypes, some of which seem to have a half-life to rival nuclear waste: the tragic mulatto in native garb and the Missing Half paradigm are alive and well. Families in historical YA fiction about mixed bloods are likely to be intact, but in contemporary stories, the nonwhite parent is usually dead. Whereas parents in fictional black-white multiracial families tend to be either high-powered artistic professionals or destitute losers with substance abuse problems, our mixed-blood characters' parents are generally employed as loggers, truckers, bookkeepers, and soldiers. Overall, the body of fiction about mixed-blood teens is meager and monochrome, seldom reflecting them or their concerns. Missing are kids whose nonindigenous heritage is not white, two-parent families, and a wider variety of settings, urban and rural. Realistic historical fiction that counters and challenges past misrepresentations and stereotypes is badly needed, as are contemporary themes on issues that concern American Indians of all heritages today.

ALL IN THE FAMILY

Virginia Hamilton's *Arilla Sun Down* is still the only YA novel focusing on black and American Indian heritage. An American Library Association Notable Book and School Library Journal Best Book of the Year, it is not among the author's best-known works. Startlingly original, it holds up well and deserves a wider audience. In it, Hamilton seamlessly integrates issues of racial and cultural identity with sibling rivalry and the personalities of family members. Hamilton asks readers to look at racial differences within a nuclear family context. Her great gifts as a stylist are on display here. Her lyrical, impressionistic prose demands a lot from readers; reading her is a kind of collaboration. Scenes are presented like puzzle pieces; it's up to the reader to place them and interpret the complex, often fragmented story they've made. Hamilton, black, was married to Arnold Adoff, a writer of Eastern European Jewish heritage, and drew from personal experience in writing the novel: "My interest in a reputed part-Indian ancestry . . . and my first-hand experience as a parent in an interracial family."[13]

The novel unfolds in a vivid mosaic of scenes interspersed with flashbacks, like the one that opens the novel. After a sledding accident, Arilla Adams and her father are rescued by Arilla's brother and James False Face, an elderly healer who comforts Arilla, telling her stories of the People. The family's stable center is Lillian, Arilla's light-skinned, black-identified mother. The family now lives in Lillian's hometown, where she teaches dance. Arilla's handsome father, Stony, is black and American Indian (quantum and tribe are not specified), but identifies as wholly Indian. He has a job, but it's unclear for how long. He tends to walk off jobs and return to Cliffville, where they used to live. Arilla's brother, Jack, then fetches him home. "Each time Dad left, he'd've squandered some pay and Mom would be good and depressed for a month," Arilla says. "I did worry some that he might go and not come back" (34).

The names that the characters use for themselves and confer on one another shift constantly. Jack is Jack Sun Run, Jack-Run, Jack-Sun, Sun, and Sun Run. Dad is Stony and Stone Father. Jack's name for Lillian is Mom or Moon Mother. James False Face is also James-Face and Old James. The net result is to make the characters' own identities seem fluid or malleable.

Racial identity divides the family. Jack adopts a larger-than-life American Indian persona. He identifies with Stony; both are flamboyant.[14] Jack sees himself as "Sun." He has designated his mother and Arilla as "Moon." Arilla resents that; why can't *she* be a sun, not merely Jack's reflection? Ordinary sibling rivalry is amplified by a racial consciousness that presents another venue for competition and comparison. Arilla is embarrassed by her brother's love of attention, as when he makes an entrance among picnicking families awaiting Fourth of July fireworks riding on a horse, naked to the waist in Indian regalia, including a headband with an eagle feather. Unlike Jack, Arilla cannot ignore the kids making "Indian war whoop" noises at him.

When Arilla invites friends from school to her birthday party, Jack exerts his considerable charm to steal the limelight from her. She is grateful that he is impressing her friends, but annoyed at how he dominates the occasion.

Family power struggles and disagreements are filtered through the prism of race. Jack's mannerisms exasperate his mother: "'Do you think you're the only one with blood of Indians in this town?'" Mom says, "'Your father is interracial. And you are interracial.' Mom says it like it's a tribe all its own." But Sun refuses to own any identity other than Indian. "'She's interracial, if you want,' not even looking at me. 'But a blood is a blood. Dad's mother was a full-blood.'" When Mom says they don't know that for sure, Sun answers, "'You look at her picture and you know.'" Mom won't concede this. The conversation degenerates into a parsing of blood quantum. "'I say she married only part colored in the first place. The rest was hers and it was blood,'" Sun says. Mom retorts, "'But your father married me. So that gives you less than a sixteenth,'" and she adds, "'or as much as three fourths.'" When Sun tells her, "'Anyway, dad and I look Amerind,'" Mom refrains from pointing out how hard they are trying to do so. "'Looks don't mean a thing,'" she says. "'It's what society says.'" Sun couldn't care less. "'Society has said it all wrong forever. And looks mean everything, and who cares what society says? A blood is a blood.'" The fight goes on, and Sun and Mom never do come to an agreement. Arilla notices "something between them not quite friendly" (131–32).

The novel is exceptional in its disregard for the rules of and homage to hypodescent. Mom does not tell Sun, "You're part black, which means you are black, period." Sun tells his mother that although modern Indians may appear to be mixed race, they are actually full bloods camouflaged in bodies that look black or white, waiting to "'reclaim what's theirs'" (132).

When the siblings are caught in an ice storm, Arilla saves Sun's life after he is thrown from his horse and badly injured. On her terrifying icy trek with the horses to get help, she arrives at her true name: Arilla Sun Down. With Sun not yet healed, their father disappears again. This time, Arilla is sent to bring him home. She tracks him down sledding in Cliffville. We learn that the memory of the sledding accident that opens the novel belongs not to Arilla but to her father. He tells her the story, and Arilla realizes that her brother saved her life before she saved his.

Arilla asks her father: If no one came to fetch him, would he come home? Stony doesn't know. She pushes him: yes or no? "'It's a circle,'" he says. "'I go and come here.'" And later, "'someone goes and comes here after me. I go back and they go back with me. You do not break the circle.'" Arilla begins to understand. "'You allow it,'" she says. "'Truth,' he says. 'You accept it.'" Arilla gets it. "'There is no yes or no. Only what goes and comes back'" (259).

Without didacticism, Hamilton presents the world as open to interpretation. We can translate what it contains as binary: yes/no, black/Indian, love/hate, trust/mistrust. Or we can replace our binary judgments with an open-ended, holistic world view. Within that framework, family members need not share the same identity, or have a permanent identity at all. Mom is interracial and black; Dad and Sun are "bloods." Arilla, like them, learns that she is free not only to choose her own identity, but to have it respected by others.

Arilla Sun Down was ahead of its time. It is rarely included in lists of Hamilton's great books, and is invariably overlooked in critical discussions of children's fiction about American Indians, yet it was the first

YA novel to present an intact biological interracial family; the first to present an interracial family outside a Euro-American context; the first to explore family members who adopt separate racial identities and the tensions that arise from their choices, as well as the accommodations each makes that permit the family to cohere.

AMONG FIRST NATIONS

Some of the best YA fiction set in contemporary indigenous communities has come from Canadian writers like Sylvia Olsen. In *White Girl* (2004), Josie, fourteen, is the daughter of a single mother who marries into a First Nations tribe. There, Josie discovers that she is white. Living in Vancouver, British Columbia, she was accustomed to belonging to the "default" race. "I lived in a white city, no doubt about it. And white people were just people. They were the people that stood in the centre and looked out. They were the background colour, the ambient noise, they blended in. It was the other people who stuck out" (9). The novel explores Josie's discovery of what it means to be a minority, along with what it takes to survive as one. She makes a few friends but most kids call her Blondie, consigning her to a "white people" category that they view with hostility. Josie finds her way into her new life with help from her stepfather and stepbrother, and especially step-grandmother, who give her the support her irresponsible mother cannot. Life is hard for people on the reserve; Olsen neither dwells on nor whitewashes the problems confronting this impoverished community. And she certainly does not ascribe mystical higher powers or "natural wisdom" to First Nations people. What interests her is how we search for and find, or fail to find, our common humanity. A blonde B.C. native of European descent, Olsen herself married into the Tsartlip First Nations. Now a status Indian, she raised her children on the reserve where she lives and works.

In *Yellow Line* (2005), Olsen paints a grimmer picture of life in an economically down-and-out coastal B.C. community, where whites and First Nations lead segregated lives. Vince, a white basketball star in grade eleven, makes it clear from the first sentence how the system works: "Where I come from, kids are divided into two groups. White kids on one side, Indians, or First Nations, on the other. Sides of the room, sides of the field, the smoking pit, the hallway, the washrooms; you name it.

We're on one side and they're on the other" (1). The segregation extends
to parents as well. Bitterness and distrust run deep on both sides.

Symbolizing the divide and giving the novel its name is the yellow
line on the school bus. "It divides the front of the bus from the back—
us at the back, them at the front. You can't see the line, but everyone
knows it's there and no one crosses over. It's just the way it is, and as far
as I can remember it's the way it's always been. Ninety minutes to school
and ninety minutes back, and no one steps a foot into the other territory. Except Dune" (3).

The one mixed-race character in *Yellow Line,* Dune is a mysterious
presence. "Twenty minutes into the trip to school, on the straight stretch
between the hairpin turn and the beach cliffs, the bus pulls around the
corner and there's Dune. He's walking down the middle of the road. I
don't know where he lives. There's nothing around—no telephone lines,
no driveways—just forests and clearcuts." Dune does not belong to one
side or the other. Talking about him, Vince sounds curious, even
awestruck. "Every morning Dune hops on the bus and plunks his butt
down dead center. Behind them and in front of us." Dune doesn't just
ignore the line, he sits on it. He represents freedom from the yellow line,
which is where Vince wants to go, too, though he doesn't realize it.
Dune's race can't be determined by looking at him. "With his black hair,
white skin and green eyes, no one knows for sure whether he's one of
them or one of us." Not knowing which slot to sort Dune into gives him
a kind of mystique: "Some people think he belongs to one of the Indian
guys. Other people think his dad is one of the men from our side. Either way he's probably somebody's half brother" (3–4).

Steve, an Indian, and Vince's friend Sherry, white, cross the invisible line that separates the two groups on the bus. Their choice roils the
community, and fault lines crack further. Through his own growing attraction to an Indian girl, Raedawn, Vince finds himself siding with the
few who choose integration, taking emotional risks and avoiding easy
choices. This pits him against his embittered, financially struggling parents, other adults, and most of his peers, especially his friends Justin and
Nick, who go after Raedawn and come close to raping her.

Vince has to make hard choices, and not all of them are good ones.
Pushed to choose sides, he discovers that there is a third choice—to
move beyond white versus Indian, to refuse to choose sides, to stop playing the game. That means there are no rules to follow. Together with

Steve and Sherry, he and Raedawn move tentatively toward the unknown.

As Vince processes what has happened to him and feels his allegiances shifting and attitudes changing, he gets on the school bus one morning and sees Dune.

> I flop into the empty seat in front of Dune.
> I turn around and just as cool as a cucumber I say, "Hey, man. How's it going?"
> "Good. You?" he answers.
> "Yeah." I nod like we're old buddies.
> "Good. I'm good too."
> I know it's just a bus seat, but all of a sudden it's like I'm left-handed or rich. It's a whole new thing. (98–99)

Those are the only words Dune speaks in the novel. After Vince joins him, Indian kids scramble onto the bus and sit around them. Dune is a living refutation of the boundaries of race, but he is not some kind of teenage United Nations, as multiracial people are often presumed or pressured to be. Dune's role is not to teach tolerance, just epitomize it. It is no accident that the first time he speaks to Vince is after Vince has chosen the third path and broken through, out of the racist prison. When he does, he discovers that Dune's been waiting for him.

In a 2007 interview, Olsen said that her own life on the reserve, to which she arrived as a seventeen-year-old newlywed, gave her an interest in exploring where different communities and identities intersect. "Authors tend to either write about First Nations or leave them out completely," she says. "My stories are mostly about how we interact with each other—different sorts of people coming together. Of course that's what I write about because that's what my life is about. I am most interested in how human beings come together and get along (or not)."[15]

A Woman of Her Tribe (1990), by Margaret Robinson, who is white, follows Annette Broadhead, fourteen, from her First Nations reserve on the west coast of Vancouver Island, B.C., where she has lived all her life with her white mother, to Victoria, the provincial capital. Annette's Nootka father died fighting in the Vietnam War. Annette is sorry to leave her godmother, Granmaw, who has raised her in Nootka traditions, and her best friend, Florence, and she is apprehensive about living in a city of white people. Her transition from the reserve's small, underfunded school to a private high school is trying and lonely, especially because her mother often works nights and sleeps days.

The ways Annette has learned to interact with others on the reserve don't work in this new setting. A gifted anthropology teacher, Miss Doud, draws her out, asking her about life on the reserve, and a Ukrainian Canadian classmate, Katie Danbor, befriends her, but the stress is overwhelming.

Annette struggles to succeed; she will lose her scholarship if she can't keep her grades up. She is harassed by racist students and becomes deeply homesick. Florence writes that she is dating a boy on the reserve and thinking about having kids. Annette's feelings of loss and divided loyalties come to a head one afternoon. She wonders if telling Miss Doud about the reserve was a kind of betrayal. She is jealous of Florence and her boyfriend, but she longs to succeed in school for her mother's sake. "Over the low hum of the insects, she heard voices murmuring within her. Vera's voice said, 'Don't forget us.' Florence's said, 'Kiki's my boyfriend now.' Mum's voice, loving and prodding, said, 'Study hard and keep your scholarship. That school is your way into the world.'" Other voices tell Annette, "'Keep your business to yourself. All we ever got from whites was sickness, cheating, war, and trouble.'" Amid the mixed messages, "Annette searched for her own voice among them. The others were important. They were part of her. But she didn't want them to drown her out. At last her own voice came, quieter than the rest but clear and just as strong. Find your own way, it said. You must find your own way" (51). And that is what Annette does.

She loves to run and turns out for sports. She makes an effort to adopt the pace and mindset needed to succeed in school. But she listens to the other voices, too. A visit to her old teacher at the reserve school helps sort out her feelings. Her mixed ancestry can be a burden, he tells her, but it is also an opportunity. "'You just have to do something that's almost impossible—keep both parts of your heritage alive in your heart'" (100). Being away teaches her how much she loves the Nootka reserve and its people, especially Granmaw. Her anthropology class awakens a new kind of interest in her culture. She grows closer to Granmaw, who tells her the history of Nootka women. Annette hears differently, "as though she'd just had ears attached to her head after years of being deaf." Before, "she'd always been eager to get outdoors, away from chores and Granmaw's mutterings, to play with Florence and Kiki." Now, she pays attention to Granmaw's account of the conquistadores. "What Granmaw had said fitted in with what she'd been learning down in Victoria with Miss Doud, out of library books. Looking at Granmaw's dark, wrinkled face, Annette realized that Granmaw was one of the women in those books" (89).

The insights run both ways. Annette looks critically at anthropological studies of First Nations, including hers, realizing that the values they express are not inherently superior to those she was raised with. "Annette's two halves, which were so often at odds, came together into a whole" (89). Annette begins to dream of a future as an anthropologist.

Granmaw tells her it is time she learns to be a Nootka woman, a process that includes a test of physical endurance, a long run, on which Annette feels the ghostly presence of past generations of Nootka women running with her. On her return, Granmaw and another elderly woman await her, and Granmaw gives her a Nootka name. "'Now you can forget that English school,' Granmaw said. 'No more white poison.'" Her friend adds, "'You can marry my grandson, Sam, and bear a Nootka child'" (125).

The women wait patiently while Annette ponders how to respond. She finds her answer in her Nootka father, who had enlisted in the military in order to finance a college education. "He had wanted a way into the world for himself. Surely he would have wanted it for her, too. She wanted it for herself. She didn't know if she could do it. But she wanted to try" (127). The two women hear her out and accept her choices. Granmaw tells her, "Maybe we wanted you to say something else. But your answers are your own" (129).

Honoring both sides of her ancestry—her foremothers and -fathers—Annette comes to appreciate each, without elevating one above the other. While she declines to stay on the reserve in the role of wife and mother, she has gained new respect and love for her heritage. The time-driven, competitive culture of school and city has no appeal for Annette, but learning does. Robinson doesn't create a bland "best of both worlds" picture of mixed heritage. It exacts a price. By refusing to reject half her heritage, Annette guarantees that she will not be included as a full member in either. She will have to fight for a place at the table as she finds her own way. This short YA novel presents a multiracial protagonist working out her identity in the context of daily life with both sides of her heritage, a rare achievement.

INSIDERS AND OUTSIDERS

Olsen and Robinson do not assume that all their readers are white. Their depiction of First Nations cultures and people are not pitched to outsiders, but to insiders and outsiders alike. They speak to nonwhite as well as to white readers, something other white authors often fail to do. Instead, they present expository cultural information for white readers through dialogue. The person conveying the information has to "step out of character and play the role of cultural tour guide," says children's book writer Debby Dahl Edwardson, whose interracial family is Iñupiaq and white.[16] Although the author's intentions may be laudable, the information is provided at the expense of authentic characterization. For example, Edwardson says, consider this line in the novel *Water Sky* (1987), by Jean Craighead George, in which an Iñupiaq woman serves her husband duck soup: "Lincoln Noah got the luscious beak; but I saved the best for you—the eyes."[17] Didacticism and factual inaccuracies aside, she says, "It uses dialogue to explain something that the native speaker would never feel compelled to explain. It would be like the wife in Chicago setting a plate before her husband and saying, 'look honey, I've broiled the luscious t-bone, prime cut of the animal, just for you.'" To avoid such a laughable result, Edwardson suggests, the author, regardless of her own cultural orientation needs to craft her words so that "her work can be read with equivalent pleasure and understanding by both those who are part of and those alien to the story's cultural setting. In order to achieve this, the writer must—to use the above example—sit right there in the tent and observe the scene from the perspective of both audiences. She must not take the easy way out by hiring a cultural tour guide."[18]

Some white authors seem to create multiracial characters precisely in order to avoid the insider/outsider problem Edwardson describes. The character has been raised monoracially as white, so he requires explanations for the nonwhite culture that is the author's true subject matter. This leads to a new problem: Where white identity exists only as a device to offer white readers a way into the story, we get a character whose white heritage is presented as valueless. For multiracial individuals, even those pressured by hypodescent to identify as wholly nonwhite, such rejection and ignorance of half their heritage is neither a realistic nor desirable outcome. To end the reign of white as the default racial norm, whites need to recognize and own all of it, good and bad.

Enchanted Runner (1999), the first of Kimberley Griffiths Little's two-book series about Kendall, son of a white father and Acoma mother, is a somewhat formulaic story. The author's good intentions are indisputable, but her failure to tackle the challenge of multiracial identity, after making her hero multiracial, deprives her work of power and depth it might have had. The principal problem is that she avoids addressing Kendall's white heritage at all. Both novels follow the "Missing Half" paradigm.

The first novel finds Kendall dealing with the pain of his Acoma mother's recent death by running long distances. Kendall's knowledge of his mother's culture is limited to stories she told. She was raised by her grandfather, Armando, who now invites Kendall to spend the summer in his mesa-top village of Acoma. Kendall accepts, but worries that his great-grandfather will reject him because he is Anglo. Armando is indeed slow to warm up to Kendall. Locating the story in Acoma, which is presented as a "living museum" of traditional Acoma culture without electricity and motor vehicles, undermines the ostensibly contemporary setting.

Cousin Trina is initially hostile, just as Armando is wary. As Kendall earns their trust, they reward him by sharing Acoma history. Kendall never questions what he is told. He has no connection with his white heritage apart from love for his father and brother. He apparently has no white extended family or friends. His white upbringing never pulls him in another direction, saying "This is dumb," or "Who do these folks think they are?" Kendall wants only to be admitted to the inner sanctum, to view the holy secrets as an insider.

Trina tells Kendall about the rain dances, ceremonies performed by men in the kivas. He wants to attend, but she says he can't: "'You're not a registered member of the tribe. You're not initiated into a society. Plus your dad is—'" Kendall interrupts her before she can say the dreaded word. "He hated feeling as though everybody was staring at him because he had Anglo blood. He'd been raised by an Anglo father that he loved. And he yearned for his Acoma mother because he loved her, too. Kendall felt like he had to straddle a thin line, two ways of living and believing, and neither one seemed easy" (76–77).

Bit by bit, Armando admits Kendall to the mysteries, including his Acoma faith. Has Kendall's white upbringing included religion? We don't know. We never see him struggle to integrate Armando's beliefs with those, if any, he was raised with. This story is not about dual status or divided identity—it is about initiation. Although Kendall is told he must learn to be both Anglo and Acoma, this never happens. The Anglo Kendall does not exist; he is an empty pitcher waiting to be filled with his Acoma heritage. Armando tells him he has a long road ahead. "'I am connected with the earth, with the gods, with all that is beautiful,'" he says. "'But you—perhaps you have the harder lot. You are both Acoma and Anglo. At the same time you are neither. There is a long road ahead of you to find out who you are. The journey on that road is never easy'" (80–81). Long yes, but both Acoma and Anglo, no.

As the last member, Armando initiates Kendall into the Snake Clan and tells him that of all the clans, the Snake Clan alone "'remembers the old way'" (82). Kendall learns he has inherited mystical gifts through his mother's blood.[19] Vague, mystical references to "blood" go unexamined by author as well as characters: "The blood of the Snake Clan, the blood of the runners was strong in him, as strong as if he were full-blooded Acoma" (111). Armando dies following an accident on a run from which Kendall rescues him. Armando tells him, "'Today, my son, you are an Acoma runner. I shed my skin on you. You are my young skin again, the last of the Snakes, until the day you die'" (131).

In *The Last Snake Runner* (2002), Kendall goes back in time to learn the old ways of the Snake Clan that were lost in the sixteenth century. Little takes literary risks that pay off in a more exciting story. Kendall is shocked and horrified when his father presents him with a stepmother, Juanita, who proudly claims descent from the conquistador leader responsible for defeating the Acoma people. He argues with Juanita about the conquistadores. She says, "'They made a beautiful place out of empty, desolate land,'" adding that "'the Europeans brought a more advanced culture and civilization, which helped everyone. They also believed it was their destiny to come settle this exciting new world and convert the native people.'" And when Kendall brings up the bloodshed this conversion involved, she tells him that "'many of the stories have been exaggerated'" (16). Readers may wonder why Kendall's father, long married to a proud Acoma woman, replaced her with the bigoted, chauvinistic Juanita, but she gets the plot moving. Soon, in Acoma regalia, Kendall is marching into Enchanted Mesa from which, after a brief exploration inside, he emerges to find himself in 1598 to witness the Spanish conquest of the Acoma people. Magically able to speak the language, he is befriended by Akish and his sister Jeneum, with whom romance blossoms. An elder, Tubaloth, recognizes Kendall as "the messenger."

The Acoma welcome the conquistadores warily at first and comply with their repeated demands for food, depleting their own reserves until, facing starvation, they resist and are conquered. Kendall witnesses the mutilation of Acoma men and the enslavement of the women. Tubaloth reassures him: "'You came to learn the ways of your ancestors. Future generations will spring from your seed,'" and "'Your message is simple. You are the hope the people need. Acoma will never die. The people will return to live again where the gods first brought us'" (168–69). Although Kendall returns to his contemporary world, how he will integrate that experience into his life is neither suggested nor explored.

Kendall is biracial in name only. The author locates the racial divide outside Kendall, which prevents the novels from achieving the thematic resonance and power that result when conflict and resolution are centered within the main character. A more interesting—not to mention realistic—scenario would have required Kendall to come to terms with his own white heritage. What if *Kendall,* rather than his stepmother, were descended from the conquistadors? What if his Spanish ancestors had killed and enslaved his Acoma ancestors? Coming to terms with a heritage of conquest, slaughter, and enslavement of other human beings might be difficult. But that heritage would have neutral and benign elements, too: ancestors good and bad with their own stories to tell. Instead, Kendall has had the weight of white history and guilt lifted from his shoulders. He has been relieved of his white identity as a reward.

MIXED-BLOOD HISTORICAL FICTION: WAR AND ITS AFTERMATH

Middle-grade fiction is crammed with historical novels about Indians, many of dubious quality. Fewer have been published for YA readers; fewer still have mixed-race protagonists. Their plots unfold during or, more commonly, soon after a war, associating American Indian mixed bloods with war's inevitable losses and unfathomable tragedies, and the period of chaotic social instability that follows. While war provides gripping material, this narrative template burdens the mixed-heritage character with a grim and sorrowful subtext.

Karen Hesse's short novel in verse *Aleutian Sparrow* (2003) is narrated by Vera, the daughter of a deceased white fisherman and an Aleut mother. Set in Alaska during World War II, the novel recounts the aftermath of the Japanese bombing of Dutch Harbor and invasion of the Aleutian Islands when Aleut people were relocated to Southeast Alaska, more than a thousand miles east, and interned in a camp outside the city of Ketchikan for three years. From the windswept, treeless islands of home, they had to adjust to a vastly different climate and lakeside landscape, crowded in by tall evergreens and steep mountains. Conditions were grim. When the Aleuts were found to have tuberculosis, they were further isolated from the rest of Ketchikan.

In the spare but evocative verse that is her hallmark, Hesse shows us what Vera leaves behind and how she copes, frightened but stoic.[20] Her relationship with her mother is tenuous and her father, whom she never knew, is disposed of in a few words:

> My mother never talks about when she was young and she / did not listen to the old ways to keep a man safe. / How she closed her ears to the Aleut tales. / She never talks about how she met and fell in love with and / married a white man, how she sent him to sea without / a seal-gut coat. She never talks about the storms / driving in and piling up the waves. How time after / time she watched from the headlands, fighting the / winds, waiting for my father's boat to come in. / She never says how I waited beside her, my fist crushing the / seam of her skirt. / And she never, never talks about the day my father did not come home. (9)

Her father's whiteness and Vera's multiraciality serve no purpose in the story. Vera does not wonder about her father's family, or if the white people of Ketchikan are anything like him. The decisions to move the Aleuts were made by white men, like Vera's father. Although Ketchikan is run by white people and Vera has had next to no contact with them, she expresses no curiosity or interest in her own background. Her biraciality makes no difference to how she sees herself or how she interprets and experiences her internment. No one else refers to it either. Vera's identity is exclusively Aleut and that is how she responds to and connects with the world. Whites are "they," not "me." After the Aleuts are settled at the camp, Vera's mother moves to Ketchikan. She abandons her daughter and people, finding work of an unspecified kind, possibly prostitution. When Vera and the surviving Aleuts are returned to the Aleutians, she stays behind.

Vera's biraciality may have been intended as a touchstone for white readers, like the biracial slaves of abolitionist fiction. Or, by giving Vera half of her own racial heritage, Hesse might be trying to inoculate herself against attacks on her cultural competence to write about Aleuts. In any case, this oddity in an otherwise graceful, polished work of fiction seems to reflect white discomfort in writing outside personal race and ethnicity.

In The Time of the Wolves (1994), whose author, Eileen Charbonneau, claims descent from Sacajawea, is set in the New York Catskills in 1824. Asher Woods, who is Métis,[21] and his wife, Ginny, who is white, are the parents of the book's main character. Both were central to Charbonneau's earlier novel *The Ghosts of Stony Clove* (1988). This semihistorical sequel with fantasy elements is centered on their offspring: twins Josh (the narrator) and Susannah, and their brother, Nathan. Thanks to the inheritance of a large estate, the family is well off. The rambling plot draws from an 1816 event, the eruption of Indonesia's Mount Tambora, that sent enough ash into the atmosphere to create a worldwide, one-year, mini ice age. Crops failed; snow fell in midsummer. Managing the very complicated plot keeps Charbonneau and her characters busy, yet the novel suffers from lack of a clear theme.

Josh and Susannah are not close. Josh, who looks like his mother, wants to follow his uncles to Harvard. Susannah, who resembles and identifies with her father, is happy at home. Asher refuses to send Josh away to school; he needs his help to prepare for the bad weather he has learned is ahead. Much is made of Asher's free spirit. "'I am Métis. Of both and neither,'" he tells Josh, who then asks: "'What am I?'" Asher says, "'That's for you to choose'" (51). The definition of Métis may be "of both and neither," but at least it is a definition. Josh is part Métis and part white. What does that make *him?* This interesting question is never answered. The author spends too much time with Asher; she is a lot more interested in him than in Josh, who spends much more time thinking about his father than he does about himself.

Asher tries to warn his fellow citizens of the disastrous weather ahead, but they do not believe him, and neither does Josh. No convincing reasons for Josh's opposition are given. Why Josh is set on going to Harvard, and why that makes him refuse to help out on the farm, are unclear, a failure of motivation that makes it difficult to care much about him.

In a melodramatic plot twist, Rebecca, a neighbor with an axe to grind against Asher, seeks out a friendship with Josh. She grooms him for her murky ends and sympathizes with his anger at his father, turning him against his family. But before Rebecca enters the picture, Josh has already pulled away from his father on his own. Why is unclear, perhaps shame for his father's uncouth ways: "I hated the smell of him when he'd come home from fishing and used that as an excuse to avoid him further" (78).

As the cold summer wears on, starving wolves come close. "My father doesn't loathe wolves, the way the other farmers do. He withdraws into the mountains, like wolves do, and hunts the same game that is their prey. But he never hunted them," Josh tells us. "To him wolves are beings very much like himself, I think—fierce, shy of civilization, protective of their young" (70). Asher fits the noble savage profile. A mystical bond with nature and perplexity at the twisted, overly complex world of the white man are his defining traits. At best a cliché, this Eurocentric trope is disconcerting in an author who claims American Indian heritage.

Poachers on the Woods property shoot and kill Susannah's beloved dog, Snow, and a litter of wolf pups. Asher chases the poachers off, then "slowly he put his hands inside the still-steaming slit underbellies, one by one. He streaked the blood down his face from his cheekbones to his jaw." Josh watches Susannah do the same. "I felt the bile rising in my throat, choking me. My father's eyes were the eyes of the wolf at the well—black eyes, sparked with glints of silver." Josh is horrified. "'Stop that!' I shouted desperately. 'You are not animals!' My father's expression was only perplexed. 'I am no part of you!' I called into the night air" (121).

Rebecca lures Josh away from home to see a wealthy friend, and there Josh discovers that he is a pawn in their plot to gain control of his family's estate. When he refuses to play along, Rebecca shrills racial epithets at him: "'You think you're one of us, boy? Decent, white? Why? Because you favor your gawking mother? You're misbegotten, do you hear me? Misbegotten, along with your red sister—bred like animals, two at a time!'" (146).

Horrified and ashamed, Josh returns home with the help of a friendly ghost and finds his father hunting the male wolf, now rabid, whose cubs were killed earlier. "'We must kill him here among the balsams,'" Asher declares. "'They're burning all around us. Making their own hell come spring, and the floods. We must kill him among the balsams where it's still holy. Where these backward people think the Devil lives. Josh, the hills are not a place without God." When Josh agrees, his father's response is "'Then I must convince your mother to send you to your fancy Boston school. Your education here is complete'" (157). As they kill the wolf, it bites Asher. Under his father's direction, Josh cuts the bites open and bleeds them. He carries Asher home who, though badly wounded, pulls through.

Her setup is promising, the plot interesting and potentially exciting, but Charbonneau doesn't take time to explore Josh's character. His motivation is weak and externally driven. Josh's change of heart and decision to return home are not based on an appreciation for his father's culture and values, but on the discovery of Rebecca's evil intentions.

Fictional mixed-heritage characters, historical or contemporary, who find themselves torn between competing or opposed identities have two choices. They must choose one or find a way to choose both. When done right, paying homage to the messiness of the process with an understanding of the conflict's source and how it works individually and socially, this produces riveting fiction, such as Senna's *Caucasia* (discussed in chapter 2). Often, however, the conflict is resolved neatly and easily. The lesson is learned, the page is turned. Our hero can put a check mark next to "figure out racial identity" and move on to the basketball tournament or apply to Stanford.

Not only are these resolutions simplistic, the writer deprives herself of great material. Writing for young adults, especially at the lower end of the age spectrum, challenges authors to express the complexity of race and heritage without oversimplification or suggesting finality exists when the reality of the subject matter is in flux. Authors can find plenty of subjects that allow for unequivocal resolution; this is not one of them.

THE TRAGIC MULATTO IN BUCKSKIN

Michael Spooner's *Last Child* (2005) is set in 1837. The engaging, unsentimental heroine is known as Rosalie to her white father, Angus, a bookkeeper at Fort Clark. Her Mandan mothers (Mandan culture permitted polygamy) and their people call her Last Child, a name given her by her grandmother, Muskrat Woman, the thematic center of the book. Rosalie divides her time between their Mandan village and the fort where her father lives. When he receives a shipment of smallpox-infected blankets, Angus tries and fails to forestall an outbreak of the disease. Spooner, who claims some American Indian ancestry, neither romanticizes nor denigrates his characters.

Rosalie views her mixed status with complacency. She is proud of her white status, of how her father depends on her, that she is welcome at the fort. The Mandans don't see her that way. When she insists she is white, Muskrat Woman asks, "'Why not red, like your mothers?'" Rosalie answers, "'It's what I want to be'" and points out that her mothers think she resembles her father, not them. "'Usually,' Muskrat Woman said, 'it's more than the seed you start with. A plant needs light and rain and someone to chase off the birds. We'll have to see how you turn out'" (42).

When Rosalie's father takes her with him on a doomed attempt to find and destroy the blankets, she is kidnapped and held for ransom, but eventually escapes and makes her way back to the village where she discovers most of the Mandans have died or are dying of smallpox.

With every turn of the plot, Rosalie reassesses her identity: is she white or red? Which is better? Not white, she decides, after she is kidnapped in order to obtain ransom from her white father. The Mandan upbringing she has taken for granted helps Rosalie free herself and find her way home, escaping a wildfire by huddling in a buffalo carcass. She remembers how her mothers, White Crane and Goes to Next Timber, criticized her. "Whiteness made me pushy and angry. Made me greedy and impatient" (90–91).

Rescued by a friend, Rosalie is taken to Muskrat Woman, who unlike Rosalie, has had smallpox. While the Mandan people die in huge numbers, Muskrat Woman initiates Rosalie into Mandan womanhood. One of Rosalie's tasks is to paint her face. This task should be guided by a Mandan women's society, but she has no model to follow. "'I'm joining a society of one, which is nothing,'" she laments. "'I'll never be any more than one, alone—half this, half that; neither one nor the other, and left outside by both.'" Muskrat Woman won't let her off the hook. "'Paint or don't paint,' she said flatly. 'But look deeper. You know who you are'" (153).

Rosalie draws a black stripe, bisecting her face, and paints one side red and one side white. Her grandmother infects her with the blood of a scab from a smallpox victim who has a mild case of the disease. "'From now on, you must not be divided in your heart—half red, half white.

You must be a whole woman, Last Child—your own color. It is a very beautiful shade'" (163).

Muskrat Woman tells Rosalie that the name Last Child came in a dream to her in which she saw the end of her people. Only one child was left. "'The sickness is sending us all down to darkness. You will be left to begin something new'" (168). Now Rosalie must integrate her two identities, she says. "'I know you feel two worlds inside you, with a sharp line between. You want to choose one or the other, but you can't.' She made a narrow gap between her hands. '*This* is where you have to walk—in this line between worlds. Your relatives will need you there, and, trust me, it will become a far wider place than you see. Plant it, walk it, build in it, and know it as your own territory'" (168).

Still recovering from smallpox, Rosalie is reunited with her father. He is leaving Fort Clark and forces her to go with him. As their steamboat pulls away, White Crane shows up, deathly ill, to try to stop it. Angus restrains Rosalie, who wants to go to her mother. "Smallpox ran down both sides of her face, turning it terrible with swellings and sores, but I knew my mother's voice." Her mother calls, but Angus is stronger. "'Let her go, Rosie!' he shouted. 'She'll die before the week is out—and trust me, you don't want to see that'" (212–13). The Mandans and White Crane are left behind. Later, Rosalie learns her mother drowned herself when she could not stop Rosalie from leaving.

Why Spooner chose to end *Last Child* this way is unclear. White Crane does not play a big part in Rosalie's story. Overall, the novel is well written, avoiding common cultural stereotypes. But this outcome is disconcertingly and eerily similar to a variant of the tragic mulatto story very popular in early silent films. The first feature-length Western ever made, *The Squaw Man,* follows an English aristocrat, James Wyn, who finds love in the American West with Nat-u-Ritch, the daughter of an Indian chief. She marries him and bears their son. When James learns he has inherited the title, he sends his son back to England to join the aristocracy, and Nat-u-Ritch kills herself in despair. "The film is a major landmark in the evolution of the American cinema. Adapted for the screen three times by Cecil B. De Mille, in 1914, 1918, and 1931, *The Squaw Man* launched both his directing career and Samuel Goldwyn's Lasky Feature Play Co., which would later become the major studio Metro-Goldwyn-Mayer."[22] The chauvinistic plots rested on familiar literary stereotypes: "In all of these films, the Indian woman's devotion to and sacrifice for a domestic and sexual liaison with a white man lead her to reject tribal bonds to pursue a nuclear, mixed-race family relationship. In the silent Western, whiteness and the reproductive family are synonymous; coherent Indian families are rarely depicted since they are presumed to be vanishing."[23] The mixed-race child may not be doomed like his mother, but he has lost his connection to his Indian heritage and will be raised as white. While the Indians may be portrayed sympathetically, like all tragic mulattos, they are ultimately victims and losers.

In other mixed-race tropes in early films, "Indian men and women ultimately choose to return to their tribes, depicting a latent, racially based 'call of the wild' that could reclaim Eastern-educated Indian and mixed-blood children from their new lives." This atavistic theme was known as "back to the blanket."[24] *In the Time of the Wolves* contains a faint echo of this theme. Captivity narratives, in which whites, usually children, were abducted by Indians, were also popular subjects for films.[25]

MULTIRACIAL HUMOR: NOT AN OXYMORON

A recent targeted search on Google for "multiracial humor" netted one hit;[26] a search for "multiethnic humor" netted seven. Adding "children" or "young adult" to the search string dropped the hits to zero. Multiculti reality, it seems, is no laughing matter. Gallows humor can be found in crossover adult fiction from authors like Sherman Alexie, discussed in chapter 5, but humor is rare among YA fiction dealing with mixed-heritage American Indian characters.

Yet, "mocking dominant beliefs or expectations about people of mixed descent is a common theme among comedians of mixed heritages."[27] A popular approach is to ridicule the annoying myths that are applied to people of mixed heritage (for example, the "best of both worlds" myth). Coping with a world in which white is the "default" race can net absurd results. Hawaiian actor and standup comic Andy Bumutai, of German, French, Hawaiian, and Filipino heritage, describes his discovery, at a film audition, that the woman organizing the event had identified him simply as "nonwhite." On asking what that meant, he was told not to worry about it; it was not official, "just my personal notes." He ponders how this might work in Hawaii, where most people are of mixed heritage: "The 'not' thing is very strange. Imagine if we did it that way: 'Hey, bro, you know Charlie, the guy who's not Chinese, Filipino, Samoan, or Portagee?' 'No, I don't know him. What else isn't he?'"[28]

Possibilities for mixed-heritage humor, as this quote illustrates, are considerable. So why is it rare in fiction? Planning a conference presentation on multicultural humor in 2004, authors Cynthia Leitich Smith, enrolled in the Muscokee (Creek) tribe, and her husband, Greg Leitich Smith, had a hard time finding any. They surveyed twenty professionals, but in response to their question asking for multicultural humor recommendations, "most left the question blank."[29] And this was *all* "multicultural" humor, not just "mixed-heritage multicultural" humor. When Smith polled colleagues, "Joseph Bruchac told us, 'It has got to change. We need laughter to survive, and our children need it more than they ever have before.'"[30]

Smith offers several possible reasons for the dearth of comedy. It gets less respect than tragedy; there is more prestige in serious books. And discomfort and uncertainty exist over where the boundaries between acceptable and unacceptable lie. "Historically and sometimes still today, reactions to diversity have not always been a source of the kind of laughter most of us would like to encourage," she notes. Writers are afraid of being accused of ethnic insensitivity. Some fear the humor of their group won't travel well, that only insiders can "get it." That's not a reason not to make the effort, Smith says. "Maybe the only way sense of humor will translate is by continued exposure, by trusting our readers to try harder when it doesn't come easily." That also means being willing to "risk the possibility of offending someone."[31] Luckily for readers, several writers have shown themselves willing to step up to the plate.

In Smith's own 2001 novel, *Rain Is Not my Indian Name,* the humor is mild but more than intermittent. The narrator, Cassidy Rain Berghoff, is a mixed-race teen in the process of defining herself. Her American Indian mother is dead and her white father, a career military man, is stationed on Guam. Rain lives with her older brother, Fynn, and his girlfriend, Natalie, editor of their small-town newspaper. Rain's feelings for her best friend, Galen, had taken a romantic turn when he was run over and killed on New Year's Eve, the day before Rain's fourteenth birthday. The narrative leaps six months ahead, the start of summer vacation. Rain stubbornly refuses to join an Indian-culture summer day camp being set up by Georgia, an old friend of her mother's. But Rain, a passionate amateur photographer, agrees to accompany the paper's reporter, known as "the Flash," and take pictures of the camp for the newspaper.

The town's native population is small; only four kids are persuaded to join the camp. Dmitri and Marie live in a trailer park; Spence, the son of two lawyers, is affluent; Queenie is black and has recently discovered her native heritage. Rain resents her for having dated Galen. The Flash interviews Queenie about her discovery that "one of my great-grandfathers was a Native American." Rain is jealous "as if stealing Galen hadn't been enough, now Queenie was barging in on my cultural territory." To give Queenie her due, "she was no guru-seeking, crystal-waving, long-lost descendant of an Indian 'princess,' but still. . . ." (70).

Inch by inch, Rain comes to terms with Galen's death and her bittersweet feelings about her Indian heritage, which are bound up with memories of her mother. The farther out she ventures, the more tolerant she becomes: of Queenie, Galen, and finally herself.

This comedy of manners milks humor from the differences between what we say and what we do. Smith doesn't exempt anyone from scrutiny. Belonging to one or more ethnic minorities that have barely survived extinction does not make us tolerant or sensitive to others in the same position. The novel plays with political correctness of all stripes. The Flash corrects Rain when she mentions Indians, telling her they prefer to be called Native Americans. She hesitates before telling him who she is. "Part of the deal with being a mixed-blood is that every now and then I feel like I have to announce it." Once she does, she has to explain. "'What are you?' people sometimes ask Fynn. It sounds like they want him to ID his entire species. Because my coloring is lighter, I usually get the next standard questions: 'How much Indian are you?' (About forty-five pounds' worth.) And 'Are you legally [or a card-carrying] Indian?' (Yes, but only on my mother's side)" (48).

Working with the Flash, Rain realizes that she has been clinging to the safety of the distant observer. As she heals, the distance that once protected her gets in her way. Like illustrations of the Heisenberg Uncertainty Principle, Rain and the Flash, by interfering with what they are observing, affect what happens as they join in the camp activities.

Smith has a good ear for the subtle ways we try to one-up each other, to prove that we are a cut above the herd. Looking for a present for the baby Natalie and Fynn are expecting, Rain asks Dmitri if he has something she could give them. He hands her a dreamcatcher and tells her to hang it above the bed. "'It's beautiful,' I said, 'but dreamcatchers are kind of . . . trendy, don't you think?'" Dmitri tells Rain his mother made it. "What with that foot crowding my mouth, I could hardly find a reply. Too bad Dmitri couldn't sell me a word-catcher to let the good ones through and trap the rest" (71).

Watching the campers build a bridge out of pasta, Flash asks Rain, "'What does bridge building have to do with a Native American youth program?'" The assumption that bridge building is unknown to Indians annoys her. "'Do you have any idea how weird it is to be an Indian in Hannesburg, Kansas?'" she snaps. The Flash responds, "'Do you have any idea how weird it is to be Jewish in Hannesburg, Kansas?'" (113). Rain is surprised and says without thinking, "'But you don't seem. . . .' Oops, I thought, sinking slightly in the chair. I wished again for that word-catcher to let the good words through and trap the rest" (114). Chastened, Rain is patient with the Flash, showing him that bridge building is just as normal for Indians as it is for non-Indians. The assumption that Indians are "about" something—probably something pre-technological— is the Flash's thoughtless contribution. "'So Indians build bridges.'" Rain says, "'Not all of us. Not me. At least not when I'm packing a camera'" (115).

After he confesses that, until this summer, he had never met an American Indian, she confesses, too: "'If it makes you feel any better,' I began, 'all I know about Jewish people, I learned from *Fiddler on the Roof*.'" All they can do is laugh. "It wasn't funny, how clueless both of us were. But laughing worked better than medicine" (115–16).

Most stories by the American Indian authors showcased in the fine YA anthology *Moccasin Thunder: American Indian Stories for Today* (2005) are bleak, set in a grim twilight world just this side of extinction, in which a happy ending consists of the hope that things can't get much worse. An important theme, as discussed earlier, is the real versus the fake, the usurpation of Indian identity and birthright by those who first stole it, then transformed it into a phony reproduction of what was stolen: caricature Indians with wigwams and squaws and sports teams. In her story, "A Real-Live Blond Cherokee and His Equally Annoyed Soul Mate," Cynthia Leitich Smith looks at this issue of authenticity with a multiculti twist and finds humor in it. A teenage Indian boy is working in a costume store in the buildup to Halloween. The rental costumes, of course, include "Indian" attire.

The narrator tells us "I'm a swear-to-God, card-carrying, respectably thick blood Oklahoma Cherokee. That's right, I said 'Cherokee.' And yeah, my hair is blond. Sandy blond. Sure, I know every 'take-me-to-your-sweat-lodge' wannabe claims he's a Cherokee. Yeah, Mama's mama is the fullblood. No, I didn't call her a 'princess,' and don't make fun of my gramma. So what if I'm not dark like her or a redhead like Dad's mama? I took after my grandpas, the Swedes" (33). In other words, we have here, appearances to the contrary, a claim of authenticity. Boys come in to the store and investigate an over-the-top Indian costume, suede and fake feathers, dyed purple. The narrator simmers with annoyance that boils over when a girl, Nika, comes in hoping to interview him. He mentally dismisses her as shallow and stereotyping, if not actually racist. He also dismisses her appearance: punk style, dyed red hair, nose ring.

One of the boys, Nika's brother as it turns out, rents the idiotic Indian costume with the dyed feathers. The narrator takes out his annoyance on Nika. She tells him she had wanted to ask him out; now his rudeness sends her away, leaving him metaphorically kicking himself. Later he goes in search of her, realizing that there is something at stake, and discovers her destroying the costume. He also notices that her hair is not dyed, but genuinely red. Touched by her gesture, he realizes that he had stereotyped her just as he assumed she was doing to him—and he learns a lesson about stereotyping in general. "When I looked back down at Nika again, I saw hints of my grandmother. Not my Cherokee grandma, my Irish one. The one with those eyes people sing about on street corners and in late-night bars. The one who was annoyed by the Celtic fad and framed four-leaf clovers. The one who couldn't stand the folks who flocked in to see Lord of the Dance. Wannabes, Gramma called them. Gramma with her iced evergreen eyes" (40–41).

Smith uses humor to explore the territory that it is best suited to: human folly and pretension. Being authentic oneself, her story reminds us, does not mean that one is able to spot authenticity or lack of it in others—to do that, we have to reach out and make the effort to see beyond the easy labels to what underlies them.

Set on the wild, rain-soaked west coast of Vancouver Island, British Columbia, Jean Davies Okimoto's *The Eclipse of Moonbeam Dawson* (1997) follows the adventures of the eponymous hero, fifteen, only child of a deceased Haida father and the white hippie mother who foisted the name on him. Freed from their rural commune, Moonbeam, awash in hormones, lands a job at an upscale wilderness resort, while his mother pursues her dream of saving the rainforest. Moonbeam knows almost nothing of his father's heritage, but that and his looks are enough to get him hired, as the resort wants to showcase First Nations employees. (His ignorance of his roots is not entirely credible. In a commune culture known for revering First Nations traditions, real or imagined, surely his Haida heritage would have had some cachet.)

At the resort, he gets to know Gloria, who is not the native she looks: "'My dad's white and my mum's Japanese, but from here. Japanese-Canadian. But most people think I'm Native or part Native, especially at the lodge since they want to hire first nation people'" (70). Okimoto pursues in more depth this theme of valuing the appearance of diversity over its reality in *Talent Night* (1995). Like Smith, Okimoto, who is white, explores the ways we assign high and low status to one another. With help from Gloria, Moonbeam looks for a name he can live with and the process awakens his interest in his roots. Gloria tells him that Haida artist Bill Reid was also half Haida, half white. So Moonbeam renames himself "Reid Dawson."

In hot pursuit of a resort guest, Michelle, whose father heads a giant timber company (the bad guys), Reid agonizes over whether to tell her about his Haida ancestry. Gloria asks if he's ashamed of it. "'No. But I didn't know my dad. I don't even know any Haida people, and the only Native traditions I know about are from the white guys who lived at Happy Children of the Good Earth. It seems so phony.'" Reid's interest in his ancestry is confined to the question of how it will affect how Michelle sees him. "'When you're mixed you have to be careful about not getting hung up on what race you are. It can make you crazy,'" Gloria says. "'Listen, Reid. You're who you are. The truth of your life is that your dad was Haida and your mother's white. Maybe you didn't know him or his people, but it's still a fact and nothing can change that'" (145).

Reid writes to Michelle, who has returned home to Vancouver, telling her he is half Haida, and follows up with an expensive visit to see her that ends disastrously. She blows him off, and he leaves. Depressed and humiliated, he heads to a museum where he listens in as a docent leads a tour of works by Bill Reid: "'Bill's quest to learn about his heritage probably began with the natural curiosity of most teenagers to know where they came from. In his case, since he had no knowledge of his father's relatives, he became interested in his mother's family'" (173). Through his namesake's sculptures, Reid feels a stirring of interest and identification with his unexplored heritage. Back at the resort, he pursues Gloria with more success than Michelle. When his mother's new boyfriend asks Reid if he would like to accompany him on a business trip to Haida Gwaii (the Queen Charlotte Islands), he says yes.

This rather slight work is heavy on setting and good on characterization, but weak on architecture. When Okimoto's environmental passions get the better of her, readers are treated to political tirades. But there is also much to like. Under the gentle humor lies a serious look at how we use and manipulate our individual race labels to achieve quite an assortment of goals.

SYMBOLS AND SIGNS

To write big stories, pessimistic or hopeful, authors must convey something of what has been lost and what remains without letting the catastrophes and extinctions and appropriations drown out everything else— and especially without losing the human being at the center. Using magical realism, working deeply with imagery and symbolism, and taking stylistic and narrative risks, a few authors have managed this feat in fiction built around mixed-heritage characters. When the author loosens conscious control, his grip on the reins of the narrative, and follows imagery where it chooses to lead rather than dispensing it in careful medicinal doses, a dialectic and dialogue, a conversation, arises between the facts, the events, of the story and the imagery that comes at meaning obliquely, by analogy. Where the artist has found the right images for his story, not only will they lend emotional color and depth, they may uncover new truths that a more linear process might have missed.

Dogwolf, a taut thriller by white writer Alden R. Carter (1994), unfolds over one hot summer in rural Wisconsin, near a Chippewa reservation. Pete, fifteen, lives with his mother, who is one-quarter Indian; his white stepfather, Chuck, who works for the Forest Service; and his two half-sisters. Pete's father, half Indian, disappeared in the woods years earlier and is presumed dead. Now forest fires threaten nearby communities. As they are reined in, new ones are sparked by lightning, but the thunderstorms bring no relief by way of rain or cooler temperatures.

On the surface, Pete is a levelheaded kid in a loving family. Chuck battles fires on the front lines, while Pete, too young to join him, watches for fire from a lookout tower and hangs out with his best friend, Jim Redwing, a full blood with a growing alcohol problem, who is increasingly engaged with his heritage and traditions.

An atmosphere of apocalyptic menace hangs over the novel. There is no room for error when battling fire, drought, and exhaustion; mistakes can be fatal. Against this backdrop, Pete becomes obsessed with blood quantum. "Until this summer, all those fractions never concerned me much," he reflects. "I don't know why, but I do know when I started trying to figure out the sum of all those fractions." Around then, he has a vision. "I felt the heat and smelled the chalky ash of my father's bones burning in that hidden place where he'd gone to die." When the vision ends, "I found myself on my knees in the dry grass, breathing like I'd run a mile. About then the dogwolf howled, and I was more scared than I'd ever been in my life, because for a minute I didn't know who I was or what was howling somewhere in the darkness beyond the trees" (7).

The dogwolf is a mysterious creature kept very firmly caged on a neighbor's property. It is reputed to be part wolf, part dog, and very dangerous, but Pete is drawn to it. The neighbor has inexplicably disappeared, leaving the animal without food or water. Pete begins to feed it. When Pete and Jim hear the dogwolf howl, Pete says it's lonely. Jim snorts, "'You're not starting to feel sorry for that damned thing, are you?'" (58). Pete protests that he's not.

The animal seems to be willing Pete to set it free. As Pete listens to it and feeds it, the bonds that tie him to family and friends loosen. Something is happening to him that he can't fathom. Pete has headaches, visions, and begins to feel a strange connection with the dogwolf. "In the trees to the southeast, the dogwolf howled. I shivered, knowing what it wanted." He gets the message. "The dogwolf wanted me to set it loose or to put a bullet through its brain" (65).

Intending to shoot the dogwolf, Pete instead sets it free. Soon rumors fly that the dogwolf is killing animals. When Jim asks, Pete denies having set the dogwolf free and a new distance grows between the boys. Through Jim and his own inquiries, Pete comes to accept that the dogwolf is an unnatural creature amplified by shamanistic power, full of hate and murderous intent. Its captivity is not unfair and immoral, but essential. The connection between them tightens as his other emotional bonds snap. "The voices of Mom, Chuck, the girls, Aunt Loretta, even Jim were growing faint, their calls weak in the static. Soon they would fade out altogether, leaving me in a howling silence where I'd have to deal with the dogwolf at last" (158).

What intervenes to pull Pete back to the world of family and emotional connection is the arrival of his grandfather, Jean LaSavage, a Métis from Flin Flon, Manitoba. Belatedly learning of his son's death, he has hitchhiked to Wisconsin to reconnect with his family. The knowledge of his Métis ancestry and Jean himself provide an anchor for Pete's sense of self. "'They're the freest race God or the Devil ever put on Earth. Sons and daughters of Cree women and French voyageurs and trappers. And some Scotch traders, too, although we French Métis aren't sure they really count,'" Jean says. "'The Métis weren't half-breeds but a people unto themselves. Buffalo hunters, traders, and fighters'" (165). Jean tells Pete the stirring story of Louis Riel, the great Métis leader who fought to secure a homeland for his people and was hanged in 1885. "'I am Métis, my son was Métis, and I think you, too, are Métis, Pierre'" (167).

Before Jean returns to Canada, Pete confesses to setting the dogwolf free. Jean says, "'Well, I think you'll have to go after him one of these days'" (170). And Pete does.

The dogwolf, unlike Pete himself, belong nowhere. "The dogwolf was never quite one thing, never quite another. I think that even in Wilson's cage, it believed that it was a wolf trapped inside the body of a dog. But outside the cage, it could never quite make the shift and got caught in some terrible nowhere in between" (230). A functional identity can't be too amorphous; it requires a definite shape, boundaries. Pete decides that when the fall comes, he'll make his way up to Flin Flon, where his grandfather lives. There is more to discover. Perhaps the answers he seeks are to be found in his father's heritage.

Dogwolf is infused with emotional power, but Carter plays his cards close to his chest. Is the dogwolf a symbol of the natural world out of balance or is it simply the condition of being neither one thing nor the other? The novel feels at times as if it has escaped from the author's control, steamrolling downhill, faster and faster, while Carter runs after it, trying to catch up. Nonetheless, the haunting and disturbing setting and imagery have staying power, especially the association of natural (the fires) and unnatural (the dogwolf) disaster with Pete's rootless disconnection from his father and his lineage. Nature out of balance runs like a ribbon through the novel, commenting on Pete's unbalanced sense of self. Jim pulls back into his monoracially defined identity, leaving Pete on the outside. Pete is in touch with his heritage in the abstract, but he needs more to go on. Jean provides a stable foundation on which Pete can build.

Ceremony (1977), Leslie Marmon Silko's unmatched debut novel, is arguably the greatest novel by an American Indian writer. Of Laguna, European, and Mexican American ancestry, Silko grew up on the Laguna Pueblo reservation, where most of the novel takes place. Tayo, son of a Laguna mother and unknown white or Mexican father, has returned to the reservation to live with his grandmother and the aunt and uncle who raised him together with their son, Rocky. Smart, ambitious, bound for college, Rocky persuaded Tayo to enlist with him to fight in World War II. But Rocky died in the Philippines and now Tayo, shell-shocked, grief-stricken, and sick at heart, has returned home, barely alive.

Great things were expected of Rocky. "He was an A-student and all-state in football and track. He had to win; he said he was always going to win" (51). Unlike Rocky, a full blood, Tayo was more drawn to Laguna traditions and culture. After the war, Tayo was hospitalized in Los Angeles and although released, remains mentally adrift and nonfunctional. He drinks in bars with Emo and other Indian veterans, but their talk about who they killed and the white women they impressed sickens Tayo. Emo has a collection of teeth from dead Japanese soldiers. "Tayo could hear it in his voice when he talked about the killing—how Emo grew from each killing. Emo fed off each man he killed, and the higher the rank of the dead man, the higher it made Emo." Tayo listens to Emo brag, "We blew them all to hell. We should've dropped bombs on all the rest and blown them off the face of the earth" (61). Despite moments of clarity, Tayo's sickness grows. His uncle Robert tells him that the Laguna men feel he needs help from a traditional healer.

Tensions between tradition and change within and outside the Laguna world run throughout *Ceremony*. At first tradition and change appear as opposites. By the end of the novel we see they are connected in an unbroken cycle of change and return. Definitions, boundaries, meanings all are in a state of eternal flux and transformation. Tradition first grounds us and later binds us. If we cannot escape these bonds and change, we die. Silko conveys this circular cycle in the structure of her narrative, weaving past into present and present into past. Old stories become new stories. Even the shapes of her poems on the page convey meaning.

The multiracial person is emblematic of how the world changes. Tayo tells a mixed-race woman with whom he had a brief, intense liaison that he was teased as a child for having "Mexican" eyes. She says that those who stigmatize difference are, like most people, afraid of change. "'They think that if their children have the same color of skin, the same color of eyes, that nothing is changing.'" She says they are fools. As they part, she tells Tayo, "'You don't have to understand what is happening. But remember this day. You will recognize it later. You are part of it now'" (99–100).

Tayo submits to seeing a healer, Betonie, who is also a mixed blood. He understands that rituals and ceremonies must be carried out with utmost care. The formality and repetition of ceremony have value. And yet, at the same time, "'Long ago when the people were given these ceremonies, the changing began, if only in the aging of the yellow gourd rattle or the shrinking of the skin around the eagle's claw, if only in the different voices from generation to generation.'" In fact, Betonie says, "'in many ways, the ceremonies have always been changing'" (126). The lesson that "things which don't shift and grow are dead things" is suppressed by those who follow the "witchery," evil that feeds on fear.

How Betonie lives—surrounded by pathetic junk, the white man's detritus—sounds the familiar theme of authenticity versus fakery. "The old man's clothes were dirty and old, probably collected like his calendars. The leftover things the whites didn't want. All Betonie owned in the world was in this room. What kind of healing power was in this?" (127).

Tayo is tempted to leave, dismissing Betonie as a charlatan. What good, he asks, can "Indian ceremonies do against the sickness which comes from their wars, their bombs, their lies?" But Betonie does not draw the line between us and them, real and fake, good and bad, Indian and white, in the way Tayo has learned to do. "'That is the trickery of the witchcraft,' he said. 'They want us to believe all evil resides with white people. Then we will look no farther to see what is really happening.'" In fact, he tells Tayo, "'it was Indian witchery that made white people in the first place'" (132).

Betonie begins the ceremony, but Tayo must work it out himself—not an event but a process, a quest to remake his connection to the natural world, the landscape of home. It is also a journey away from hate and oblivion toward respect and love for every living thing. At one pole is life, the generous earth, the lesson that "nothing was ever lost as long as the love remained" (220). At the other pole is the discovery Tayo makes in the New Mexico mountains: a uranium mine. "Human beings were one clan again, united by the fate the destroyers planned for all of them, for all living things; united by a circle of death that devoured people in cities twelve thousand miles away, victims who had never known these mesas, who had never seen the delicate colors of the rocks which boiled up their slaughter" (246).

Tayo's mixed blood, like the ceremony itself, manifests wholeness, completion arising from the status of being mixed itself. Uranium mined from the homeland of American Indians is made into bombs that destroy in a flash cities and thousands of human beings across the world. In a shrinking world, the definition of wholeness has to be bigger than one people, one culture. Tayo, like the mixed-race woman, like Betonie, bridges worlds that tradition says are separate islands. The world has changed. Recognizing that allows Tayo to return to what is eternal and does not change: life itself and the love that keeps us hoping for one more sunrise.

NOTES

1. The 100 percent full-blood antecedent from whom descent is calculated is identified from sources such as tribal membership lists and records of past governmental efforts to count the native population. There is no way to guarantee how "pure" the original "full-blood" ancestor's blood actually was. As many have pointed out, this system does not reflect how indigenous peoples defined themselves before European conquest. Sorting out tribal enrollment issues is a high priority among tribes, but not close to resolution.

2. Louis Owens, *Mixedblood Messages: Literature, Film, Family, Place* (Norman: University of Oklahoma Press, 1998), 199.

3. Terry P. Wilson, "Blood Quantum: Native American Mixed Bloods" in *Racially Mixed People in America*, ed. Maria P. P. Root (Newbury Park, Calif.: Sage, 1992), 122.

4. Pearl Fuyo Gaskins, *What Are You? Voices of Mixed-Race Young People* (New York: Henry Holt & Co., 1999), 41.

5. Wilson, "Blood Quantum," 109.

6. The character of the South African bushman in the film *The Gods Must Be Crazy* is a contemporary version of the noble savage.

7. Such themes are especially common in fantasy; for example, see the "Wild Men" in J. R. R. Tolkien's *Lord of the Rings* trilogy who guide the "civilized" warriors through a forest, speak a pidgin dialect, and are able to read the weather.

8. Gaskins, *What Are You?*, 6.

9. Rhonda Harris Taylor and Lotsee Patterson, "Getting the 'Indian' Out of the Cupboard: Using Information Literacy to Promote Critical Thinking," *Teacher Librarian* 28, no. 2 (Dec. 2000), www.teacherlibrarian.com/tlmag/v_ 28_/v_ 28_2_feature.html (24 Sept. 2007).

10. Credited to songwriters Al Capps and Mary Dean, the song rose to the top spot on record charts in the United States, Canada, and some European countries. Although Cher performed the song and was photographed in American Indian garb, and is often identified as part Cherokee, a genealogical investigation by William Addams Reitwiesner failed to turn up any record of American Indian ancestry. www.wargs.com/other/sarkisian (16 July 2008).

11. In 1999, Nasdijj, who claimed a white father and Navajo mother, published an essay "The Blood Runs Like a River Through My Dreams" (*Esquire* 131, no. 6 [June 1999]: 114). It and the book based on it were nominated for national awards. In 2006, Nasdijj was unmasked as a white writer, Tim Barrus. In March 2008, *The New York Times* (Motoko Rich, "Gang Memoir, Turning Page, Is Pure Fiction," March 4, 2008, 1) disclosed that Margaret Jones, the American Indian–white author of a searing memoir, *Love and Consequences,* detailing an excruciating foster-childhood during which she sold drugs for a street gang, was actually Margaret Seltzer, an affluent white suburbanite, and the story was entirely fabricated.

12. Debbie Reese, a teacher of American Indian Studies and tribally enrolled at Nambe Pueblo, posts book reviews and critiques on her blog, American Indians in Children's Literature: americanindiansinchildrensliterature.blogspot .com/.

13. Virginia Hamilton, *Arilla Sun Down* (New York: Dell, 1976). Quoted in front matter.

14. Jack's interpretation of American Indian identity seems to consist of parading in regalia; other American Indian characters, including his father, James, and Shy Woman, are more nuanced.

15. Olsen was interviewed February 25, 2007, for the British Columbia Teen Readers Choice Stellar Book Award website. www.stellaraward.ca/2008/interview .php?id=12/ (5 April 2008).

16. Debby Dahl Edwardson, "Worldview in Contemporary Indigenous/Native American Literature: Language, Landscape and the Spiritual Geography of Story" (MFA critical thesis, Vermont College, Union Institute and University, 2004), 15–16.

17. Jean Craighead George, *Water Sky* (New York: Harper and Row, 1987), 38.

18. Edwardson, "Worldview," 15–16.

19. Kendall's mother is said to have ended the Snake Clan. "She was the last woman to bear Snake Clan offspring, and clans were passed on by the women. When she married Reid Drennan, she gave a death sentence to her clan. She had fallen in love with the wrong man." However, in this matrilineal society, surely the real problem was that she had no daughter.

20. Some literary critics consider portrayals of indigenous people as lonely stoics, such as in Scott O'Dell's *Island of the Blue Dolphins* and Jean Craighead George's *Julie of the Wolves,* to be objectionable stereotypes. See Georgia Johnson, "The Colonized Child on the Tundra," *Journal of Children's Literature* 21, no. 1 (1995): 24–30, and C. Anita Tarr, "An Unintentional System of Gaps: A Phenomenological Reading of Scott O'Dell's *Island of the Blue Dolphins," Children's Literature in Education* 28, no. 2 (1997): 61–71.

21. The term "Métis" originally referred to those whose ancestry included First Nations and European heritage. Over time, the Métis came to be viewed as a distinct ethnicity and are named, along with First Nations and Inuit peoples, as one of Canada's three official aboriginal categories in the Canadian Constitution of 1982.

22. Joanna Hearne, "'The Cross-Heart People': Race and Inheritance in the Silent Western," *Journal of Popular Film and Television* 30, no. 4 (Winter 2003): 182. The thirty-two mixed-race Indian dramas explored here were all made between 1909 and 1926.

23. Hearne, "'The Cross-Heart People,'" 189.

24. Hearne, "'The Cross-Heart People,'" 191.

25. Hearne, "'The Cross-Heart People,'" 182. For an analysis of captivity narratives in young adult literature, see Paulette F. Molin, *American Indian Themes in Young Adult Literature* (Lanham, Md.: Scarecrow Press, 2005). Plots involving abduction and escape or return are often forms of the "changeling" narrative in which one's child is stolen, and a fairy changeling is substituted. After the changeling is discovered, a quest to restore the true child to the family and return the changeling to Faery ensues.

26. April 6, 2008. It was an article identifying quixotic results from the 2000 U.S. Census.

27. Darby Li Po Price, "Multiracial Comedy as a Commodity in Hawaii," in *The Sum of Our Parts: Mixed-Heritage Asian Americans,* ed. Theresa Williams Léon and Cynthia L. Nakashima (Philadelphia, Pa.: Temple University Press, 2001), 123.

28. Price, "Multiracial Comedy," 124.

29. Cynthia Leitich Smith, "Multicultural Humor, Seriously," *Cynsations,* 27 July 2004. cynthialeitichsmith.blogspot.com/2004/07/multicultural-humor-seriously.html (6 April 2008).

30. Smith, "Multicultural Humor, Seriously."
31. Smith, "Multicultural Humor, Seriously."

FICTIONAL WORKS CITED OR CRITIQUED

Note: An asterisk denotes works critiqued as well as cited in the chapter.

Lori Marie Carlson, ed., *Moccasin Thunder: American Indian Stories for Today* (New York: HarperCollins, 2005).*

Alden Carter, *Dogwolf* (New York: Scholastic, 1994).*

Forrest (Asa) Carter, *The Education of Little Tree* (New York: Delacorte, 1976).

Eileen Charbonneau, *The Ghosts of Stony Clove* (New York: Orchard, 1988).

———, *In the Time of the Wolves* (New York: Tor-Doherty, 1994).*

Jean Craighead George, *Julie of the Wolves* (New York: HarperCollins, 1972).

———, *Water Sky* (New York: Harper and Row, 1987).

Virginia Hamilton, *Arilla Sun Down* (New York: Dell, 1976).*

Karen Hesse, *Aleutian Sparrow* (New York: Simon & Schuster, 2003).*

Will James, *Smoky the Cow Horse* (New York: Scribner's, 1926).*

Kimberley Griffiths Little, *Enchanted Runner* (New York: Avon, 1999).*

———, *The Last Snake Runner* (New York: Random House-Laurel Leaf, 2002).*

Nasdijj (Tim Barrus), "The Blood Runs like a River Through My Dreams," *Esquire* 131, no. 6 (June 1999): 114.

Jean Davis Okimoto, *The Eclipse of Moonbeam Dawson* (New York: Tom Doherty, 1997).*

———, *Talent Night* (New York: Scholastic Trade, 1995; Reprint, iUniverse-Authors Guild backinprint.com, 2000.).

Sylvia Olsen, *White Girl* (Custer, Wash.: Orca, 2004).*

———, *Yellow Line* (Custer, Wash.: Orca, 2005).*

Margaret Robinson, *A Woman of Her Tribe* (New York: Scribner's, 1990).*

Leslie Marmon Silko, *Ceremony* (New York: Penguin, 1977).*

Cynthia Leitich Smith, *Rain Is Not My Indian Name* (New York: HarperCollins, 2001).*

———, "A Real-Live Blond Cherokee and His Equally Annoyed Soul Mate," in *Moccasin Thunder: American Indian Stories for Today,* Lori Marie Carlson, ed., (New York: HarperCollins, 2005).*

Michael Spooner, *Last Child* (New York: Henry Holt, 2005).*

· 4 ·

Divided Loyalties

Immigrant Mixed Heritage

$\mathcal{M}$ost Americans came to the United States as immigrants. Driven by famine, war, and social conflict as much as they were drawn by dreams of wealth and prosperity, they came in waves. In the years between 1815 and 1860 alone, five million immigrants arrived. Even for those driven by desperation, leaving home was a hard decision: family, tradition, language, food, everything familiar was left behind. The only way to keep the memory of home and cultural identity alive was to re-create them as closely as possible in the new land. Countless permutations of this journey have appeared as history, memoir, and fiction—including children's and young adult literature—detailing waves of immigration, the diasporas, what was lost and what was gained in the struggle to adapt. Regardless of the cultures involved, YA fiction has focused most often on the cultural and generational gaps between the first and second generations of immigrants. For example, Amy Tan's *The Joy Luck Club,* published as adult fiction, but considered crossover YA, depicts the struggles and conflicts between mothers raised in China and their daughters born and raised in the United States. These narratives explore the gap between parents, who were shaped by the culture they left behind, and their children, who know only the new culture. The characters struggle to bridge the gap, not always successfully. The family unit itself, however, is not of mixed heritage.

That classic YA immigrant narrative centers on the generation gap. When we add another generation, we reframe the story. Our young married couple from China has immigrated to the United States. They have a son; he grows up and marries a black American woman, whose own family dates from the African diaspora. The children of that couple, of mixed Chinese and black American heritage, blend two strong cultures. This scenario, depicted in Sherri L. Smith's *Hot, Sour, Salty, Sweet* (2008), is becoming more commonplace every day. It differs from the classic immigrant parent/acculturated adolescent scenario because the parents are not the immigrants. The grandparents or their forebears made the immigrant journey. Now we have two sets of grandparents, each of whom wants to see its culture preserved in younger generations. Whose traditions prevail? What if the cultures are historically in conflict, as the Chinese and Japanese have been? What if they represent different faiths, such as Jews and Christians? What happens when a teen raised interculturally gets romantically involved with a teen whose family is monocultural? These scenarios are hard to live through, but great to read about. Until very recently such families were rarely reflected in YA fiction, but this is starting to change.

In this chapter, we look at mixed-heritage characters for whom culture and ethnicity, including religion, define identity more than race does. This identity may be visible to the observer, as in half-Asian identity, or invisible, as in interfaith Jewish and Christian identity. Each presents its own problems and opportunities.

Definitions of race and ethnicity have been most variable in the context of immigration. Jews, considered an ethnic group in Europe and pseudo-scientifically identified as a race by the Nazis, became a white religious group in mid-twentieth-century America.[1] Immigrants from China, Japan, Korea, and Vietnam were not Asian until they came to the United States. The boundaries of race, culture, and ethnicity are permeable, and more adolescents than ever before in American history are living proof of this fact. As our society becomes more diverse, as multiracial individuals marry other multiracial individuals, as technological change continues to shrink the world, cultural definitions and identities can be expected to shift even more.

FICTIONAL FAMILY DEMOGRAPHICS

Young adult novels about mixed-heritage characters from nonwhite or non-WASP (White Anglo Saxon Protestant) immigrant backgrounds tend to be upbeat, contemporary tales told with more than a dash of humor. Issues arising from mixed heritage, ambiguous physical appearance, and racial classification are secondary to the embarrassing-immigrant narrative: weird, non–English-speaking relatives who cook gross, un-American foods and have strange ideas about how teens should dress and act. Multiracial identity may be central or it may function mostly as a trendy narrative hook. Five of our mixed-heritage protagonists are being raised monoracially, ignorant of half their ancestry. The missing half in these narratives is usually white (*Kim/Kimi* is the exception), and although missing, it is seldom sought out. The tragic mulatto makes an appearance, in exotic dress. But the often exasperating issue on which many of our adolescents are focused is their all-too-evident immigrant heritage. If they could send Grandma back to Taipei or Dad to New Delhi, they would.

These works rarely explore or even acknowledge the grim history of mixed heritage in America. Historical novels are rare, even though many immigrants, such as the Chinese, have a long history in the United States; by 1867, fifty thousand Chinese Americans were enumerated in California alone. Gary Nash, in *Forbidden Love*,[2] his YA history of mixed-race unions in America, provides abundant evidence that they weren't confined to black- or American Indian-and-white couples. This reality is not reflected in YA fiction, which, almost always contemporary, follows familiar plot paradigms. Interfaith families, other than a few Jewish-Christian combinations, are almost nonexistent. Consequently, hundreds of years of mixed-heritage stories have yet to be told.

Of our sixteen interracial fictional families, nine are intact: two parents living with their biological children. In the remaining families, one father (Japanese American) is deceased. Six sets of parents are estranged or divorced; of these, five custodial parents are mothers and one is a father. Family social status and income range from marginal to affluent. Overall, these families are more diverse in makeup and social class than those we saw in earlier chapters.

WHITE NOISE

In YA fiction, characters of immigrant mixed heritage often disown or disregard their white ancestry. In the Cuban-Polish American and Japanese-Polish American families in this chapter, for example, the only heritages discussed, much less celebrated, are Cuban and Japanese. The characters in the Missing Half stories in chapters 2 and 3 sought and/or were enriched by discovering their missing heritage. Heritage is missing here, too, but no one cares. Rodney, protagonist of Jean Davies Okimoto's *Talent Night* (1995), describes how, after his Japanese American mother's divorce from his white father, she changed her name. "No longer was she Helen Suyama-Delenko. Whack! Off went the Delenko . . . back to good old Helen Suyama" (7). Okimoto celebrates cultural diversity in all its forms except European American white identity. She is not alone. Our authors may assume that white "mainstream" American culture is so dominant, it hardly needs more exposure. *But that homogenized whiteness is not about culture at all.* It does not reflect Polish American or Norwegian American or Greek American traditions; it simply reflects the dominant white caste. Just as white authors may forget that their multiracial characters are not members of that dominant caste, authors in this chapter—and not all are white—often render their characters' white heritage invisible or dispose of it with a few derogatory comments.

Beyond our social constructs of race lie a multitude of complex cultures and ethnicities, including white heritage. Whether derived from southern slave owners, Irish indentured servants, Norwegian fishers, or Polish farmers—their European American ancestry belongs to these characters every bit as much as their Chinese or Japanese or Cuban heritage. Dominant-caste ancestry is still ancestry. Recognizing and acknowledging the failings and achievements of one's forebears is important. We are here because of them. Their choices, good and bad, set the stage for our own. In fiction, as in real life, we can't heal past evils by pretending they don't exist. To produce authentic fiction, novelists need to start depicting the white ethnicities of their mixed-heritage families.

TRAGIC MULATTOS: EAST ASIAN DIVISION

Kim/Kimi, a 1987 novel set in rural Iowa, turns up regularly on multicultural and school reading lists. The author, Hadley Irwin, is actually a nom de plume representing the collaboration of two white women authors, Lee Hadley and Ann Irwin, both now deceased. Kim, sixteen, is the daughter of a white mother and Japanese American father who died when she was an infant. Three years later, her mother married a white college professor. Their child, Kim's half-brother, Davey, is twelve. Kim's mixed heritage is presented as a wound that never heals, a kind of racial birth defect. At risk for failing in school, tardy and inattentive, Kim neglects homework to immerse herself in vapid romance novels about popular blonde, blue-eyed Stepford teens. What is the cause of all this alienation? Let's put her on the metaphorical psychiatrist's couch:

"It hadn't always been that way," Kim recalls. In grade school, she rushed home to tell Mom about her day. "Mom would listen and laugh or look serious, depending on what I was saying. It was as if she were my best friend and there was nothing I couldn't tell her and she always understood." It changed in sixth grade. "Heidi Hansen wanted me to give her my answers on a geography test, and I wouldn't do it. When the teacher wasn't looking, she leaned across the aisle and whispered 'dirty Jap.' She didn't say it loudly enough for anyone else to hear, but she might as well have shouted it." Kim kept this a secret. "From then on, I didn't tell Mom a lot of things, and it got to be a habit. That's also when I started reading romances" (11–12).

Kim has an affluent, loving family: "I suppose I had about anything anyone could ever want. Mom and Dad were great, and Davey was a really super little brother, but I didn't belong . . . even in my family" (13). Her father is "exactly the kind of person that anyone would want for a dad—funny and gentle." In fact, "only when something came up like Pearl Harbor was I reminded that he wasn't my real father" (38).[3] When Kim wonders why she hasn't been asked out on a date yet, Davey tells her to look in the mirror. She's different, Japanese—no further explanation needed. If racism is responsible (we aren't given enough information to know), nothing that happens in the novel is likely to help.

What prompts Kim's odyssey is the annual December trauma: "It had happened every year since junior high whenever December 7 came around or anyone mentioned the attack on Pearl Harbor. There was no way I could deny being Japanese—half Japanese, that is, thanks to a father I'd never known" (18). When a film is shown in her history class about the bombing of Pearl Harbor, she walks out, telling Davey later: "'Everyone looks at me as if World War II were my fault. This isn't 1941, is it? And I'm not a Jap. I'm an American. I can't take it anymore'" (22). For 1987, this hypersensitivity seems a tad neurotic. After all, the Korean War and Vietnam War have taken place in the interim. Neither is mentioned in the novel.

It's not that she doesn't want to be Japanese, Kim says; she just doesn't want to be "different." To recap: Kim's experience of being Japanese is: a) hearing a girl whisper "dirty Jap" in sixth grade, b) being forced to hear about World War II in history class, and c) not being asked on dates. She has experienced her Japanese ancestry in no other way. Her motivation to learn about her missing half is that she "can't take it anymore." The only time Kim wonders about her "Japanese part," as she calls it, is after an incident of perceived or anticipated bias.

Although her parents are presented as loving, even doting, and her stepfather is a college professor, neither has talked about her ancestry to Kim. She never experiences her Japanese heritage as something to celebrate. No one says: "You should be proud," or "You have an interesting background," or "What is it like to be half-Japanese?"

With abundant financial and emotional support from Davey, her best friend Jav, and an adult family friend, Kim flies to California because—the only reason she gives for going—her father's relatives may be there. When Jav wants more details, Kim says, "'What am I supposed to be? I'm half and half. I look Japanese—'" (18–19). We never get a clearer articulation.

In California, Kim is billeted, chauffeured, and helped by Japanese Americans to whom she has been referred by friends in Iowa. Their motive for helping Kim is kindness and empathy. She accepts their help as her due, expressing no gratitude or interest in those who help her. Kim's expectations of Japanese Americans are wince-provoking stereotypes. She speculates on what she'll find at the home of the woman who has volunteered to put her up: "The house would probably have paper walls and pillows to sit on or else legless bamboo chairs." She worries that she'll have to sit on the floor, that she'll "probably be served raw fish and green tea" (71). Even when it has to do with her father's life, Kim reacts to what she learns with impatience and boredom. After Mrs. Enomoto volunteers to spend a day driving her to the site of the camp where he was interned, Kim thinks: "Rats! Here I was wasting a whole day. What did Mrs. Enomoto expect me to find at Tule Lake? Footprints in the sand? I was searching for my father. What could I find in an old prison camp?" (134).

Through the help of many people she does not thank, Kim finds and contacts her father's sister and mother. After an inconclusive visit, having learned a bit about Japanese American history, she flies home,

with a vague possibility of future contact. Finding her missing half does not enrich Kim's life. She returns to Iowa the same glum, self-centered girl who left. Her only sign of progress—if that is what it is—is that she can no longer keep straight the various plots of her dreary romance novels. As a measure of self-esteem, this leaves a lot to be desired.

We have to go back many decades to find a novel that presents as biased and negative a picture of mixed heritage as *Kim/Kimi* does. The book rests on a mountain of unexamined, insulting assumptions and stereotypes. The novel makes Kim's mixed-heritage experience—a subject about which the authors are unforgivably ignorant—define her totally. Kim was intended as a tragic mulatto; she is merely a whiny one. Her character, motivation, and behavior throughout the novel rest on one assumption: not being all white is a tragic cross to bear, one that justifies any amount of failure, rudeness, lack of empathy, and self-centeredness.

One need only attend a panel discussion at a Society of Children's Book Writers and Illustrators conference to hear horror stories about the awful manuscripts editors turn down every day. Why wasn't *Kim/Kimi* one of them? What is done is done; the question to answer now is why this insult to readers' intelligence and humanity remains on book lists, multicultural or otherwise.

With relief, we turn to Sherry Garland's *Song of the Buffalo Boy* (1992). Set in Vietnam in 1989, this was an American Library Association Best Book for Young Adults. Loi, seventeen, is the daughter of a white American GI and Vietnamese mother. Born during the Vietnam War, Loi has only vague memories of a kind soldier and a snapshot to associate with her father. She and her mother live with her mother's brother, a widower, and his children. Loi's appearance reminds villagers of the American soldiers in the disastrous war that brought ruin to many of them, of the leftover chemicals from the war that have seeped into the groundwater, causing horrific birth defects. It makes her the target of bitter bias and mistrust.

Unlike Kim, Loi longs to know about her father. Her mother is no help: "'Never, never speak of that man again to me or in front of anyone else. As far as I am concerned, that horrible man is dead and forgotten,'" she says. "'You must remember that if it hadn't been for your kind, generous uncle we would have starved after the war. And we would not have a home now. His life has been full of woe because he took us in'" (24).

Loi is in love with a village boy, Khai, who returns her feelings, but his family won't permit him to marry a *con-lai* (half-breed). Instead, Loi's uncle accepts an offer of marriage for her from an aging alcoholic widower with five children. "'Officer Hiep may not be a perfect man, but he has a good government job and he is the *only* man who is willing to marry a fatherless *con-lai*'" (34). Loi is horrified, but her mother says Loi is lucky to have any marital prospects. The village is extremely poor and options for such a girl are severely limited.

Loi is determined not to marry Officer Hiep. She and Khai search for a way out. When she meets an American, Raymond Smith, searching for his half-Vietnamese daughter, they verify that Loi is too young to be his child, but he tells her that as the child of an American, she can immigrate to the United States. The government will find her sponsors and housing. Her husband and children, if any, can come, too. Smith's interpreter adds, "'You might even be able to locate your father,' because he can see the division number on the soldier's left sleeve in the photo" (116). Loi and Khai concoct a plan to take a bus to Ho Chi Minh City and marry and then, Loi hopes, immigrate to America to find her father (Khai resists that part of the plan). The scheme goes awry when Khai misses the bus. Loi arrives in the city alone with very little money and no urban survival skills. Joe, a Vietnamese street urchin posing as half-American, takes Loi to the Foreign Office to apply for a visa. Without money to pay for bribes, the process is slow. Every day, Loi goes to the bus station, but Khai does not come. She and Joe live in a crowded park close to the Foreign Office. After Joe is beaten up and out of money, Loi, in desperation, decides to try prostitution but cannot go through with it. She and Joe are saved when they run into Raymond Smith. Unable to find his daughter, he offers to bring Loi and Khai to the United States with him. When Khai shows up, he refuses to go. Loi stays with him, and persuades Smith to take Joe back to the United States with him instead.

The romance between Loi and Khai is the book's central theme (the novel won Best YA Romance for 1993 from Romance Writers of America). The setting is strong and Loi is engaging and sympathetic. Khai, who along with tending buffalo plays the flute and carves wooden animals, is appealing, so that Loi's choice is believable. Unlike Kim, Loi's biracial status *is* a kind of birth defect. She is Vietnamese culturally, but her appearance symbolizes what other Vietnamese despise or at least would rather forget. Loi knows very little about America. Her motiva-

tion is to find her father, the smiling man she remembers, the man in the photo. What leads Loi to stay in Vietnam is not just Khai's reluctance to leave, but a letter she receives from her mother, saying the man in the photo was not her father. "'He was just a kind soldier who found my mother after she had given birth to me. He felt sorry for her and took us under his wing for a long time. But my mother didn't sleep with him; he already had a wife and children.'" So who was her father? "'Má didn't know my father's name. He was just a boy, lonely and scared like her. She slept with him once and never saw him again'" (270).

Loi is a tragic mulatto precluded from passing. Her ancestry is clear for anyone to read. It may be a stretch to believe she and Khai would turn down the opportunity to emigrate, but they are not destitute and neither has much of a sense of what life would be like in America. Even with napalm residue, arranged marriages, anti-American bias, and extreme poverty, there is no place like home. This, Garland successfully persuades us, is a happy ending.

Raspberry Hill, protagonist of Sharon G. Flake's *Money Hungry* (2001) and *Begging for Change* (2004), is the feisty narrator of these novels celebrating the power of friendship in a largely black, inner-city community. Two important characters in both books are multiracial siblings, Mai and Ming, children of a black mother and Korean immigrant father. Raspberry's best friend, Ja'nae, is dating Ming. In *Money Hungry,* Ja'nae tells Mai she should be proud of being mixed. "'I ain't mixed. I'm black . . . like you,'" Mai says. Raspberry thinks, "I don't know why Ja'nae even goes there. She knows how Mai feels about her mixed race, and how Ming feels about being mixed, too. Ming don't want to be called black, African American, or Korean. He says he's biracial. Mai don't want to be called Korean or biracial. She's black. Call her anything different, and she will go off on you" (40). Mai's touchiness is irresistible, guaranteed to get a rise out of her. She has a tattoo reading "100% BLACK."

Mai's parents operate a food cart that sells Korean and soul food. Most, but not all, of the community is delighted to be able to order collard greens with their *bibimbap* and *chajang mein*. "Mr. Kim is a proud man. A nice man," Raspberry says. "He wouldn't hurt or cheat anybody. But the kids around here are just plain mean to him. Mai don't treat her father no better. But she checks herself when she's around Ming, 'cause he don't play that" (97).

The sequel finds Mai no more resigned. When her all-Korean cousins Su-bok and Ling visit her in *Begging for Change,* little Ling takes to her cousin and tells people that she, too, is black, just like Mai. During the visit, the girls enter a store whose owner assumes Mai is up to no good. "The man with the broom sweeps at Mai's legs and feet like she's dirt. 'You go. Fore I call police'" (213). When he calls her trash, she hits him, he calls the police, and they call Mai's father, who insists that Mai apologize to the storekeeper. When she refuses, her father grabs her by the arm. Her father orders her to apologize; if she does, the man won't press charges. "Mai is talking a mile a minute," Raspberry reports. Mai tells her father the shopkeeper has called her "black trash."

> Mr. Kim keeps his back turned to her. He repeats himself. "Apologize." When he turns around, I see tears running down his face. "You too," he says, pointing to the man with the broom.
>
> I don't know what Mai and the man say, 'cause they're speaking in Korean. When they are done, Mr. Kim whispers something in Mai's ear. She shakes her head and says, "No, Daddy. No." He holds her, rocks her from side to side.
>
> "You look in the mirror and all you see is a little black girl," he says, pushing curls out of her eyes. "I see my sister and my mother. People I love, just like you."
>
> Mai points to the store owner and his wife, then to the people all around us. "They don't see what you see, Daddy. All they see is this," she says, pulling at the skin on her arm. "And this," she says, shaking out her hair. "And they can't figure out what I am." (217)

Mai tells her father that everyone wants her to choose sides: black, biracial, Korean. "'I did choose,'" she says. "'Only nobody likes the side I picked . . . not the kids at school, or the boys at the mall, not even you.'" They talk quietly and Raspberry overhears Mr. Kim say "that the next time someone asks what she is, she should tell 'em that she's Kim Sunghee's daughter. 'Sweet as honey and brown as fresh baked bread'" (217–18).

Mai is a tragic mulatto for our time: she has chosen an identity that doesn't match her phenotype. No rule of hypodescent or certificate of tribal enrollment can help. Mai will have to find a way to be happy in her own skin. Flake leaves us with the hope that by seeing her father's love for her, finally understanding that he shares her pain, she has taken a step in that direction.

FOREIGN RELATIONS

Mai is ashamed of her father because he is not black, but compared to the parents and relatives of some mixed-heritage teens, Mr. Kim blends in beautifully. In *Nothing but the Truth (And a Few White Lies)*, Justina Chen Headley's 2006 debut novel, Patty Ho is finishing her freshman year of high school as a serious underachiever, while her brother, Abe, has been admitted to Harvard. Patty is jealous of Abe, who is not only high-achieving, but looks Chinese. Patty's looks are more ambiguous. The book's emotional center is Patty's relationship with their driven, upwardly mobile Taiwanese immigrant mother who works as a bookkeeper, burning the midnight oil to create opportunities for Patty and Abe. She is estranged from their white father. All Patty knows of him is that he met her mother when he came to Taiwan to study, and left the family when Patty was two. This is no Missing Half narrative. Apart from a few vague references, Patty does not refer to him unless he is brought to her attention by someone else. She and Abe appear to have no connection to his extended family. Patty makes several speeches about feeling crushed between Asian and white identities, but they are unpersuasive, in part because she shows no interest in her father's heritage. Her behavior, and the book's strongest, most deeply felt and realized scenes, involve Patty's relationship with her mother. Their troubled relationship is the engine that drives this story. Her mother is proudly Taiwanese. Correspondingly, Patty longs to be all-Chinese, not half. Her whiteness is a barrier to that goal.

In an incident that would have put Kim in a coma, a racist boy spits on Patty who, shaken, walks on to school, after registering that the passenger in his car is a boy she has had a crush on. While she changes her shirt, which has gobs of spit on it, she thinks, "No matter how much I scrub, no matter if my skin is rubbed raw, no matter how much cover-up and concealer I wear, I can't erase who I am. I feel like I'm stuck on some infinite teeter-totter: too-white, too-Asian; too-white, too-Asian" (45). This caught-in-the-middle tirade doesn't fit the incident. The boy's racism was directed at her because she was Chinese, not because she was half-Chinese.

Where Patty feels awkward is not at school but at the Taiwanese Family potluck suppers. One of the best and funniest scenes in the book takes place during one of these, where the kids post eavesdroppers to listen in on "the adults who were playing a ruthless game of My Kid Is Better than Yours." At these suppers, Patty's mixed ancestry is a painful contrast to the monoracial "China Dolls" who, she notes, are "identical twins a year older than me whose claim to potluck fame is their glossy, jet black hair and porcelain skin. My whitened skin gets no such looks of envy. I've cheated by adding white to my gene pool whereas the China Dolls are pure-breeds, superior for producing such light skin on their own" (60–61). The person Patty most wants to impress is her mother. Highly competitive Mama, however, wants to impress other Taiwanese Americans. Scattered through the book are her scoldings, transcribed as a lecture series with titles like "You Have It So Easy" and "You Shame Family Honor."

Patty's power struggle with her mother colors the choices she makes at school. The book's organizing conceit flows from a "truth statement," an assignment that Patty has blown off. Nagged by mom, Patty has applied and been accepted to math camp at Stanford University. At the airport, preparing to board her flight to California, Mrs. Ho's behavior gives new meaning to "embarrassing." Watched by Patty's fellow camper Anne Wong and the handsome Chinese boy with her, Stu, Mrs. Ho goes ballistic when Patty's suitcase proves to be overweight. Mama lightens it by tossing out Patty's clothes and underwear (Anne packs the extra in her duffle bag).

While Patty enjoys camp, she has to be coaxed by Brian, in charge of the campers, to exert herself. Patty has avoided working up to her math potential ever since, as a seven-year-old, she disappointed her mother after solving a Rubik's cube, "the one and only time Mama had actually talked herself into believing that I was a certifiable genius. Her smiles at me have never been wider. That just made her disappointment so much more acute when I walked out of the IQ test, labeled above average but nowhere in the heady realms of potluck envy" (100).

Romance buds between Stu and Patty; she goes "buildering" (scaling campus buildings) with her roommate Jasmine, and finally applies herself at math. Despite the action, these scenes are the book's weakest. We need Mrs. Ho. The topic of Patty's white father finally comes up when Brian, who is dating a Chinese girl, asks her whether it was hard for her parents to cross the racial divide. She has no idea. "Forever, it seems, I've sketched out scenarios for how Mama drove my father away, how she harped on him until he couldn't stand it anymore. But honestly,

I have no idea what really ended them, just as I don't know what brought them together. All I know is that life in the scorched aftermath has made me parched for love" (131). This isn't convincing, since these feelings aren't reflected elsewhere in the book.

Patty has many conversations with her mother in her head, but fails to keep in touch with her in the real world. When her letters and calls go unanswered, Mama shows up unannounced. The sight of Patty and Stu together infuriates her. She makes a scene in front of Patty's peers. "'You think you know everything. Big fifteen-year-old girl. But you know nothing. You throw yourself away like cheap *ho-lee-jing* garbage'" (154). Mama adds, "'You make bad decision. All the time.'" She drags Patty off to her sister, intending to take Patty back to Seattle, but Aunt Lu brokers a cease-fire: Patty can stay with her while she finishes math camp.

At Aunt Lu's home, Patty finds a pair of tiny slippers, "Lotus shoes," Lu says, that belonged to her great-great-grandmother. Having never heard of bound feet before, Patty thinks they look like doll shoes. Lu says these "dolls" had their feet broken and bound to keep them from growing more than three or four inches long. When Patty asks why, Lu says that scholars believe women bound their feet in order to look sexy, on the same principle as wearing stiletto heels. Headley, like other authors noted in this book, delivers this historical exposition in a kind of journalistic question-and-answer dialogue. Once again, the protagonist has been kept ignorant of what she ought to know, so that another character can instruct her and, thereby, readers.

Along with the tiny shoes, Patty discovers old family photos. One shows her mother's face bruised and swollen. Her aunt won't discuss it, so Patty calls Abe, who tells her their father beat their mother and that she nearly left the family when Patty was an infant. She returned to them only because she heard Patty crying. Though Patty has thought Abe is their mother's favorite, he, it turns out, is convinced that Patty is the favored one.[4] Patty returns home and turns in her assignment. "We are all hapas, in one way or another. Not necessarily half-Asian, but trust me, we are all half-something" (240) she philosophizes in her A paper.

However, it is Mama readers will remember. Not only a powerful character, she is a powerful symbol, the umbilical cord connecting her immigrant children to the world left behind. Early in the book Patty, unable to sleep, goes downstairs and discovers "Mama using a huge pile of spreadsheets as a pillow, one hand on her big calculator and the other grazing her laptop computer. Her hangnailed fingers twitch like she's trying to crunch numbers even in her sleep" (37). Readers of Amy Tan's *The Joy Luck Club* have received a crash course in driven Chinese mothers, and Headley's is a card-carrying member of the club. As in Tan's novel, the tension between immigrant mother and the daughter on whom her hopes for the future rest makes for riveting fiction. She may be part monster, but Headley owes her: Mama rescues this novel from the novelty-chick-lit bin.

Maya Running (2005), by Indian American author Anjali Banerjee, is set in 1970s Manitoba, Canada. Another debut, it joins the modest surge of fiction about multiracial teens of Indian descent (Mitali Perkins's novels are discussed in the next chapter). Old world/new world culture clashes provide most of the plot points, conflict, and humor in this light, humorous fantasy. Maya, thirteen, is an only child of immigrants from India, an Indian father and half-Anglo Indian (of English colonial extraction) mother. Maya is lighter skinned than her father and most Indians, but is called "nigger" in white, rural Manitoba, where "there are no black people in our town, so I guess I'm the next best target. When I die, I'll become an exhibit at the local museum" (18). Maya is not ignorant of Indian culture and customs; she just wishes they would go away. She blows off questions about her Indian heritage, even from Jamie, a boy she likes. Maya's survival strategy is to try to fit in, without fighting back. Despite this, Maya doesn't want to move to California where her mother's career is going to take the family. Nominally Hindu, Maya's father "doesn't pray to or worship Hindu gods. He worships the universe and Einstein's theory of relativity" (20). Her mother is equally secular.

When her beautiful Indian cousin Pinky comes for a visit, Maya's carefully crafted self-image and the hard-won perch she has staked out for herself in the social pecking order fall apart. Maya studies Pinky's photo before she arrives. "The girl in the picture radiates fairy-tale beauty, every molecule molded just so. Her hair is night flowing rich and bold past her shoulders. Her wide Indian eyes are the brightest stars, her lips red and full. Her creamy skin—one could almost touch it—gives off a vibrant life." Maya compares herself to Pinky. "Suddenly, my fingers look plain. I remember the metal in my mouth. The sharp braces push at my tongue." Her house, her life suddenly seem boring. "The only mysterious element of life is this girl's smiling face" (22).

Pinky fulfills Maya's worst fears. In monochrome Manitoba, she stands out as exotically beautiful, secure in her sense of self. She fascinates Maya's friend Psycho, and Jamie is soon smitten. Maya feels invisible next to Pinky. The trouble with camouflage is that sometimes you want to be seen. Pinky enjoys sharing Indian culture and is a hit with everyone. Maya's friends want to know why *she* doesn't wear saris or have a bindi on her forehead. And when Pinky borrows "typical Canadian clothes" from her, Maya compares herself to Pinky on her own turf and falls short. "The shirt hangs on Pinky just right. Desperation tugs at my insides" (78).

Pinky prays to a statue of Ganesh, the Hindu deity who removes obstacles, that she has brought with her. One night Maya wakes up to find the statue alive, munching on candy in her closet. She asks him to remove her obstacles—the move to California, being eclipsed by Pinky—and Ganesh obliges. The next morning Maya is beautiful; her braces are gone, her figure is womanly. She is no longer clumsy, has a dream wardrobe, and can speak French. Meanwhile, Pinky has "lost her starlight glow of charisma" (112). Jamie is now smitten with Maya; her parents are her acquiescent robot-like servants. Spooked, Maya complains to Ganesh, but is stuck with what she asked for. Pinky returns to India, taking the statue of Ganesh with her.

Desperate to reverse course, Maya talks her still-compliant father into making an impromptu family visit to India, where she tracks down the statue of Ganesh and accomplishes her mission. Back in Canada, Maya is finally comfortable in her skin. "I am changeable, as transient as the seasons. My mother and father, my ancestors, the dust and heat of India, the northern lights and the snow melting on the prairies—I am all of this and none of this. I am special in a way that is bigger and older than this town" (209), she rhapsodizes.

Maya's motivations don't always make sense; the trip to India feels rushed, but Ganesh is a lively presence, and the gentle "be careful what you wish for" lesson is entertainingly taught. Banerjee is a rarity among YA authors: she presents a culture likely to be unfamiliar to readers and does so without saddling her innocent characters with reprehensible negligence and ignorance. Banerjee shows it can be done. The only quibble is that the legacy of Mom's Anglo heritage is undetectable, except in skin color.

Marie Lamba's *What I Meant . . .* (2007) portrays an interracial extended family that includes a relative who is not merely embarrassing, but downright toxic. The protagonist Sangeet, fifteen, is a smart, level-headed teen with a younger sister, Doodles. Their Indian father has left his monotheistic Sikh religion behind along with his turban; their white mother is a lapsed Catholic. Rounding out the family is Chachi, Dad's disagreeable, thieving sister-in-law from India, his brother's widow. Family tensions run high. Mom arbitrates the many points of contention. While Mom is not religiously observant, her upbringing, as recorded in her girlhood diary, is central to the plot and we get a stronger sense of her than of most white parents discussed in this chapter.

There is much to enjoy in this first novel, which, like *Maya Running,* is played for laughs. Lamba, white, who is herself in an interracial family, doesn't recycle tired plots. Refreshingly, the boy who pines for Sangeet and whom she ignores does *not* prove to be her true love in the end. Nor does Sangeet make up after a fight with her best friend, Gina; they remain estranged, as sometimes happens. Unlike Patty and Maya, Sangeet is at home in her skin. Her story is more about the immigrant experience mediated by race than bifurcated racial identity. Chachi, however, can only be described as a monster. Had she been a more rounded character, had her conniving been more nuanced or relieved by positive traits, the story would have been more compelling.

Sangeet's personal journey becomes a subplot of the Chachi drama. Chachi steals food from the kitchen, but when caught, blames Sangeet, which causes her parents to worry that she has an eating disorder. This plot complication is meant to be humorous but Chachi is too horrible to be funny. "This is the way it should always be in our home. It's what is right. But Mom only wants to see the good in people, and won't even listen to the truth about Chachi," Sangeet laments. "Dad's so wrapped up in tradition and family values that he refuses to see how bad things are. Or maybe he does see, but just can't deal with it. He never will tell Chachi to go" (122). Sangeet worries that permanent damage is being done to the family, especially to Doodles, who "is already forgetting how to be relaxed and happy at home. In two years' time, she won't even remember what it was like before Chachi came. She'll have almost no recollection of how much fun we used to always have together" (122).

Chachi tries to divide Sangeet's happily married parents, railing at both of them, especially Dad, for not honoring Indian customs. "'Her, I don't blame. She doesn't know any better. But you. You are no good'" (179–80). When both take her abuse patiently, Sangeet is driven to spy on Chachi herself, but a scheme to videorecord Chachi's machinations falls apart and their war escalates. Chachi shreds Sangeet's prized poster, steals money from Doodles (Sangeet is blamed), and reads their mother's girlhood diary. Sangeet's parents have forbidden her to date; when she defies her family by sneaking out to attend a concert with a boy, Chachi makes sure she is discovered on her return.

The climax of the novel occurs at a Sikh Gurdwara, the temple where Chachi has nagged the family into arranging a special service of remembrance for her long-dead husband. Lamba paints a vivid picture of the family group: "Dad looks funky, with a blue bandanna knotted on his head. Sort of a Springsteen-meets-Gandhi look" (286–87). Each family member kneels before the altar. When it is Sangeet's turn, fearful her skirt will rise up too far, she does not touch her head to the ground. Chachi notices this. "'Disrespect,' she says, and crawls beside me. Before I can again start my silent prayer, my face is slammed onto the ground. I grasp my nose. Blood drips onto my hand. I move to rise, but her hand is strong on my neck." In front of this crowd of people, "I stand as Doodles and Mom are lifting their heads from the ground. Chachi yanks my hand from my nose and pulls me by the wrist downward. I throw her off me." No one comes to Sangeet's aid. "Now I'm stumbling between worshipers to the carpet pathway, blood pooling in my hands. The music pipes up as I run. My chuni drops to the ground, women gasp, and all eyes are on me" (288–89). She makes her way to the ladies' room and eventually stops the bleeding. After the service, the family goes to an Indian restaurant where Chachi, still going strong, tells Sangeet she is "'turning out just like that mother of yours.'" Sangeet stands up for her mom as Chachi reveals that she has read in the diary how her mother "'did the filthy sexual act'" (295). Only when Chachi attacks Sangeet physically do the adults finally get it. At last, Sangeet's parents recognize that she is neither bulimic nor a thief, and Chachi is sent back to India.

Like the bad fairy at a royal christening, Chachi shadows what ought to be a lighthearted romp. Her attacks on Sangeet are truly vicious. Dad's Indian upbringing may be intended to explain why he fails to stand up for his wife and daughter, but why does American-raised Mom go along? Lamba assembled the ingredients to bake up an excellent mixed-heritage story, but she added too much Chachi to the batter.

A plot thread concerns the Indian festival of Diwali, one of the most important of the Hindu calendar. When a relative calls to wish the family a happy Diwali, Sangeet does not know what it is. Like Patty Ho, Sangeet is ignorant of important aspects of her nonwhite culture and history. At the end of the novel, the family—Chachi-free at last—celebrates Diwali, the festival of light, inviting the goddess Lakshmi to bless them with badly needed good fortune.

Jean Davies Okimoto's comedy of manners, *Talent Night* (1995), is set in multiracial south Seattle. Rodney Suyama lives with his Japanese American single mother and his older sister, Suzanne. Their Polish American father is long gone. Artist, environmentalist, and unreconstructed peace child, Mom creates aluminum sculptures of slugs. Rodney fantasizes about being a rap star, although he's been told that as half-white and half-Japanese, he doesn't qualify racially. (The event that gives the book its name, a talent contest, is a secondary plot thread that gets the story rolling; it follows Rodney as he chooses a name, figures out what he wants to rap about, and finally performs.) Rodney has a crush on Ivy Ramos, who is Filipina and black. His best friends, David Woo and James Robertson, are respectively Chinese and black. The latter's passion is karate and film—he dreams of making movies that combine Lee sensibilities (Spike and Bruce); whenever the boys rent videos, James steers them to *The Seven Samurai*.

The world Rodney and his sister and friends move through without noticing is multiracial and multicultural. The mental constructs they use, the vocabulary and cultural markers, date from an era in which races and cultures were assumed to be separate and immutable. Okimoto shows but resists the temptation to tell us that Rodney's world is a cultural smorgasbord. She sets it in front of readers, asking us to pay attention to what we are consuming.

Rodney seldom mentions his father or his heritage. They have seen him only once since he moved to the East Coast. Like Patty Ho, Rodney has a white missing half that he is not inclined to seek out. The unexamined devaluation of white ethnic heritage works against an otherwise powerful portrait of cultural diversity.

The Suyama family is turned upside down when Mom's Uncle Hideki makes a proposal to will his reparation money (U.S. government compensation for having unjustly interned Japanese Americans in World War II) to Rodney and Suzanne. The gift will be conditional on their demonstrating to him that they value their Japanese heritage.

Soon, both kids are daydreaming about how to impress Uncle Hideki and what they'll do with the money. Suzanne takes up ikebana and writes haiku. Rodney reads Basho. They solicit help from friends, including Ivy and Brent Hanson, Suzanne's white boyfriend. The kids list the "real" Japanese Americans they know, or could get to know, and introduce to Uncle Hideki. Ideas include raiding the local Buddhist church youth group, and reaching out to the few Japanese Americans and exchange students they know from school. Mom is disgusted. "'You kids can't just ask Brent and Ivy to disappear for a few days,' Mom snapped. 'It's not right!'" (69). Undeterred, Rodney and Suzanne continue to brainstorm ways to demonstrate to Uncle Hideki how Japanese they are. They make a list of all the Japanese words they know—less than a dozen, it turns out. "'We've got to do better than sayonara, arigato, and sushi!'" (71), Suzanne says. But the only other words they know are names of major Japanese multinationals, car manufacturers, and popular foods. In the end, they decide to cook an authentic Japanese meal. Rodney copies a poem of Basho's out to memorize; meanwhile, Suzanne has written a haiku of her own. She reads it to Rodney, first in English, then Japanese. Impressed, he asks how she learned it. She says her boyfriend Brent translated it for her. "'The white guy!'" Rodney exclaims. "'Brent studied Japanese at the U'" (87), Suzanne tells him smugly.

Rodney goes to a school dance with James, who tells him he'll have to leave early because he has a karate tournament the next day. "I don't know why this had never even occurred to me before, but right here was one of my two best friends, and he was practically an expert at something Japanese!" Rodney asks, "'Hey, man, could you show me some karate moves and stuff, and maybe loan me your outfit?'" James says, "'Gi, it's called a karate gi.'" Rodney explains about Uncle Hideki. "It struck us both funny. James is African American and I'm half Japanese and I've got to learn about this stuff from him. It's like Brent being the one to translate Suzanne's poetry" (88–89).

One evening, while showing off karate kicks James taught him, Rodney slips and overturns Suzanne's ikebana and breaks the vase. Amid the recriminations, Mom comes out to see what's going on; they see she has been crying. Mom has been looking through a family photo album because, she says, Uncle Hideki's proposal has brought up old issues for her. What bothers her is that the kids are focusing on the money, with no thought to what the reparations mean. She shows them pictures of the Santa Anita racetrack, where she was born, shortly after Japanese Americans were first rounded up. She shares the history of the 442nd Regimental Army combat team, the most highly decorated in U.S. history, all Japanese American soldiers.

While Okimoto takes this opportunity to educate her characters and readers on an important episode in U.S. history, readers are left wondering why Mom has left them ignorant of what her family and community went through. She tells them, "'If you didn't learn this in history, you should have'" (112). Whose responsibility is it, however? Okimoto makes clear that—like war veterans and Holocaust survivors—many Japanese felt deeply shamed as well as traumatized by the internment. However, Mom was a toddler when her internment ended. She has since grown up to be an outgoing, iconoclastic, environmental and peace activist. The idea that she would feel too traumatized to teach her own children about what internment meant to her family and other Japanese Americans goes against what we know of her, so her long silence needs explanation. If it is true, as she tells them, that "the internment camps are at the core of what it means to be Japanese American," why has she waited until now to tell them?

Later, Suzanne tells Rodney some of what Mom has now shared with her, about what happened after the war was over. A gang of white boys would scream "Jap" at her, hurling rocks at her on her way home from school, scaring her so much she "soiled herself" (119). Withholding this kind of personal information from children is believable. After all, we censor and edit personal anecdotes of our own childhoods before we share them with our children. It's Mrs. Suyama's failure to discuss the internment overall, the effect on three generations of loyal Americans of being treated as national enemies, that doesn't fit.

In any event, as we follow the characters around we begin to ask: What does ethnic heritage mean in such a world? Are we valuing the right things? Which is more authentically ours, the culture we inherit by birth or the one we choose because we love it?

Rodney and Suzanne find cultural authenticity can clash with other values. Mom doesn't want them to buy Japanese-made disposable wooden chopsticks because they are bad for the environment; but the reusable plastic ones are made in China, not Japan. At an Asian market, they hunt for ingredients that are 100 percent Japanese. But what *is* 100 percent Japanese? They want to make Japanese *gyoza,* but Suzanne tells Rodney her cookbook says "'gyoza was originally a Chinese dish.'" Rodney says, "'David Woo always reminds me that everything was originally Chinese.'" But at least "'it'll go with the plastic Chinese chopsticks'" (120).

Unique among mixed-heritage fiction, *Talent Night* asks us to think about what makes something culturally authentic and what kinds of ingredients add up to cultural identity. Is it artifacts—chopsticks, kimonos, cuisine, art? Is it the collective experience shared by individuals, such as internment during World War II? Okimoto does not answer this for readers. She makes the questions and their complexity clear, then leaves them for readers to ponder.

Welcoming Uncle Hideki on the big day, they exchange gifts and make small talk. After looking at the kids, Uncle Hideki says to Mom, "'They don't look hapa'" (137). This strikes Rodney as rude, as well as odd; he had thought Japanese culture valued politeness.

Uncle Hideki is surprised that Mom is not cooking. At dinner, he points out that the reusable chopsticks aren't Japanese, nor are the California rolls. What interests him is abstract authenticity, not the fact that his never-before-met niece and nephew have done their best to honor him. Ivy, now Rodney's de facto girlfriend, has been invited to eat with them. As they sit down to dinner, Ivy is introduced to Uncle Hideki, who tells Mom: "'*Kuronbo.*'" No one else knows what that means, but "Mom turned bright red, and she looked like she was going to explode" (142). Uncle Hideki continues to stare, while Mom glares at him, speechless. The social temperature drops, and Uncle Hideki soon leaves, barely saying goodbye. When asked what *kuronbo* means, Mom tells them it is a derogatory epithet meaning "black." Regardless of the fact that they won't get his reparations money, everyone is happy to see the last of Uncle Hideki. Sometime later, Mom shows Rodney an article in the local Japanese American community newspaper that says Uncle Hideki judged a calligraphy contest and had to award the first prize to a white boy.

Uncle Hideki looked a lot like her father, Mom tells Rodney, but "'it's like he wanted to keep all the traditional things about Japanese culture, but he missed how you should treat people'" (160). Whatever we decide culture is or is not, it is just one element of life and identity. Those who elevate it above universal human values—love, honesty, kindness, ethical behavior—that all cultures share, end up with nothing but culture to hold onto.

LATIN ROOTS

There are few prominent characters of mixed heritage with Latin American roots in YA fiction. One appears in Ann Brashares's series, *Sisterhood of the Traveling Pants* (2001). The high-profile conceit of this popular series is that four friends share a pair of jeans between them that fit each girl perfectly, although they are of widely different sizes.[5] Carmen, fifteen, is the daughter of a Puerto Rican Catholic mother and white WASP dad. Brown-skinned and generously proportioned, although not seriously overweight, Carmen lives with her mother and looks forward to brief visits from her idolized father. When he finally invites her to visit him, Carmen is stunned and upset to discover that he is engaged to Lydia, a blonde WASP with two teenagers, Paul and Krista. Carmen sees Lydia's lifestyle and customs as a rebuke to her Roman Catholic mother. At dinner, Carmen "submitted to handholding and an unfamiliar grace. Her father was the one who'd refused to convert to Catholicism to please Carmen's maternal grandparents. Now he was Mr. Grace?" (78).

Krista tells Carmen, "'You don't look at all like I was imagining'" (78). Carmen interprets this as a dis: "'You mean, I look Puerto Rican?'" She stares Krista down, who giggles nervously. "'No, I just meant . . . you know . . . you have, like, dark eyes and dark wavy hair?'" Carmen thinks, "And dark skin and a big butt?" but refrains from saying so out loud. "'I look Puerto Rican, like my mother. My mother is Puerto Rican. As in Hispanic. My dad might not have mentioned that'" (78). She is right. Is the tension due to new-blended-family awkwardness or Carmen's ethnicity, or both? Readers are free to choose. Other incidents are similarly vague. Carmen's bridesmaid dress is too small and doesn't suit her. However, after the introductory scenes, most of the difference Carmen experiences is appearance-related, only skin deep.

Carmen's personal blended identity is not explored as an issue in itself; it's subsumed in the context of family breakup and formation of a new blended family. Carmen's behavior and culture, like that of all the sisterhood, is pitched to the series' urban, middle-class, mass-market target audience. The author has the skill to go deeper, but the book's format—each chapter consists of short scenes that cut from one girl to another—works against depth.

For a more insightful look at part–Latin American identity, we have Nancy Osa's *Cuba 15,* a 2004 Pura Belpré honor book that made several national "best of" book lists. Osa's protagonist, Violet Paz, is strong-armed into having a *quinceañera* by her Cuban American abuela. Like others before her, Osa finds the "quince" ideal YA fictional terrain; only a wedding consumes more resources, hopes, and dreams. The fifteen-year-old star makes her debut, attired like a fairy princess, at a huge party. Violet is not thrilled by this prospect at first. "How could I tell my own grandmother that I hated dresses, wouldn't be caught dead onstage, and didn't even think of myself as Cuban? I had green eyes and practically blond hair, for God's sake—the same coloring as my Polish American mother" (11). Violet's appearance, however, is all we see of that heritage. Violet's father works at a pharmacy; her mother runs a thrift store in a church basement. Violet's younger brother, Mark, is a believable pesky sibling.

The novel introduces readers to facets of Cuban American culture: food, playing dominoes, family social dynamics. Violet herself, though engaging and good company, is a little too self-assured to be consistently believable. Wresting control of the quince planning from her strong-willed family, she makes a speech. She would have preferred to go on a trip to Spain, she tells them, but was not given the choice so has accepted the status quo. "I eyed each of them in turn. 'And I'm making it my duty to see that every one of you'—I gave Dad an extra-hard stare—'looks presentable.'" When her father tries to protest, she interrupts. "'And we are going to have one person, and one person only, in charge: me! Is that clear?'" To further cow them into submission, she declares, "'Listen up, people! This quince planning means war, and I need to know whose side you're on. Are you with me?'" (48). Not many adult children can toss off that kind of speech to their elders; for a teenager to do so requires a fair suspension of disbelief.

The entertaining buildup to the quince includes a graceful introduction to Cuban culture. Like Violet, Osa is the daughter of Cuban American and Anglo American parents. The clash in *Cuba 15* is not between Cuban and Polish or even Cuban and mainstream Anglo culture: it's between Cuban exiles with conflicting views on Cuba and how to deal with the Castro regime. Dad refuses to talk about Cuba, where he was born. When Dad discovers Violet has gone to a Peace with Cuba benefit and bought a raffle ticket, he is so furious he wants to cancel the quince. Mom's Polish culture, on the other hand, is invisible, apart from Violet's eyes and hair color and the mention of a few family recipes. Although well integrated into the Cuban side of the family, her character is the least developed of the family. Mom surprises everyone by going back to school, while continuing to play the time-honored role of enabler and smoother of ruffled feathers. Where is her Polish heritage? How does the family combine the two? If not, why? Do they have a tacit agreement that the family will identify primarily as Cuban Americans? If so, how does that make Mom feel? Did the marriage cause a rift with her extended family? (Total rifts are the most common way authors get white culture out of the picture.) Abuela tells Violet that her Dad knows little of the quince because "'it is the mujer who makes the tradition, always. For the men, no tenemos expectaciones. For why do you think the quinceanero exists only for the girls?'" Violet doesn't know. "'Because it is the woman who carries the tradition forward'" (246). But no one mentions any Polish traditions Violet's mother might have had to pass on. The loud voice of mainstream Anglo American culture can drown out just about everything else, but this quarrelsome, loving, vivid Cuban American extended family is strong enough to stand up to white-bread culture, and it would have been entertaining to watch them do it.

"HALF-NESS": INTERFAITH IDENTITIES

Because we view race, culture, and ethnicity as beyond volition—things we are born with—we are not held responsible for them. Religious identification is another matter. All religions involve individual choice and affirmation. "Americans see race as a greater barrier between people than religion, when, in terms of cultural conflict between individuals, just the opposite is true."[6] When mixed heritage includes two different faiths, each with its own beliefs, calendar, and traditions, integrating them into a family culture becomes a major challenge.

This conflict may be why, although nearly four in ten Americans live in interfaith families,[7] only a few YA novels portray them. Those that do border on middle-grade fiction. Since Judy Blume's *Are You There God? It's Me, Margaret* appeared in 1970, there has been little appetite for focusing on religion directly, in the context of multiple or conflicting faiths. Timidity has often been the authors' watchword. A character's religious observance may provide background detail, but rarely receives indepth scrutiny. Of YA novels that explore religion head on, many do so in the context of extremist religious cults that do not resemble any known religion.[8]

A century ago, L. M. Montgomery gave us *Anne of Green Gables* (1908). Almost everyone in Anne's world, apart from an occasional French Canadian servant, is not just Protestant, but Presbyterian. Today, while 62 percent of American adults age seventy and older are Protestant Christians, the figure goes down to 43 percent among Americans ages eighteen to twenty-nine, and a quarter of that younger age group is unaffiliated with any religion.[9] The growing Muslim and Hindu population also is vastly underrepresented in YA fiction, and is virtually undetectable in children's literature, despite the growing number of such interfaith families. Some queasiness over addressing interfaith issues directly is understandable, given the multiplicity of faiths contemporary readers adhere to, nearly all asserting a monopoly on truth. However, if we believe that YA fiction ought to speak to the experience of modern adolescents, this is a silence that needs to be broken.

The issue of interfaith marriage and families is of special concern to American Jews, among whom between one-third and one-half of all marriages are interfaith. For Orthodox Jews and some other sects, Jewish identity is defined as biological, inherited through matrilineal descent; if a Jewish man marries a non-Jewish woman, she and their children are not Jews. Even if they convert to Judaism, they will not be recognized as Jews. Similarly, even when both parents are Jews, their adopted children cannot be Jews unless their biological mothers were Jews. Like American Indians who define tribal identity by a minimum blood quantum, those who support a matrilineal definition of Jewish identity see outmarriage as a countdown to extinction. When a Jewish man forms a family with a non-Jewish woman, a potential biological line is extinguished.

Even among those who accept converts as "real" Jews, interfaith unions are often perceived to result in a loss or dilution of Jewish tradition because the loud voice of superficially mainstream Christian culture is overwhelming. This experience is shared by Greek Orthodox, Muslim, Hindu, Buddhist, and atheist Americans, too, but the suppression of Judaism by Christians has a longer, clearer, often horrific history. Of the few YA novels that focus on interfaith families, most are Jewish and Christian.[10]

The modest growth in YA fiction with teens from nominally Hindu and Muslim homes is welcome. But stories with contemporary settings, like most YA fiction intended for a general audience, aren't much interested in the role of religion in characters' lives. Maya is not raised as Hindu, but in a more "secular humanist" tradition. Sangeet attends the Sikh Gurdwara on special occasions, but family religious observance is primarily social. She does not know what Diwali is until an uncle wishes her "happy Diwali," nor does she appear to follow her mother's Christian faith. Patty Ho is culturally Taiwanese, but we don't see her embrace a religious faith. We are told nothing about Mai's religion. The unspeakable Kim seems to have been raised faith-free as well. Rodney mentions the Seattle Buddhist Church, but we don't see it play a role in his life. Only Loi, raised monoracially in Vietnam, follows a faith. Of course, we can't read too much into these omissions, since YA fiction overall tends to treat religion as wallpaper.

The first YA novel to tackle the interfaith family, Blume's *Are You There God?,* is a perennial favorite of adolescents and censors. While its frank discussion of puberty has aroused more comment, good and bad, what was and remains groundbreaking is its interfaith family. Margaret's mother, a Christian, was disowned by her parents for marrying a Jew. Her dad's mother, Sylvia, who helps the family out financially, wants Margaret to identify as Jewish. (Although Margaret's mother is not Jewish, Sylvia sees Margaret herself as Jewish. The issue of matrilineal descent never surfaces in the novel.) Margaret, who is eleven and an only child, is feeling the pressure. She loves her grandma, but "she's always asking me if I have boyfriends and if they're Jewish" (2–3). The family has recently moved to New Jersey in part, Margaret suspects, to get away from Grandma in New York. Margaret presents her many questions about life and religion to God, but whether she receives a definitive answer is left up to the reader to determine.

At the start of sixth grade, Margaret's class fills out a questionnaire about themselves. Under "I hate," she writes "religious holidays." Her new friends are surprised that she is being raised without faith. "'If you aren't any religion, how are you going to know if you should join the Y or the Jewish Community Center?'" Margaret says she might not join either one. When told "*everybody* belongs to one or the other" (35), she says it will be up to her parents. But in her prayers (she is covering all the bases), she asks God to send her, along with a bra, direction as to which group to join. For a year-long school project, Margaret decides to investigate religion, so she can figure out "which religion to be" (52). Her grandmother misunderstands Margaret's request to accompany her to temple. "'I knew you were a Jewish girl at heart!'" (55) is Sylvia's ecstatic response. But Margaret just wants to see what it's all about. She goes to church with friends and notes what she finds. She is also interested in her approaching puberty, and that journey is interwoven with her religious exploration.

Margaret is resentful that her mother's parents' first visit dashes her plans to visit Grandma Sylvia in Florida over spring break. Dad isn't too happy, either. "'They want to see us.'" Mom says. Dad retorts, "'They want to see *you*, not me! They want to see Margaret! To make sure she doesn't have horns!'" (121). Family tensions run high before the visit and higher during it. Her grandmother questions Margaret, her only grandchild, about Sunday school and is shocked to learn she doesn't attend. "'A person's got to have a religion,'" she says, Margaret's mother explains, "'We're letting Margaret choose her own religion when she's grown,'" and her dad adds, "'If she wants to!'" The grandparents don't accept this. "'A person doesn't choose religion,'" Grandmother says, and Grandfather agrees. "'A person's born to it!'" Like Grandma Sylvia, they believe that religion is inherited. Irritated, Dad says, "'Margaret is nothing!'" Margaret is shocked. "I didn't want to listen anymore. How could they talk that way in front of me! Didn't they know I was a real person—with feelings of my own!" (133). Later, Grandma Sylvia asks Margaret if her grandparents tried any "church business." Margaret admits they did. "'Remember, Margaret,'" Sylvia says, "'no matter what they said . . . you're a Jewish girl'" (140).

Summing up her religious experiment for her project, Margaret says she didn't enjoy it much and doesn't plan to make up her mind for a long time. "I don't think a person can decide to be a certain religion just like that," she asserts. "It's like having to choose your own name. You think about it a long time and then you keep changing your mind. If I should ever have children I will tell them what religion they are so they can start learning about it at an early age. Twelve is very late to learn" (143). By the novel's end, Margaret has gotten her period, but she is not even close to figuring out her religious identity.

This picture of pressure from extended family is reiterated in more detail in Ilene Cooper's 2004 novel *Sam I Am,* which is remarkably similar to Blume's earlier novel, even down to the unanswered questions posed to God and the enlightening school assignment (on the Holocaust, in this case). Again, Dad is Jewish and Mom is Christian (Episcopalian). Like Blume, Cooper takes a mostly humorous look at waffling parents and dueling grandmas. Sam Goodman, twelve, is our narrator. He has a sister, Ellen, eighteen, and brother, Maxie, six. In the Goodman household, "interfaith" has amounted to an uneasy conflation of Hanukkah and Christmas: the "Hanukkah Bush." When the family dog knocks over the bush and Mom's cherished Christmas ornaments are broken, the repressed feelings of each parent—that the compromise has slighted their own traditions—rise to the surface. Stress builds as the grandmas arrive for Christmas Eve dinner, also the first night of Hanukkah. Christian Nana gives Sam and his siblings Christian-themed gifts (Sam gets a WWJD key chain). Dad's mom, Grandma Sally, brings Hanukkah gelt and disparages the cheese fondue that is a Christmas Eve tradition in mom's family, while Nana calls Grandma Sally's kugel "heavy." The kids, alarmed, feel stretched and torn.

Like Margaret's family, the Goodmans have dealt with interfaith conflict by avoiding religion per se, focusing on cultural tradition instead. As a result, the children are ignorant of both their religious heritages. While this makes sense in the family context, Cooper goes farther. The first time Sam encounters the Holocaust in school is in seventh grade (many schools introduce the topic earlier). Cooper asks us to believe that Sam's own family, including an observant Jewish grandmother, has failed to mention the killing of six million Jews to him. Is the benefit derived from having characters learn about history through dialogue and plot, rather than being assumed to know it already, worth the cost of suggesting that interfaith families routinely keep their children ignorant of important cultural and historical realities?[11]

For the Holocaust project, Sam interviews people who lived through it. Grandma Sally tells him how a cousin escaped from Auschwitz; Nana condemns the Holocaust as horrific genocide. As in Blume's novel, surging hormones are part of the plot. The object of Sam's interest is blonde, blue-eyed Heather Daniel. This thread remains separate from the Jewish-Christian identity thread until the end, when Heather trivializes the Holocaust and Sam sees through her at last. The novel ends as Maxie is off to Hebrew School and Ellen is going to church with Mom. Sam isn't quite sure where he will end up. All want to make this interfaith family work somehow and they love each other enough to try.

Much is made of the fact that the Goodmans don't practice any religion. How did their dad get to be so "'un-Jewish,'" Ellen wonders. Sam insists he *is* Jewish. He says he is, after all, and he loves Grandma Sally's Jewish cuisine. That's not what being Jewish means, Ellen says. Sam reminds her they go to Passover dinners. "'Haven't you ever noticed how uncomfortable Dad is with all the prayers that are said at the table?'" Ellen asks. And Mom is no better, attending church only a few times a year and rarely taking the kids in order, Ellen suspects, to avoid upsetting dad. When Sam says they could go if they liked, Ellen says, "'Yes, but we usually don't. It's sort of an unspoken rule in this house: Don't talk about religion'" (16–17).

It is unclear whether Mom misses Christian religious practice or the opportunity to pass on traditions. She loved going to church as a kid and feels they are "missing something" (103). But just what *are* they missing? The same lack of clarity surrounds Dad's upbringing, but sorting out Jewishness is easier. Unlike Mom's religious identity, his is not set precariously on a set of personal beliefs but on historical cultural and ethnic identity. When Sam interviews him for his Holocaust project, Dad reminisces about collecting money for Israel, "'so that the Jews would always have a safe place to live.'" Sam says Israel doesn't seem very safe. "'But at least we have a homeland'" (157), Dad replies. Sam is surprised his father says "we." Dad admits he was scared hearing about the Holocaust as a kid, and, like Sam, angry at the Jews for not resisting harder. Sam responds: "'So is that why you don't like being Jewish?'" His father snaps, "'Who says I don't like it? I'm proud to be Jewish'" (159). Sam is really confused now. "'But you don't—'" His father stops him. "'I'm happy I'm Jewish. Just because I don't go to synagogue regularly [Never, Sam thinks] doesn't mean that I don't consider myself Jewish'" (159).

Cooper is a fine writer with a sense of humor and gift for revealing complex family dynamics, blatant and subtle. That very honesty makes it clear, however, when she reaches a point beyond which she can't or won't carry her exploration. One of those times is when Sam raises the Big Issue of all religions: "'If everybody worships the same God, they should all believe the same thing,'" Sam tells his mother. "'They do, in a way,'" she says. "'All religions teach if people are good to one another, are charitable, and try to be the best they can be, the world becomes a better place.'" Sam replies that if so, it doesn't seem to be working. Mom tells him it happens "'one person at a time'" (104). But in that case, why do we need structured religion at all? If we follow these questions too far in fiction, we find ourselves in philosophical quicksand. But Cooper's difficulty is that she's made her characters so vivid and believable, when she punts on the tough issues, it really stands out.

The solution she arrives at is for each parent to become more observant in his and her religion. Mom says, "'Your father and I haven't made any commitments to our religion. No wonder you children are confused.'" She wants all of them, herself and Dad included, to spend some time thinking about what they believe, "'because it's important to know where you get your comfort'" (139–40). The presentation of religion as primarily a source of comfort comes out of the blue. How this will help the children decide what they believe is not clear.

Sam does not get answers to his big questions, but he does learn that Heather is a shallow bigot, and that neither grandma is going to stop lobbying his family to follow her religious path. Near the end of the novel, Dad is injured in a serious car accident. He pulls through, and "gets religion" in a low-key, ecumenical way. He tells the family he wants them all to attend Easter services this year. "'I've gone to synagogue with my mother since my brush with death, but I want to say thank you to Whoever is up there in every religious building that I can.'" Maxie asks, "'Does this mean we're Jewish or we're Christian?'" Both, his father tells him. "'We're mixed. I guess in this family it's going to be up to each one of us to decide what we believe and how we put those beliefs into practice.'" Mom adds, "'I'm sure some people think we've done it all wrong, but this is who we are'" (251–252). Cooper doesn't go farther than this because, in her realistically conceived world, to do so would require her to venture out of the safe zone of cultural consensus into murkier, more confrontational waters. *Sam I Am* is only a first step into interfaith family exploration. But this still puts her way ahead of the pack.

Although some interfaith families do deal with religion by avoidance, evidence suggests that just as many choose one religion to follow or incorporate a totally different religious practice. The picture of the hapless, isolated Jewish-Christian interfaith family Cooper gives us suggests that nothing has changed in nearly forty years. But since Blume's novel was published, interfaith support networks for every religion have arisen to help families negotiate these issues, offering hands-on help, courses, and counseling.[12] It would be interesting to see an interfaith story unfold in a truly contemporary context as well as among other faiths and older teens. But with the meager supply of interfaith fiction available, we can be thankful that what exists comes from gifted writers who at least see a complicated subject for what it is.

Why should we assume that being raised in an interfaith family is significant enough to require fictional exploration? *Half/Life: Jewish Tales from Interfaith Homes* (2006), edited by Laurel Snyder, discussed in more depth in chapter 6, provides eighteen answers in the form of personal essays by professional writers, all children with one Jewish parent. "It's a hard thing, the interfaith home. It leaves a taste in your mouth," says Jennifer Traig. "Even now I feel strange about it and I tend not to tell people about my background. It makes them uncomfortable." And Traig adds, with considerable bitterness, "In the Orthodox community, it's sometimes considered bad form to reveal your gentile origins; you might put someone in the awkward position of subconsciously thinking less of you, and sometimes, when people find out—they do."[13]

The terminology itself hurts. "This is a problem of essentialism," says Danielle Pafunda, "Do all Jews have certain traits in common? Do half-Jews have half of these traits in common?" The identity suggests something incomplete: "To understand this qualifier half, I must consider terms such as octoroon, half-breed, mulatto, multiracial, and race itself. How many drops of Jewish blood make a Jew?"[14] Several essayists describe being told they are not Jews because their Jewish parent is male. Some stretch their Jewish "half" into a whole identity, converting to Judaism and searching for a community that will accept them as legitimate. Others turn to Christianity. And some are still puzzling it out while raising their own half-Jewish children. The variety of experience and pain expressed in this anthology provides abundant proof that many interfaith stories have yet to be told.

Naomi Shihab Nye's *Habibi* (1997) was an American Library Association Notable book and Best Book for Young Adults. Liyana, fourteen, is the daughter of a Palestinian father, Poppy, a doctor raised in Jerusalem, and a white, American-born mother. With Liyana's younger brother, Rafik, they move to Jerusalem from the United States where Liyana's father has lived since attending medical school. "Only recently he grew hopeful about Jerusalem and his country again. Things started changing for the better. Palestinians had public voices again" (31). Liyana does not want to leave the United States. As she packs, she ponders her identity. "I'm just a half-half, woman-girl, Arab-American, a mixed breed like those wild characters that ride up on ponies in the cowboy

movies Rafik likes to watch. The half-breeds are always villains or res-
cuers, never anybody normal in between" (20). In Jerusalem, the children meet Sitti, their grandmother, and their huge extended family. To
visit them requires crossing Israeli checkpoints to and from the West
Bank. In Jerusalem, they befriend kids from a nearby Palestinian refugee
camp and Liyana meets a boy, Omer. Their friendship is complicated by
the fact that he is a Jew.

Nye excels at portraying Liyana's discovery of a world for which her
American upbringing has not prepared her: poverty, injustice, armed soldiers, refugee camps, the kindness of individuals, the cruelty of institutions. She looks for places to fit herself in, ways to make sense of what
she sees. She hears her father tell relatives, "'We are *Americans*,'" and it
sounds odd coming from him. "Even Poppy, who was always an Arab
before? Of course there was never any question about their mother being an American, but Rafik and Liyana walked a blurry line. Liyana
tipped from one side to another" (124–125).

Liyana does not realize Omer is Jewish until their friendship has become a part of her life. He asks if it bothers her. She says no, "'I'm an
American,'" then adds, "'Mostly.' But that sounded ridiculous. He hadn't
asked for her passport. 'I mean, this fighting is senseless, don't you think?
People should be able to get over their differences, by this time, but they
just stay mad'" (165). She hears herself babble on about the sufferings of
the Palestinians and adds, "'Of course I know the Jewish people suffered
so much themselves, but don't you think it should have made them more
sensitive to the sufferings of others, too?'" And Omer says, "'I do'" (166).

At Christmas they go to Bethlehem's Church of the Nativity where
as a child Poppy attended services with Arab Christian friends. "Liyana
liked to remind herself: Jesus had a real body. Jesus had baby's breath.
And Jesus did not write the list of rules posted on the stone wall. There
were many, but Liyana's eyes caught on the first: NO ARMS AL-
LOWED INSIDE THIS CHURCH" (174). Liyana's great-grandparents
raised her grandmother, Peachy Helen, to believe that only those belonging to their denomination would be "saved." But her grandmother
did not pass on that view of religion to Liyana's mom. "Peachy Helen
had often taken Liyana's mother to the art museum instead of to church.
They would stare into blue and green paintings by Monet. 'Look at the
wavery edges of things! *That's* how we could live,'" she told her. When
her daughter had measles, Peachy Helen had made up prayers of healing
for her, as she did for Liyana and Rafik. She took them to museums but

also to "a rich assortment of Sunday schools—Methodist, Presbyterian, Episcopalian, Unity, and Unitarian—where they signed in as 'visitors'" (181). Their own ecumenical upbringing allows Liyana and Rafik to accept and respect the rights of others to their own beliefs.

Liyana wants to bring Omer to the West Bank to visit Sitti, but Poppy says his family wouldn't appreciate it. "'What good is it to believe in peace and talk about peace if you only want to live the same old ways?'" Liyana asks. "'Didn't you say . . . that it would be great if people never described each other as 'the Jew' or 'the Arab' or 'the black guy' or 'the white guy?'" (240–41). Poppy gives in, and they bring Omer to meet Sitti. Omer reminds Sitti of a young shepherd she once knew, and the two forge a strong connection.

Habibi is about dismantling walls that hide us from one another. Cultural, national, ethnic differences are important, beautiful costumes worth great effort to preserve and honor, but to recognize and appreciate our common humanity, sometimes we need to lay them aside.

GRACE NOTES

Mixed heritage serves some YA fiction as a kind of literary diacritical mark designed to enhance other character elements. When done well, this technique enhances and illuminates other narrative elements while prompting the reader to consider racial identity and ethnic heritage in a new way.

In Nancy Werlin's *Black Mirror* (2001), the racial status of the protagonist, Frances, is an essential, but minor note—an accent or analogy. She attends a New England boarding school, one of a token group of low-income townies on scholarship. She feels ugly, out of place, lost, and alone. Her Jewish father is remote. Her Japanese American mother has abandoned the family, retreating to a Buddhist monastery in Japan from which she will not return, even when her son, Frances's brother, Daniel, dies of a heroin overdose. Daniel was Frances's hero, her one connection to a world from which she now feels completely alienated. Frances's physical identity and racial history inform her character and comment on the world she inhabits. Her racial identity affects her self-image, but it's the ambiguity, not the difference that she can't tolerate: "I'd seen the discreet double takes. I'd been asked countless times: 'Where are you from?'

I certainly didn't appear Caucasian—that is, typically 'American'—and I didn't fit a single stereotype of what a Jew ought to look like." That would have been manageable, if she had simply looked Japanese, but "there was also something about my looks that didn't fit what people expected from a child of Asian ancestry. Something that seemed a little . . . off" (4).

Frances has covered her mirror with black silk to mourn her brother and remind her that she failed to understand him. It also allows her to avoid her reflection. Frances's interaction with her image marks her progress. "Jews put black over mirrors during times of mourning so they wouldn't think about themselves. But I never did look in mirrors anyway, because I disliked myself. No, wait. I disliked my appearance" (151). This crucial qualification signals Frances's struggle to value who she is. All elements of this taut suspense story work together, as Frances uncovers the ugly secret of what's really going on in this school. The stakes are high—life or death. Both her adversaries and her allies use Frances's low self-esteem, her self-hatred, to manipulate her. Frances and readers come to recognize that not only her self-esteem but her survival may depend on her ability to accept and appreciate herself for what and who she is.

Throughout the novel, Frances takes hesitant steps toward self-acceptance, eventually uncovering the mirror that hides her from herself. Her sense of physical dislocation and her mother's abandonment are informed by her multiracial status, but neither is a symbol for the other. It's an excruciating and difficult journey, like watching a butterfly break out of a chrysalis in real time, but ultimately satisfying to the reader.

Japanese American author Cynthia Kadohata, winner of the 2005 Newbery Award for *Kira-Kira,* takes intriguing creative risks in *Outside Beauty* (2008), set in 1983. Japanese American Helen Kimura supports her daughters—Shelby, our narrator, and her three sisters—by acquiring boyfriends and banking their lavish gifts to her. Each girl has a different father: Italian, Chinese, Japanese, and Anglo American. Narcissistic and selfish but also loving, Helen is unique in YA fiction. Her relationships with men are symbiotic; she is not a prostitute or call girl. The girls adore her, even Shelby, who at thirteen has discovered that there are ways of looking at the world in which physical beauty doesn't matter much. When a serious car accident puts Helen in the hospital, the girls are parceled out to their respective dads.

Despite the title, the book's subject is all kinds of beauty, especially the beauty of love. Shelby's shy, plain, immigrant father, struggling to make a living selling chewing gum, is a horrible dresser, but a wise and loving father. Kadohata does not look at beauty as an either-or proposition, but both/and. What holds the sisters together before and after Helen's accident is their love for one another and their mother. Everyone accepts Helen's selfishness; it is part of who she is, just like her positive traits. Helen has raised her daughters to look on life as an adventure, to be open to surprises. "One year when my mother decided she wanted to develop her mind, she bought a subscription to *Psychology Today,* and I read an article about how the dead of night was a frontier to some people, similar to the way the western United States had once been a frontier," Shelby tells us. "You learned a lot when you had a mother like ours" (226). Shelby's father, Jiro, reminds her "of one of those nearsighted Japanese men with cameras who moved in clusters throughout Chicago tourist attractions. But he was different from those men. They belonged somewhere. He didn't seem to belong anywhere on the planet" (99). With their mother in the hospital, Shelby plots ways to reunite as a family; she worries that Maddie's repressive father will crush her spirit. When Helen gets a life-threatening staph infection, fathers and daughters return and gather in the Kimura apartment. "Over time our fathers had grown more what they were," Shelby notices. "Mr. Bronson had grown more stiff, my father had grown both more Japanese and more Southern, Mack more emotional, and Larry more wonderful, handsomer, stronger" (173). Later, Shelby realizes "that there was one thing my father, Mr. Bronson, and Mack had in common: they were all outsiders, just like my mother was. And they were all lonely" (261). Helen's ability to appreciate beauty in others is what makes her lovable. Each odd dad, even Mr. Bronson, is beautiful in his own way. The multiracial daughters are the proof of the pudding: beauty exists in myriad forms. The trick is learning how to see it.

REFRAMING THE ISSUE: FASHION AND CUISINE

Carrie Rosten, a multiracial writer with a weighty pedigree (her greatuncle was William Steig), made her debut with *Chloe Leiberman (Sometimes Wong)* in 2005. This unique novel set in an upscale, gated community in Orange County, California, has charm, but to find it, readers must forage through bins of brand-name references and stylistic tics.

Hidden among them is the story of a high school senior whose social-climbing Chinese American mom and Jewish tax-attorney dad have high academic expectations for her. But Chloe's genius lies in designing clothes; she achieves personal and creative synthesis by combing through vintage clothing shops, cutting up and spray-painting brand-name attire, and putting together a "look" with its own identity and purpose.

Our introduction to Chloe is abrupt: "So Chloe Wong-Leiberman was a senior without a plan. She was also a Chinese Jewish WASP with a fashion disorder" (3). This fashion disorder (FD) manifests as a compulsion to tell people what they should wear and to zone out and mentally make them over. Her closet is huge and well organized: "All her blue jeans were hanging on a solo rack—a wave of dark indigo turning into the palest shade of Pacific blue. Colored cords hung directly opposite white cargos—a crisp wave of buttercream fading into paper white." The intriguing suggestion is that her obsession with fashion reflects a need to bring the disparate facets of her self and heritage into harmony: "Her closet had a rotating theme each season and, was, like, a color-coded shrine" (21–22). Chloe's ability to dress herself is the basis for her self-esteem—the only thing she feels she does right.

Rosten makes fashion the vehicle through which Chloe works out her identity issues, and she has plenty. She has been told she is cute, but feels "something got lost in translation." She has shiny black hair and almond eyes (Chinese Mom); but the hair is coarse textured and her eyes light brown (Jewish Dad). "Basically, she was split down the middle, or rather, in thirds. She likened herself to a three-part picture puzzle she assembled and took apart constantly, rearranging the disparate pieces trying to make them feel whole. She never quite did feel like a whole person until she got dressed" (34).

Despite the novel's chick-lit feel, it explores a serious issue in a highly original way. Chloe deconstructs a "look" and rearranges it, not so much as a fashion experience but as an experiment in integrating elements to create a harmonious visual whole. When the look is complete, she takes a Polaroid snapshot of herself in it, creating a record of who she was, is, and how she has evolved. This is not about conspicuous consumption, but about identity and self-esteem. Like Frances, Chloe avoids looking at her face; the photos are from the neck down.

Armored in fashion, Chloe joins the family for a Chinese New Year dinner that includes her younger brother, Mitchell, a stock broker in training who is hitting all the high-achieving notes, and her Chinese grandmother, Pau, a secret Chloe sympathizer. When Chloe lets slip that she has not applied to any colleges, her father calls her a quitter. "That was valid. Chloe Wong-Leiberman was an avid quitter. Viola, dance, track . . . and field. A borderline C student when she could've got As, she was a quasi-underachiever fully comfortable with being average," Chloe admits. "Neither a leader nor a follower, she never quite lived up to her much-touted 'potential.' She had always been smart according to teachers but never 'applied herself' seriously" (46).

Chloe doesn't feel part of her family, not because she is multiracial, but because of who she is as an individual. "They didn't even try to understand who she was so why should she bother telling them the truth? Plus, it was all too apparent she was a *part* of a family she'd never feel a *part* of at all. Like, Chloe was convinced she was more space alien than Wong-Leiberman. Sorry, folks, we DON'T do returns or exchanges. *Not* store policy" (61). Race-based expectations don't help. The school counselor calls her in when she is put on academic probation. Mistaking her for a more academically successful student, he tells her: "'You're a smart girl, Chloe. I mean, you're part Asian, right? It says right here in this memo. *Other*—Asian and other stuff. I have every bit of faith that you'll figure out a plan'" (133).

With a few detours through boyfriend troubles and in between clothing riffs, Chloe shapes her fashion disorder into a career path. Echoing Frances, Chloe's progress is signaled when she begins to include her face in her snapshots, but Rosten doesn't go deep enough in exploring Chloe and her gift. The introduction of the "countess," a wealthy, eccentric neighbor with a regal lifestyle, takes the initiative away from Chloe. The annoying countess makes oracular pronouncements on Chloe and on fashion: "'This eye of yours is like magic. It is your window into a world so beautiful, so unique, soo filled with endless wonder you can't possibly begin to seeee. Your quest for the best will be a noble one indeed.'" Chloe plays Plato to the countess's Socrates: "'So then making clothes can be noble?'" she asks. "'Why yes, because creation is noble!'" (166). Encouraged, Chloe summons the nerve to apply to a London design school.

Excesses aside, Rosten is trying something new in a genre whose practitioners tend to stick closely to formulaic plot and character development. That she only partially succeeds is not surprising—she is a new writer—but one hopes she will continue following the countess's advice to Chloe. Creation is indeed noble.

In Sherri L. Smith's *Hot, Sour, Salty, Sweet* (2008), food provides an inexhaustible cornucopia of images with which to represent multicultural and multiracial reality. Ana Mei Shen, our Chinese-and-black protagonist, looks forward to the eighth-grade graduation dance with her heartthrob, Jamie Tabata. When a school plumbing disaster cancels the festivities, Ana's best friend Chelsea suggests inviting Jamie to an impromptu family dinner instead. She does, and he accepts. The guest list expands to include Chelsea, her little sister Dina, and her single father, all European Americans; Jamie and his Japanese American parents; even Mandy, the snobbish blonde whom Mr. Tabata wants his son to date instead of Ana, and her single mother. The mayhem starts long before the guests arrive.

The novel unfolds over the rest of that afternoon and evening. Shopping, cooking, eating with them, we get to know Ana's family: her younger brother, Sammy; her loving parents; and the grandparents who outbid one another for Ana's affections, using expensive graduation gifts as currency. As they rush around pulling dinner together, Nai Nai, Ana's Chinese grandmother, and Grandma White, her black grandmother, collide, each carrying sacks of rice: Ana rushes up to help, asking if they are okay. "'No we are not okay. But you are okay. You are plenty okay. Go get me some ice,'" Nai Nai shouts. Ana's other grandmother says, "'Get me some ice too, honey. I swear this woman's trying to kill me'" (67). Yi Yi, Ana's Chinese grandfather, resolves the argument, telling Ana to clean up the spilled rice, but when she wants to throw it away, both grandmothers insist she save it.

Roles reverse: parent to child to parent and back. Tired of her grandmothers' bickering, Ana complains to Grandpa White, who tells her, "'The two of you kids are our common ground, and that is a beautiful thing'" (83). In between cranky comments and frantic cooking (the menu includes potstickers and gumbo), Ana provides that common ground. Both grandpas are inclined to go with the flow, while their wives—more alike than they'd ever admit—go at one another. Grandma White tells Ana that in the fifteen years she's known her, Nai Nai has never called her by her first name. Ana says her father thinks Nai Nai is embarrassed that she can't pronounce the word "Lillian." Grandma White isn't ready to be that generous. "'Well, I guess I should be grateful that she calls me anything at all.'" Ana says, "'You guys aren't rivals,'" to which Grandma White says, "'Aren't we, though?'" (90–91).

Family stories, cautionary tales, reminiscences are shared. Amid the beat-the-clock food prep, nonstop competition, and her fears about Jamie and his father coming, the grandparent competition gets to Ana. She tells her dad she feels like Switzerland, a neutral country caught in the middle of a war. This problem of being forced to choose sides also exists at school. "'Your mother and I knew it might be hard for you and Sammy to grow up biracial. But it's not about taking sides. You are the best of both of us, the best we have to offer as human beings,'" her dad tells her. "'Our cultural differences only enrich us and make us stronger'" (102).

Ana is not convinced. Casting around for a way to explain, her dad picks up a jar of Szechuan peppercorns. Their differences are like the different flavors in Chinese cooking, he says. "'Some are hot like this pepper, or sour like vinegar, or salty like dried shrimp, or sweet like melon. They're all so different from each other, but take a bite of one of those dumplings dipped in vinegar and soy sauce, and it's delicious. Ana, it's perfect'" (102–3).

The dinner comes together at last, and the guests arrive, adding more flavors to the complicated human stew. Nai Nai tells Mr. Tabata, "'You look very Japanese,'" and before he can respond adds, "'My husband fought the Japanese.'"[15] As Ana tells Nai Nai that "'war is not exactly an ice breaker'" (125), Sammy mentions to everyone that Grandpa White fought in Korea. Mr. Tabata points out that in Korea, the Americans were fighting the Chinese. "'I was fighting whoever my country told me to fight,'" Grandpa White says. "'Have you ever been a soldier, Mr. Tabata?'" (126). The answer is no. Grandpa White asks who wants to say grace. A pregnant pause ensues. Grandpa and Grandma White are very Christian, Nai Nai is Buddhist, Chelsea's family is nonreligious, and the others could be anything. Luckily, Grandpa White knows what to say. "'Bless this food we are about to receive. May it help our children grow strong and wise and comfort us old people too. Amen'" (126). The dinner is delicious, although Ana gets in trouble with her grandmas for having mixed up the two kinds of rice, but as it proceeds, Mr. Tabata reveals himself to be rude and manipulative, trying to bring his son together with Mandy, deliberately slighting Ana.

Two climaxes occur: one expresses unity, the other disunity. In the first, Grandpa White describes how, during the Korean War, he came to prepare and share Southern fried chicken with a Chinese soldier in a deserted farmhouse. Neither could speak a word of the other's language, but both were hungry. Food was the language they shared, and while speaking it, they could not be enemies. The second climax is a rejection of the beauty of multiraciality and multiculturalism. Everyone ignores Mr. Tabata's slights until he goes too far. Having offered condescending praise for the "multicultural" menu, he compares the dinner to a food court at the mall. Ana calls him the rudest person she's ever met. "'I may not be a hundred percent Chinese or black or a hundred percent anything, and God knows I'm not a blonde, but this is still my family, and my dinner and my house. And you can respect us or you can leave.'" When Ana's mother says faintly that this is not how to make friends, Ana has a moment of understanding: "All the years her mother has held her tongue against the judgments of family and strangers, too. All the times her father has kept quiet or joked and pretended it didn't matter what people thought of his black wife and half-breed kids." Ana looks back a generation earlier: "All the times Grandma White has had to listen to jokes about marrying a black man named White. Every barb and insult Grandpa White endured in a newly desegregated army while serving his country at war. And all the doors shut in Nai Nai's face when they first came to the United States, trying to rent an apartment or buy groceries with the wrong accent and the wrong skin" (148). Ana does not apologize or back down. Mr. Tabata leaves; Jamie stays.

Mr. Tabata may be racist,[16] although not a strict monoracialist (he is trying to get Jamie and Mandy together), but he cannot appreciate the multiple races and jumble of cuisines, despite the fact that they are delicious. Ana loves her crazy, sometimes dysfunctional but always devoted family and recognizes, honors, what they represent and share. Mr. Tabata's slights remind Ana of that combined history: enduring slights and institutionalized racism, struggling to survive and make better lives for their children and grandchildren. *Hot, Sour, Salty, Sweet* slights neither Chinese nor black American heritage. Neither is dominant, better or worse than the other. Smith, who is black, offers living proof that stories in which neither heritage is lost or missing or subordinate can not only be told, but make for powerful, evocative fiction with vivid characters that speak of the world pressing in on us, a world that so much fiction continues to ignore.

NOTES

1. David Schoem, "Teaching an Interracial Issues Course," in *Multiracial America: Resource Guide on the History and Literature of Interracial Issues,* ed. Karen Downing, Darline Nichols, and Kelly Webster (Lanham, Md.: Scarecrow Press, 2005), 16.

2. Gary Nash, *Forbidden Love: The Secret History of Mixed-Race America* (New York, Henry Holt, 1999).

3. This novel is insensitive to adoption and blended-family issues. When Kim asks, "'What was my real father like, Mom?'" (39) her mother does not call her on this and ask, "Do you mean your biological father as opposed to your cardboard stepfather?" Even though her stepfather has legally adopted Kim, evidently only biological parents are real parents.

4. This rationale for dropping all contact with their father and his family is insufficient. Even in bitter family breakups, permanent severance from one parent's entire family, including grandparents, is not routine.

5. What prevents this novel, "shaped" by the packager Alloy, from being more than a mass-market beach read is the very motif that branded it. The pants work against the imperative that characters must be responsible for their own insights and the changes that move them toward their goals. These characters are doing fine on their own when the tiresome pants show up. The girls mail them to each other at critical times, but what the pants do to earn their world travels (Greece; Baja, Mexico; across the continental United States) is unclear. Serious problems that arise—Bridget, for example, shows signs of the bipolar disorder that prompted her mother's suicide—seem out of proportion to the solution that looking good in a pair of jeans is likely to offer.

6. S. T. Frazier, *Check All That Apply: Finding Wholeness as a Multiracial Person* (Downers Grove, Ill.: InterVarsity Press, 2002), 120. Frazier credits Paul Spickard, *Mixed Blood: Intermarriage and Ethnic Identity in Twentieth-Century America* (Madison: University of Wisconsin Press, 1989), 358.

7. "Interfaith" is a term most often associated with families in which one partner only is Jewish. However, the word simply means "between faiths," and in the absence of a clearer term, is used here to mean any family in which the parents come from different religions.

8. For YA fiction about religious cults, see Bruce Brooks, *Asylum for Nightface* (1996); Margaret Peterson Haddix, *Leaving Fishers* (1997); Kathryn Lasky, *Memoirs of a Bookbat* (1994); Sam Mills, *The Viper Within* (2008); Richard Peck, *The Last Safe Place on Earth* (1995); Judy Waite, *Forbidden* (2004); Beckie Weinheimer, *Converting Kate* (2007); Ellen Wittlinger, *Blind Faith* (2006); and Jane

Yolen and Bruce Coville, *Armageddon Summer* (1998). Among YA novels for teens that tackle religious themes see Han Nolan, *When We Were Saints* (2003), and Heather Quarles, *A Door Near Here* (1998). Often, fantasy offers the more innovative takes on religion as in the works of Madeleine L'Engle, David Almond (especially *Skellig* [1999] and *Clay* [2005]), and Diane Duane.

9. Pew Forum on Religion & Public Life, "The U.S. Religious Landscape Survey Reveals a Fluid and Diverse Pattern of Faith," 25 Feb. 2008, pewresearch .org/pubs/743/united-states-religion (27 March 2008).

10. Mark London Williams has authored the middle-grade, science-fiction Danger Boys series. The protagonist, Eli Sands, has a Jewish mother and Episcopalian father. Set in the near future, the books involve time travel to the past, including to ancient Jerusalem.

11. Many studies have been conducted of interfaith Jewish families in the United States. Depending on where the community is located, between 30 and 60 percent appear to be raising their children as Jews, following traditional religious observances. How data are interpreted varies widely. (Shmuel Rosner surveys recent findings in "The Passover Test: What the Passover Seder Reveals About Interfaith Couples," *Slate*, www.slate.com [17 April 2008].) However, no data suggests that children raised in interfaith families are routinely kept ignorant of the Holocaust. To suggest that they are plays into the hands of those who argue that interfaith unions result in a severing of Jewish identity in their offspring. Researching the Holocaust, Sam reads about *mischlings* (legally defined as half-Jews in Nazi Germany) whose separate treatment by the Nazis remains contentious. For discussion see Daniel Klein and Freke Vuijst, *The Half-Jewish Book: A Celebration* (New York: Villard, 2000). For a fictional view of mischling status, see David Chotjewicz, *Daniel Half Human: And the Good Nazi*. This German novel, translated by Doris Orgel, concerns a German's discovery that his mother is Jewish.

12. Articles archived on the interfaithfamilies.com website describe how Jewish and Hindu families, Jewish and Buddhist families, and even Jewish and Muslim families are going about integrating their respective cultures within their families.

13. Laurel Snyder, ed., *Half/Life: Jewish Tales from Interfaith Homes* (New York: Soft Skull, 2006), 137.

14. Snyder, *Half/Life,* 100.

15. Hostility between Japanese and Chinese American immigrants, based on the Japanese invasion and occupation of China, is also the theme of Lensey Namioka's delightful novel *Mismatch*. One source of its humor is that white Americans don't, can't distinguish between different Asian peoples. In *Nothing but the Truth (And a Few White Lies),* Patty's white friends expect her, like them, to see Vietnamese people and Chinese as identical to Taiwanese people, fitting into the category, invented by white people, called "Asian."

16. Two novels do not a trend make, but it is worth noting that Mr. Tabata and Okimoto's Uncle Hideki are portrayed as shallow, bigoted, judgmental men who display racism against blacks. Each is the villain of his novel; each is sexist. Uncle Hideki wonders why Mom doesn't cook dinner for him. Mr. Tabata bullies his silent wife. When characters are underrepresented in fiction, the few who appear receive heightened scrutiny.

FICTIONAL WORKS CITED OR CRITIQUED

Note: An asterisk denotes works critiqued as well as cited in the chapter.

David Almond, *Clay* (New York: Delacorte, 2005).
——, *Skellig* (New York: Delacorte, 1999).
Anjali Banerjee, *Maya Running* (New York: Random House, 2005).*
Judy Blume, *Are You There God? It's Me, Margaret* (New York: Atheneum, 1970; reprint, New York: Dell, 1991).*
Ann Brashares, *Sisterhood of the Traveling Pants* (New York: Delacorte, 2001).*
Bruce Brooks, *Asylum for Nightface* (New York: Laura Geringer, 1996).
David Chotjewicz, *Daniel Half Human: And the Good Nazi,* trans. Doris Orgel (New York: Atheneum, 2004).
Ilene Cooper, *Sam I Am* (New York: Scholastic, 2004).*
Sharon Flake, *Begging for Change* (New York: Hyperion–Jump at the Sun, 2004).*
——, *Money Hungry* (New York: Hyperion–Jump at the Sun, 2001).*
Sherry Garland, *Song of the Buffalo Boy* (New York: Harcourt Brace, 1992).*
Margaret Peterson Haddix, *Leaving Fishers* (New York: Simon & Schuster, 1997).
Justina Chen Headley, *Nothing but the Truth (And a Few White Lies)* (New York: Little, Brown, 2006).*
Hadley Irwin, *Kim/Kimi* (New York. Puffin-Penguin: 1987).*
Cynthia Kadohata, *Outside Beauty* (New York: Atheneum, 2008).*
Marie Lamba, *What I Meant . . .* (New York: Random House, 2007).*
Kathryn Lasky, *Memoirs of a Bookbat* (New York: Harcourt, 1994).
Sam Mills, *The Viper Within* (New York: Knopf, 2008).
Lensey Namioka, *Mismatch* (New York: Delacorte, 2006).
Han Nolan, *When We Were Saints* (New York: Harcourt, 2003).
Naomi Shihab Nye, *Habibi* (New York: Simon Pulse–Simon & Schuster, 1997).*
Jean Davies Okimoto, *Talent Night* (New York: Scholastic Trade, 1995; reprint, iUniverse–Authors Guild backinprint.com, 2000).*

Nancy Osa, *Cuba 15* (New York: Delacorte, 2003).*

Richard Peck, *The Last Safe Place on Earth* (New York: Delacorte, 1995).

Heather Quarles, *A Door Near Here* (New York: Delacorte, 1998).

Carrie Rosten, *Chloe Leiberman (Sometimes Wong)* (New York: Delacorte, 2005).*

Sherri L. Smith, *Hot, Sour, Salty, Sweet* (New York: Delacorte, 2008).*

Judy Waite, *Forbidden* (Oxford, U.K.: Oxford University Press, 2004).

Beckie Weinheimer, *Converting Kate* (New York: Viking, 2007).

Nancy Werlin, *Black Mirror* (New York: Penguin-Speak, 2001).*

Mark London Williams, Danger Boys Series (Cambridge, Mass.: Candlewick).

Ellen Wittlinger, *Blind Faith* (New York: Simon & Schuster, 2006).

Jane Yolen and Bruce Coville, *Armageddon Summer* (New York: Harcourt, 1998).

• 5 •

Finding Home

Mixed-Heritage Adopted Characters

Children are our future. They carry our genetic and cultural genes. A child adopted out of her birthfamily and birth culture loses one set of those genes. Adopted into a new family, she acquires a new cultural profile, but not a biological one. Parentage—unlike race, nationality, or ethnicity—is biological. How we view this process depends in part on how we view race and culture. For example, if we are racial essentialists, we will view transracial adoption differently than if we believe race is irrelevant to character and identity. How we weigh the health and survival of ethnic and cultural traditions relative to the health and survival of individuals also affects how we view this kind of adoption. In short, mixed-heritage adoption raises the questions we have looked at in this book already, along with new ones.

Transracially or transethnically adopted characters in fiction offer a means of exploring racial conflict and healing and the relative value of community and individual identity. Adoption itself, among the most ancient of human institutions, can serve as a potent metaphor for becoming an adult, acquiring the sense of self and of belonging to a wider community beyond the shelter of family. Writers may use adoption as a subtle—or not so subtle—vehicle to convey their views on race and what constitutes a good upbringing. To explore characters in search of their missing half, writers can do no better than to pick an adoptee. Transracial and international adoption have been around for more than fifty years, but until recently neither has played much role in YA fiction. Of the fourteen novels explored in this chapter, five were published before 2003, and only one before 1994.

WHAT IS LOST AND GAINED
IN MIXED-HERITAGE ADOPTION

"Mixed-heritage adoption" in this chapter means children whose race or ethnicity differs from those of the white adoptive parents. These adoptions are most often international, but can be domestic, usually children of color adopted by whites. There is no reason legally why parents of color cannot adopt white children. While this happens occasionally, it is extremely rare. The dominant white caste has historically controlled the system of child placement and adoption and has been unwilling to place its children in the homes of families of subordinate caste.[1] The belief that children and adoptive families should be matched by race still governs the thinking of many social services professionals.

About 2.5 percent of American children under eighteen are adopted. In addition, millions of children are being cared for by extended family or others in informal adoptions; more than half a million are in foster care. Blended families cement their status by stepparent adoption. From the peak of 175,000 adoptions in 1970, the number has dropped to 135,000 annually. This number includes stepfamily adoptions and around 20,000 international adoptions.[2]

In developing countries, millions more children need families than there are families to care for them. The flow of children for adoption worldwide moves from poor, often war-torn, chaotic societies—most of them nonwhite—to affluent, developed countries with white majority populations. Advocates and opponents of international adoption alike sometimes oversimplify the complicated and varied situations of children in need of parents. The issues are complex and multifaceted. People in countries that fail to provide for their vulnerable children feel torn when they see their children sent away. "Approximately 500 American children are adopted annually by foreigners, mostly in Canada and Europe, but in comparison to this country's status as a 'receiving country,' we know practically nothing about the United States as a 'sending country.'"[3] Not surprisingly, this fact is not well known. No country, including the United States, wants to be seen as unable or unwilling to care for its own children.

Adoption saves children from early death or growing up in barren institutions and places them in loving families. Adoption has also eroded cultures. As many as one-third of all American Indian children may have been removed from their families and placed in boarding schools and foster or adoptive homes before passage of the Indian Child Welfare Act (ICWA) in 1978.[4] Some argue that adopting children from countries long colonized and exploited by rich ones is a form of trafficking that ought to be prohibited. Picture a Korean child adopted by a white family and raised as the only nonwhite person in rural Minnesota. He has been stripped of his birthright—family, language, culture, community, country—while racism and bias prevent his full acceptance in the United States. Plenty of autobiographical accounts, some discussed in the next chapter, bear witness to the difficulties adoptees have faced over the fifty years during which Americans have adopted from other countries.[5] There is more truth in these allegations of cultural incompetence than many of us, especially adoptive parents, care to admit.

But these views are also dated and rely on racial essentialism in their most extreme form. The profile presented of the communities in which children find themselves is often out of date.[6] Many small American communities are far more diverse today than in the 1970s and 1980s. Also, those who oppose all transracial adoption seldom acknowledge the millions of interracial biological families around them. Domestic transracial adoptions, particularly of black children by white parents, have declined since the 1970s and after the National Association of Black Social Workers passed a resolution opposing white adoptions of black children in 1972.[7] Federal law now prohibits use of race as a qualification for adoption, but numbers have never risen to earlier levels. However, domestic transracial adoption, especially of children two years or older or with special needs placed in white homes, continues. Four of the YA novels discussed in this chapter feature teens transracially adopted by white families within the United States.

It is not the duty of fiction writers to express an opinion on the debate, but when they create mixed-heritage adoptive families they enter it, regardless of their intention. Influential children's books have helped to shape how adoption is seen, portraying the joy of adoptive families welcoming their child, discussing how and when to tell a child that he is adopted. "Telling emerged as the central purpose of a growing children's literature, including classic books like *The Chosen Baby* (1939) and *The Family That Grew* (1951). These books, sometimes accompanied by detailed instructions about when, how, who, and what to tell, literally made adoption go down as easily as a bedtime story, a tradition that continues to this day."[8]

Adoption is never a win-win or lose-lose proposition, but a complicated calculus that affects and is affected by our beliefs about family, race, culture, and children. Too often, books for children of all ages have presented simplistic and distorted pictures of adoption. Fortunately, this is changing for the better, especially in YA fiction. Writers of all races have crafted powerful narratives that honor the complexity of international and transracial adoption—including portrayals of birthparents as human beings with limited, difficult choices.

FICTIONAL FAMILY DEMOGRAPHICS

Although single parents of both genders adopt, only one of our fourteen families is headed by a single parent. All but two of our adopted characters were adopted as infants or toddlers and have no recollection of the birthfamily. Only one family has more than one adopted child. Although many adoption agencies and placing countries require medical proof of infertility as a prerequisite for parents to adopt, eight of our families have biological children, too. If the issue of fertility is raised at all, these biological younger siblings are depicted as "surprises," not the result of concerted medical intervention. Several mothers have miscarriages, but only one undergoes infertility treatment. Even where there are no biological children in the family, the parents are almost never infertile. Of our fourteen sets of adoptive parents, only two are identified as infertile. In fact, writers often go out of their way to make sure readers know the parents are fertile, but have chosen to adopt for other reasons, usually exceptional ones.

Most of our fictional adoptive parents are heroic. They may have a few flaws, but these are invariably the result of how deeply they love their adopted child. If they resist Susie's decision to search for her birthparents, it is only because they don't want to see her get hurt. Birthparents are seldom mentioned. If they are, they are either angels who selflessly gave up their children so they could have a better life, or they are pathetic victims or deplorable deadbeats, unfit to care for children. More recently, writers such as Dana Reinhardt, Ting-Xing Ye, and Marie Myung-Ok Lee have represented birthmothers as complex individuals, neither selfish monsters nor selfless heroes. Birthfathers make few appearances. Only one author, Rose Kent, invests much literary effort in closely depicting the adoptive parents as characters. While hers are ultimately sympathetic, they are not heroes and have plenty of blind spots.

The 2000 U.S. census confirmed that adoptive families have higher incomes and more education than the average American family. Many adoptive families are not middle class, much less high-powered professionals, but only Kent gives us a working-class adoptive family. Each set of adoptive parents is white except those in Mitali Perkins's *Monsoon Summer,* but that novel is a special case in that the adoptee is the mother of the teen protagonist. Unfortunately or not—depending on one's view of transracial adoption—fiction reflects reality in this case. Few nonwhite families adopt white children.

PASSING FOR BIOLOGICAL

In Barbara Ann Porte's *Something Terrible Happened* (1994), discussed in chapter 2, biracial Gillian is befriended and mentored by her older, adopted cousin, Antoine, who was born in the Philippines, placed in an orphanage at age three, and adopted at six. When Gillian observes that neither of them has "real parents," Antoine disagrees. His adoptive parents *are* his real parents. Gillian asks if he minds looking different from his folks, "'like, for instance, when you go places together and people stare?'" Antoine says, "'I don't pay attention. Unless someone brings it up, it isn't anything I think about'" (139).

Gillian asks about his birthfamily. Did they die? Were they in an accident? Antoine doesn't know. "'I try to keep that whole side of my life out of my mind. I like to think of starting out for the first time the day my mom and Aunt Corinne came and got me'" (140). He gently lectures Gillian. She should be grateful for being so well cared for. He understands her life hasn't been easy, but "'you have to get over it. People do, you know; otherwise they'd never get on with their lives'" (144).

Gillian has watched an expert on TV assert that adopted children can have an especially hard time during adolescence. "His specialty was what he kept calling 'cross-cultural' adopting, meaning when parents are a different race from their children. 'Often, such children feel out of place in both the society in which they were born and the one in which they were raised,' he said. All I could think was, it's a good thing Antoine doesn't know that" (178–79). Porte is using Gillian, her POV character, to show readers that Antoine is right and the expert is wrong, that it is normal to forget the birthfamily, to pretend the adoptive family is the biological family. This vision of adoption reflects a still-common misunderstanding of what adoption means to the individuals it affects.

In 1964, sociologist David Kirk published *Shared Fate: A Theory and Method of Adoptive Relationships*,[9] the result of a decade-long study of two thousand adoptive families in the United States and Canada. By the mid-twentieth century, adoption had evolved into a system for forming families by matching infants and small children with infertile married couples. Kirk found that these infertile couples suffered from "role handicap," a sense of failure and sadness that they were unable to fulfill their role as biological parents. Role handicap included the social stigma of infertility. Society delivered the message that the inability to reproduce biologically is pitiable and that adoption is inferior to biological reproduction as a way to build a family. Adoptive parents chose one of two methods to cope with this handicap. The first, Kirk labeled "rejection of difference." Parents pretended their family was formed biologically. The placement process supported and reinforced this rejection of difference. Agencies took care to match adoptive parents to children not only by race and religion, but by hair and eye color. To underscore the fantasy that the adoptive parents were the biological parents, a new birth certificate was issued, replacing the names of the biological parents with those of the adoptive parents. Records were sealed, ensuring no contact of any kind between birth and adoptive families. Kirk compared these transactions with their racial equivalent: passing.

The earlier in the child's life placement occurred, the better. "Aside from the personal satisfactions usually derived from caring for a child during his early infancy, having an infant also helps the adoptive parents to 'pass' for biological parents."[10] Parents were advised to tell their children of the adoption, but the suggested narration minimized the role of the birthparents. "The story of the adoption is made into a myth of origin, implying that the parents chose the child out of all others. In a social-work-approved version, the parents chose the child after the agency had judged that they would suit the child. The myth is primarily, as one parent put it, 'to take the sting out of an unpleasant situation.'"[11] Adoptive parents used a variety of methods to dispose of the birthparents, saying, for example, "'We feel we are the real parents and we refer to the (original parents) as 'the lady and the man who had you.'"[12] Some parents cited divine authority, telling the child his adoption was God's plan for their family. Some said they often forgot they *weren't* the biological parents. Yet Kirk found that rejection of difference did not overcome role handicap in practice. When something happened to undermine this myth—such as being asked about the child's birthparents—adoptive parents expressed anger and distress.

Families that coped by "acknowledging difference," Kirk discovered, were happier and better adjusted. They did not "forget" they were not the biological parents; instead they acknowledged the birthparents, expressed empathy for them, and thought about them. These parents discussed the birthparents with their children and shared their feelings about the adoption and encouraged their children to do so.

Kirk's theories have become conventional wisdom in the adoption community over the forty-plus years since *Shared Fate* was published. Most adoption professionals accept as a given that in adoption *every party loses something*. The birthparents lose the child; the child loses the birthparents; the adoptive parents lose the biological connection to the child. It was this common loss that led Kirk to use the term "shared fate." By acknowledging their shared losses, families could go on to build family relationships on a foundation of honesty. Although the stigma of not bearing children has lessened considerably in the United States, the fact that adoption is based on loss is constant. Even when adoptive parents are not infertile, the losses are the same.

Before Kirk, adopted children who did not support their parents' effort to reject difference were labeled as troubled. "For decades around midcentury, adoptees who expressed desires to learn more about their natal relatives, or find them, were considered maladjusted products of less than successful adoptive families. According to this way of thinking, children whose adoptive parents offered true love and belonging would have no reason to search."[13] This is the attitude that Kirk's research found invalid. "The expectation that adoption could erase and should replace natal families completely, which gave rise to the practice of matching, turned any curiosity about origins into a sign of trouble."[14] When children persisted in asking questions and expressing concern about birthparents and being adopted, parents sought counseling for them. Well-adjusted children did not need to rehash the past.

Antoine represents David Kirk's "rejection of difference." Although this attitude has long been discredited in the real world, Porte is by no means alone among authors in misunderstanding how adoptees process their experience. Authors of books for all ages continue to portray happy adopted children blissfully forgetful of their birthparents, all needs fully met in the bosom of their "real" families.

WICKED BIRTHPARENTS

Although published in 1987 as a contemporary novel, Pat Costa Viglucci's *Cassandra Robbins, Esq.* feels closer to 1965. Cassandra, seventeen, is the only nonwhite person in her adoptive family. All we know of her birthparents is that they were teenagers—one white, one black. Her older brother, Todd, is also adopted; their younger brother, Sam, is their parents' biological son. When Todd brings his black roommate Josh home for the summer, Josh and Cassandra are drawn to one another. Viglucci's not-very-hidden agenda is to show Cassandra making the "right" decisions about sex.

Cassandra reflects, "Being the only brown person in a white family is no big deal. Being the only girl is" (4). Being adopted is so unimportant it isn't even mentioned. Cassandra's remarks about her birthparents are offhand and breezy. She reflects that she and Todd don't know how tall they will get "or what our biological families looked like except for some sparse details the adoption agency had given Mom and Dad" (16). Her mother has always told her she is pretty because "a brown infant in a white family had to feel good about herself." It worked. "I was proud of my color, my background, my heritage and, most of all, myself" (20). She'll need that self-esteem later, to drive off hormone-addled suitors. In church, Cassandra notices a black father, white mother, and their two children, and thinks, "If my natural parents had not been teenagers and had stayed together, that could have been me ten years ago" (55). But she quickly moves on to another thought, and that's the last we hear of the birthparents. Given her abstinence agenda, Viglucci misses a golden opportunity here. During romantic interludes that might lead to sex, Cassandra never thinks of her birthparents who, presumably, found themselves in a similar situation.

While Cassandra has to deal with a mild incident of racism or two—unpleasant, but she's up to the challenge—she is happy with her adoptive family and aside from a few emotionally neutral mentions of birthparents, she might not be adopted at all. Although she experiences racism, she does not experience the bias against adoptees that is sometimes directed at children. Here, adoption is a non-issue for everyone.

Lee McClain's fantasy novel *My Alternate Life* (2004) stars Trinity B. Jones, biracial foster kid placed with a single mother, Susan, who has a teenage daughter, Kelly. Delivering her to Susan's house, the social worker hands Trinity a present, a computer game, which proves to be magical; it shows her what she asks to see. Trinity asks to see her birthmother, who left her at an orphanage when Trinity was eight. No one has told Trinity whether her mother is alive or dead. The fantasy game is confusing. Is what Trinity sees real? Is she seeing the consequences of choices she has yet to make? The first time Trinity asks to see her mother, the game shows her attending a fancy party. "She was the prettiest person there. She was laughing and talking and seemed to be having a great time." Trinity is relieved that she is not sick or dead. "My throat was all choked up. I wanted to go and bury myself in her arms. At the same time I was wondering: How could she be so happy when she'd given away her daughter? Did she know I'd been put out and had to find a new family in the sticks?" (15).

The novel loses credibility quickly. Trinity learns through the game that her mother is now married and living in luxury in a mansion. Trinity develops a convoluted plan to persuade her mother to take her back. Tucked in among the nonsense are moments that resonate. Trinity pictures her mother chatting with her maid, living the life of Riley. "Something dark and ugly twisted in my stomach. Suddenly I felt about five years old. *Can't get mad at Mommy, don't let her see you're mad, she hates that*" (31). Trinity worries that her mother won't want her because she is white and Trinity, whose father was black and American Indian, is brown. "For all I knew, she hated my color. Or maybe she hated how I didn't have movie star looks like she did. . . . Would I stand out in her world now, a world that was rich and probably all white? Would she be ashamed of my light brown skin, my super-curly hair, my full lips?" (32).

Adding to her pain, she discovers that her mother is apparently trying to get pregnant. "My mind raced. If Mom was trying to have another baby, then she must want to be a mom. Maybe she didn't know where I was." Or worse, "Maybe she wanted a new baby, a little tiny baby," Trinity thinks, "rather than a teenager who dressed and acted like a slut" (65).

The game, whose logic only gets fuzzier, shows Trinity her mother and herself as they would have been had her mother not abandoned her. Her mother is a slutty waitress, abusive to Trinity, and Trinity is a junior version of Mom. Trinity is given a chance to choose this life instead of her own. She has only seconds to decide. "Did I want to be the poor-trash child of a miserable waitress . . . but a regular, normal biological child living with my mom? Or did I want the nice bedroom, the computer, Kelly, Susan?" (135–36). Although she chooses Susan, "I was left with a cruel, bitter ache in my heart. I'd had a chance to be with my mom. To never have been a foster kid. To wipe out all the hurt of the past eight years . . . and I'd turned it down" (137).

When Trinity finally meets her face to face, her mother says, "Don't I know you from somewhere?" (96). Among nightmare adoption-reunion scenarios, this has to be near the top of the list. This encounter teaches Trinity that Susan is more of a mother than her own, who doesn't love her. (It doesn't help that Mom's husband is a white racist.) Trinity herself is a tough cookie but an engaging one, and the scenes set at her old orphanage feel authentic. The book's breezy tone is not suited to the tragedy of child abandonment. McClain's message that parenting is what we do, not who we are is worth making, but she never quite closes the deal.

Chris Crutcher received glowing reviews for *Whale Talk* (2001), which made the American Library Association Top Ten Best Books for Young Adults. The engaging storyline concerns a high school swim team cobbled together by the narrator protagonist, Tao Jones, known as T.J.[15] Aside from T.J., all team members are kids with disabilities and problems. The school in eastern Washington lacks a pool, so the kids practice swimming at the fitness club. With help from a homeless man and a sympathetic teacher, T.J., who is a brilliant athlete, fabulous student, and extremely mature senior, molds his motley crew into a workable team.

Adopted at age two, product of a one-night stand between a black-Japanese father and white drug-addicted mom, Glenda, T.J. comments on his origins with remarkable sangfroid. "I know next to nothing about the individuals who contributed all that exotic DNA, so it's hard to carve out a cultural identity in my mind. So: Mixed. Blended. Pureed. Potpourri," he tells us. "Adopted. . . . Big deal; so was Superman" (1). And T.J. himself is depicted as a kind of superman. Crutcher drapes his hero in a mantle of impeccable progressive credentials. Surrounded by small-town bigots and right-wing idiots, T.J. can, without fear of being labeled bigoted himself, excoriate them with his lacerating wit.

T.J.'s adoptive mom comforted Glenda after her Nordic American husband abandoned her when he realized baby T.J. was not his child. Two years later Glenda tracked her down and handed over T.J. They never heard from her again. "Sometimes I find myself longing for her, just to see or talk with her, discover more about the unsettledness within me, but most of the time that ache sits in a shaded corner of my mind, a vague reminder of what it is not to be wanted." This rings true and conforms to what is known about how kids think of their birthparents. He remembers nothing of her, "not what she looked like or the sound of her voice or even the touch of her hand" (3).

Later, Mom delivers a lecture about his birthmother to T.J. She tells him that even though Glenda had neglected him as a baby, he was inconsolable when left with his adoptive parents. "'You had diaper rash so bad your butt looked like a crater. And thrush, my God. You'd been left unattended for hours on end, sometimes days. You ate when your mother felt hungry, which was the only time she was reminded that you might be hungry, too, and she was eating darn little, because she was *launched* on meth.'" Nonetheless, T.J. cried for days after his birthmother left, and when she came back to say goodbye, "'you stopped crying the instant you saw her. She held you and cried, and you didn't utter a peep.'" T.J. interrupts Mom's story, which he's heard before. What's the point? he asks. The point, Mom says, is "'that you didn't respond to what was good for you, you responded to what you knew, what was familiar'" (147).

This scene is problematic. All adoptees, not just teens, harbor complicated feelings about their birthparents. These can change over time and are often contradictory. T.J. was adopted because his troubled mother gave him away as a toddler to his adoptive parents. Here, Mom, not for the first time, denigrates his birthmother, telling T.J. that he was crying inconsolably for her because he didn't know what was good for him.

Adoptive parents are in a bind when it comes to talking with their kids about birthparent issues. This birthmother has a drug problem; she is a mess. Mom is a lawyer. Taking children of color from impoverished parents—even when parents initiate the process—and handing them to dominant-caste professionals who have abundant resources to expend on the child is a serious, bitter, and heavily debated issue in the adoption world.[16] But even if Glenda were an heiress, for an adoptive mother to talk to her child about his birthmother in those terms is deeply insensitive. However wonderful the adoptive family, however much love flows between them, the child has lost the most fundamental biological connection human beings have to one another.

Georgia Brown, the black psychotherapist who straightened T.J. out as a child, practices a brutal form of play therapy that encourages victims of abuse to act out on others the abuse that has been inflicted on them. We are told her system works, but how and why are unclear. If Georgia were white, these scenes might well resonate differently with readers. Georgia often invites T.J. to help in this endeavor. "Play therapy, as practiced by Georgia, is done live and full scale, meaning she will drag in anybody available to play the roles that allow the kids to work out their life traumas," he says. Ignoring fussy rules about patient privacy and confidentiality, Georgia asks T.J. to act out a scenario with a multiracial patient, Heidi, who is about four or five years old. She directs him to be the "bad dad" and yell "nigger" at her. "In a calm voice Georgia tells me I'm supposed to yell at Heidi for letting the black dolls in the house, and I finally piece together from Heidi that I'm also supposed to find them one by one, scream at Heidi for letting each one in ('Get these nigger babies out of the house! They stinky!'), and throw them out, and it wouldn't hurt if I kicked or punched them while I'm at it" (70). During the session, T.J. helps Heidi try to wash her brown color off. It's hard, but Georgia knows what she is doing. By the end of the session T.J. and Heidi are dancing to a Bob Marley CD. Georgia makes T.J. sign a confidentiality agreement predated two weeks earlier. If we can buy the idea that a strange young man screaming racial epithets at a preschooler has therapeutic value, then perhaps we won't mind that Georgia has involved T.J. in a child's therapy session without parental consent.

In the four novels discussed so far, birthparents are variously nonexistent, irrelevant, selfish, incompetent, abusive, and uninterested in contact with their child. They display no positive qualities beyond having had the good sense to turn their children over to the noble adoptive parents who have much more to offer. All the authors are white; all the adoptive parents are white and middle class. All the children are nonwhite. Open adoption, in which some degree of contact exists between adoptees and their birthparents and extended birthfamilies, has been widespread since the 1980s. Yet none of these adoptions involves any contact: exchange of photos, letters, or visits. The bias displayed in these novels went unchallenged by reviewers.[17] The trend is slowly moving away from such stereotyping toward portraying birthparents as individuals with hard choices to make. They may not be heroes, but they are at least human.

THE KIMCHI MOMENT: ETHNIC AWAKENINGS

A popular theme in fiction with internationally adopted protagonists concerns the arrival of a character from the adoptee's home country. Previously ignorant about and uninterested in her country of origin, the adoptee is helped by the newcomer to first confront, then embrace the culture of her birth country as part of who she is. In this paradigm, the adoptive parents are not all-wise—far from it. They may be doing the best they can, but they make mistakes, sometimes serious ones.

The Korean American author Marie G. Lee, who now uses the name Marie Myung-Ok Lee,[18] has written two novels with protagonists adopted from Korea and raised in white families in the Midwest. Alice Larsen, protagonist of the first, *If It Hadn't Been for Yoon Jun* (1993), was adopted from Korea by a Lutheran minister and his wife, lives in a small town in Minnesota, and attends a middle school where she is the only Asian. She identifies as white and rebuffs her parents' faint efforts to introduce her to her birth culture, refusing to attend a Korean culture camp. Her sister, Mary, is her parents' biological child. When an immigrant family from Korea moves to town—a single mother and her geeky, overweight son—Alice must confront her own issues of race, racism, and adoption head on.

The novel is more commercial middle-grade than YA fiction, which plays against depth. The genre's standard-issue plot and narrative conventions are too thin and too pat for such complex subject matter, all but forcing characters to find easy solutions to hard problems. Lee returns to this subject matter more successfully in her crossover YA/adult novel *Somebody's Daughter*, discussed later in this chapter. But her insightful, sly depiction of adoptive-family denial is worth a look. Alice's father acknowledges difference; Alice and her mother reject difference and pretend she is their biological child. When Mr. Larsen extends a dinner invitation to a Korean family, new to town, Alice is mortified. "'The kid is a real dweeb. I don't want to eat dinner with him. Please, please can we skip this?'" Mom says they'll see what they can do, but Dad won't cancel the invitation. Alice overhears her parents argue. Mom says, "'I'm telling you, our daughter is happy as she is without our foisting a foreign culture on her.'" Her father disagrees. "'A lot of kids don't like what's unfamiliar,'" he says. "'She ought to at least give this family a chance.'" And, he adds, "'I thought perhaps Alice could become friends with the boy and learn a little more about her culture on the way.'" This hits a nerve. "'What do you mean, *her* culture?' said her mother. 'She's my— our daughter'" (28–29).

This textbook example of denial is played for both humor and insight. Mom says: "'Her biological mother gave her up. I think that gives us the right to bring her up as our own, as an American.'" Dad reminds her that Alice's birth country and culture are part of her, regardless of what her birthmother did. Mom won't budge. Alice has just made the cheerleading squad; she's popular; she's as pure Minnesotan as they come. Dad is not about to give in. "'She's old enough that we can start showing her both sides of the coin,'" he insists. "'We owe it to her'" (29). Alice's denial is equally strong. When her best friend asks if she ever thinks about her real parents, Alice is stung. She says the Larsens *are* her real parents. (And, indeed they are, but so are her birthparents.[19])

Dad learns Yoon Jun is unhappy and doing badly at school and asks Alice to befriend him. "Now, this was going way too far," she thinks. "No one should link her with Yoon Jun Lee just because an accident of nature made them look somewhat similar. That wasn't fair!" Hoping to put him on the defensive, she asks her father, "'Does this have something to do with my slanty Chinaman eyes?'" Later, Alice is pleased to overhear her mother tell him, "'I wish you would just ease up on poor Alice . . . the poor girl's going to have an identity crisis.'" Dad is adamant, however. "'Look, Yoon Jun Lee could use a little human kindness. It won't kill Alice. You saw how shy he is'" (62–63).

When Yoon Jun and Alice are paired together for a school project on Korea, Alice, at first reluctant, warms up to him. She goes to dinner at his house and his mother serves traditional Korean food, including kimchi. Alice begins to see her Korean heritage as something valuable that belongs to her. Now that she is no longer in denial about who she is, she uncovers bitter feelings of her birthmother's abandonment. Yoon

Jun shows her another way to look at that: "'Al-ice,' he said. 'They not give you up because they not want you, because they not love you. For some babies, there is no life in Korea, and is much better to grow up somewhere else. The parents suffer so child can have better life.'" That perspective opens Alice's eyes to a new possibility: "*Maybe one day,*" she thinks, "*the people at the adoption agency could help me find my Korean parents so I could write to them and tell them I'm okay, that I'm happy. Maybe Yoon Jun could act as a translator*" (128–29). This scenario that ends Alice's story is the starting point for Sarah in *Somebody's Daughter*.

Rose Kent's lively and very funny *Kimchi & Calamari* (2007) is unique in several ways. The family that adopted Joseph Calderaro from Korea is working class. Dad washes windows for a living. Mom works in a hair salon. The Calderaros, deeply proud of their Italian heritage, are bringing up Joseph just as any good Italian American family raises its firstborn son. They also have biological children, twin daughters younger than Joseph. One of Kent's achievements is to make these flawed, sometimes delusional parents sympathetic and lovable, without ever letting readers lose sight of who Joseph is and what he needs. The novel is marketed as middle grade, but is crossover YA. Kent, who is white, has biological children and adopted children from Korea.

On Joseph's fourteenth birthday, his class is assigned a heritage project,[20] for which they are to research and write about their ancestors. Joseph, who has begun to think about his own lately, tells his friend Nash that he doesn't need fifteen hundred words for his project. Two sum it up: "'I'm adopted'" (5). That evening, at his birthday dinner featuring Joseph's favorite eggplant Parmesan, his father presents him with a gold chain with a tiny gold horn, a *cornu,* worn by Sicilian men to ward off the evil eye and bring good luck. Joseph is dismayed. Wearing this will not only make him look dorky, but weird, since his biological ancestry is Korean, not Sicilian. Joseph is a nice kid and acutely aware of how important their Italian heritage is to his parents, especially his dad, and wants to spare him the pain of having to acknowledge that Joseph is anything other than Italian American himself. These two events set the plot in motion.

When he was a small child his mother made Joseph's adoption into a bedtime story. Teary eyed, she would say, "'Once upon a time, Mommy and Daddy wanted a baby to love.'" Mom's story includes the birthfamily. "'Meanwhile, in Korea, a special mommy was growing you in her tummy, but she couldn't care for a baby. Still, she loved you so much that she did something very hard. She allowed you to travel all the way to America, to be Mommy and Daddy's little boy. And that is how we became the Calderaro family'" (19–20). Joseph realizes that to his parents, his life began when they met him. But he is interested in what happened before that. He does have a little more to go on. For his first family tree project back in third grade, she told him his Korean name "Duk-kee," and the surname the adoption agency added to it: "Park." That is all he has to go on.

When Joseph tells his dad he doesn't know what to write, Dad launches into reminiscences about how Grandma and Grandpa Calderaro came from Siena in 1947. Joseph is at first sympathetic, then impatient with his father's obtuseness. He finally blurts out that they're not *his* ancestors. Dad is hurt: "'That's a heck of a thing to say about your grandparents,'" he says reproachfully. Joseph backpedals. "'They're great, Dad. But I'm asking you about my Korean relatives, and you're not helping'" (40). Dad tells him to ask his mother.

A new Asian kid at school proves to be Korean. Yongsu Han is somewhat geeky, but nice, and they become friends. Yongsu's mother is downright cold when Joseph admits he doesn't speak Korean and is adopted. "Obviously Mrs. Han thought I was a cheap Korean imitation, maybe even a troublemaker who needed watching." This hurts; usually, his friends' mothers like him. Yongsu's mother tells her son that it is not natural for Koreans to raise other people's children. Joseph tries to shrug it off. After all, his parents aren't exactly helping him with his heritage project. Clearly, they don't understand adoption either.

With zero information on his own forebears, Joseph gets creative. Researching Koreans of renown, he reads about the runner who won a gold medal in the 1936 Berlin Olympic Games. Joseph decides to claim him as his grandfather. For all he knows, it could be true. His research makes Korea come alive as a country for the first time. The more contact he has with the Hans, the more Joseph wonders about his own birthfamily. Yongsu has an older sister. Might Joseph have a sister in Korea? He thinks about the ways he differs from the rest of the Calderaro family. Is there someone in Korea who shares his lifelong passion for hot peppers?

When his teacher wants to submit his essay to a national contest, Joseph confesses it is made up. Dad can't understand why Joseph refused to write about Grandpa Calderaro. "'How can you say this isn't your *real family*? I've tried to be the best father I can for you, Joseph,'" he says. "'Every day I go out there and break my back for you and your sisters. *That's* family.'" Joseph is fed up with his father's denial. "'It's not just about what you know, Dad! Why can't you deal with who I am? I couldn't count on you to help me write one lousy essay. Last time I checked, being adopted wasn't a crime, but you sure act like it is!'" (112). "Essaygate" has other consequences. Like so many of our younger heroes, Joseph has a crush on a snooty blonde; this one rejects him when she learns he lied on his assignment.

The turnaround moment for Joseph comes when Mrs. Han thaws enough to invite him to dinner. There, he has the quintessential "kimchi moment," discovering a passion for the addictive hot, garlicky, cabbage pickle Koreans love. Connecting spontaneously with something so strongly associated with his birth country makes him feel Korean, too.

Joseph's insistence that his identity is more than simply Italian American finally touches a chord in his father: "'I'm not you, Joseph, and I can't imagine how it feels to be adopted. But I know how it feels to wonder if I'm doing what I was meant to do. I ask myself that almost every night as I rinse out my sponges and load my ladder back on the truck'" (156–57). This insight pays off. When Dad breaks his arm on the job, he takes it as a sign to go after the college education he has always longed for. Dad researches tours to Korea that help Korean American adoptive families search for birthparents. He and Joseph will go when they have saved the money.

The questions Jean Davies Okimoto raises in *Talent Night* are echoed in *Kimchi & Calamari*. When you are adopted, which is your true culture? Your true ethnic heritage? For adopted individuals the only answer that makes sense, Kent shows us, is "both." But even though it's the right answer, it does not always *feel* right, and there is no guarantee others will agree with it. Much of who Joseph is has nothing to do with the Calderaros. And much of who Joseph is has nothing to do with Korea and his birthparents. Joseph himself is the connection between them. Working that out is a lifelong task. It can be sad, even heartbreaking. But to be embraced by two cultures is also enriching and wonderful, a rich gift as lasting as the pain that accompanies it.

Julia Alvarez has written for all age groups. She received the Pura Belpré award for *Before We Were Free*. Her family immigrated to the

United States from the Dominican Republic when she was a child, and Alvarez draws on her full heritage in her work. Milly Kaufman, the protagonist of *Finding Miracles* (2004), was adopted from an unnamed Latin American country where her parents were living after their stint in the Peace Corps, and just after the birth of their first biological child, Kate. Their son, Nate, was born in the United States. The Kaufmans speak Spanish, know Milly's birth country, and are well-educated on adoption issues. The extended family is another story. Mom is a lapsed Mormon. Dad is Jewish. His notoriously difficult mother, Happy, is miffed because Dad did not carry on the family business. Kate and Milly's sibling rivalry is augmented by Milly's adopted status.

While this fine novel has believable characters and treats adoption intelligently, one element is problematic. Milly's feelings about her adoption are confused and conflicted. She has told only her best friend that she is adopted and is very anxious that no one else at school know. When Pablo Bolivar, a new student whose family has emigrated from Milly's birth country, shows up at school, she snubs him and pretends she doesn't understand when he speaks Spanish to her. The point that adoptees can be in denial about their status is valid. But it is hard to accept that Milly does not stand out as physically different from her family. Vermont is about as white and northern European a state as any in the United States. Most Latin American families who are so impoverished that they are forced to place their children in orphanages are *mestizo,* of mixed Hispanic, indigenous, and sometimes African heritage. Few adoptees from Latin America resemble their white adoptive parents and from a very early age they discover that fact; a few years later they realize that others perceive it as well. These children have no choice about whether, when, and with whom they share the fact of their adoption. While plenty of Latin Americans could pass as northern European American, most are from more privileged backgrounds; among adoptees they are rare. There are very few Latin American adoptees in children's or YA fiction. By making Milly's appearance atypical, Alvarez lost an opportunity to reflect their image to them.

Milly's parents rightly leave it to her to decide when and how to share her personal story and even whether to talk about it with them. After she learns that Pablo comes from her birth country, Milly becomes morose and anxious. Her mother says, "'You've always chosen to be very private about this.'" Mom is a therapist. "'It might be good to talk about it, don't you think?'" (35). But Milly can't.

Milly overhears her mother talking about Happy's plans to treat Milly differently in her will from her other grandchildren. "'How can she think we'd accept a will that doesn't treat all our kids the same? A stipend for Milly instead of a share!'" (46). Hearing that her grandmother does not consider her equal to her other grandchildren forces Milly to recognize that she *is*, in fact, different. Although it hurts, it helps her reach out to Pablo—if she is not 100 percent Kaufman after all, maybe she needs to think about the culture she shares with him. When the Kaufmans befriend the Bolivars, Milly's friendship with Pablo is reinforced. Milly's birth country, long governed by a brutal military dictatorship that has jailed Pablo's two brothers and killed an uncle, is holding elections that may restore democracy. As the country transitions to democracy, the Bolivars plan to return and reunite with family freed from jail. Instead of going on a family vacation, Milly wants to visit her birth country, but with the Bolivars, not with her family. Dad is hurt. Why does she want to go alone to a foreign country? "'It's not a foreign country,'" Milly says. "'It's my native country'" (109). Kate turns on her angrily. "'It's my native country, too, you know,'" she says and bursts into tears, adding, "'I feel like you're giving up on us as a family'" (110). And she struggles with feelings of rejection throughout the novel. Kate's sense of loss and abandonment is as much a part of the adoption experience as Milly's own search. Their relationship is insightfully and beautifully depicted, rare in YA fiction about adopted teens.

Milly summons the courage to look inside the little box containing a few items from her birthfamily that the nuns at her orphanage gave to her parents: a coin, two strands of hair—one fair, one dark—braided together, and a scrap of paper with the word "Milagros" (miracles) on it. That was Milly's name at the orphanage, and her parents have kept it as her middle name.

The remainder of the novel takes place in Milly's unnamed birth country. By making it an amalgam rather than specifying a real country, Alvarez can't describe actual places and events. The outcome is a setting that is more integrated with the story than it might have been. Her strategy gives Alvarez freedom to match the details of history, landscape and climate, food, and social customs to the needs of Milly's story.

Milly's journey to her birth country parallels the country's awakening from years of nightmarish military rule. Many died trying to bring freedom to their country. Truth and reconciliation hearings are held; the family watches these on TV obsessively. The mood of the country is sad, grieving the loss of beloved family and friends who will never return, and at the same time joyful and festive: a new day has dawned that brings hope for a better future. This mood subtly echoes Milly's own loss of the opportunity to grow up in her birthfamily and culture, and her joy at discovering it now, getting to know the people and places that are her heritage, and experiencing a blossoming romance with Pablo.

Milly accompanies the Bolivars as they return the body of Pablo's uncle, killed in the struggle for freedom, to the mountain village he was born in, Los Luceros. Throughout the novel, Milly is told that her eyes are just like the eyes of people who live in Los Luceros (readers need to buy the suggestion that eye color is town-specific) and she is curious to see for herself. Could this be where her birthfamily is? In Los Luceros, Dulce, Pablo's widowed aunt, takes Pablo and Milly to see an elderly woman who might know of any babies born in the village at the time of Milly's birth. Dona Gloria remembers three. One of them was a freedom fighter who gave birth to a little girl. She returned to fighting, was soon captured, and never heard from again. Milly is sure that is her mother. She asks, "'Do you think she really didn't want me?'" Dona Gloria says, "'Without our children, we lose the future. We lose our stories. Our dreams die!'" (223).

Milly never discovers which, if any, of the babies she was. Some losses are permanent. But she has recovered a seedling of identity to nurture and grow, here and back home in Vermont. Milly takes Milagros back as her first name.

Not every child adopted from another country has such opportunities, supported and encouraged along the way, to recover her heritage. But it is a goal worth reaching for. In the end, Milly's entire adoptive family, even Kate, is enriched by her dual identities.

Mitali Perkins's 2004 novel, *Monsoon Summer,* looks at adoption from a different angle. Perkins, Indian American, was born in India and immigrated to the United States as a child. Her South Asian narrator, Jazz, is not adopted—her mother is. Jazz, short for Jasmine, and her brother, Eric, are biracial; their father is white. Jazz resembles their dad, Eric their mom. Home is Berkeley, California, where Dad is a computer geek, and Mom works with refugees. She was adopted from an orphanage in Pune, India, at age four. When she is invited to set up a prenatal and obstetrics and gynecology clinic there, the family accompanies her.

This novel is more a privileged American teen's discovery of how the rest of the world lives than a "back to your roots" story. Because

Mom was raised in the United States by white parents, she has not been able to experience her Indian heritage or pass it on to her own children. She is as much a stranger in India as the rest of the family. Nonetheless, she has done her best to give the kids some cultural grounding, as her own adoptive parents had done. "We ordered take-out curry all the time. My grandparents took us to see every Indian-made film that came to the Bay Area. And two evenings a week, rain or shine, since I was ten years old, I'd conjugated verbs with an ancient Hindi tutor" (9).

Like Milly's sister, Jazz feels threatened by her mother's interest in her roots. When Mom brings up the possibility of searching for her birthparents, "Mom's parents are Helen and Frank," Jazz protests. "She's not going back to India to find her birth family." Jazz turns to her mother for confirmation, "but she didn't meet my eyes" (24).

When they settle in Pune near her mother's orphanage, Jazz tries to avoid it. Because Jazz is fair, she draws attention when she goes out. Worse, when they go shopping, Mom is assumed to be Jazz's servant. "I hated the way people overlooked her and catered to me, curiosity obvious in their faces." Mom's behavior makes Jazz uncomfortable. "It did something to my insides watching her study the face of every older, darker-skinned woman, as though waiting for one of them to recognize her" (102).

Jazz first attends a school nearby, but she soon switches to volunteering at the orphanage, where she befriends an orphan, Danita, who at seventeen is preparing to leave the orphanage and hopes to bring her two younger siblings with her, if she can find a way for the three of them to stay together. This friendship gives Jazz a way to understand her mother's background. As the summer wears on, Jazz becomes more comfortable in India and with her own Indianness, and like her mother, reclaims her birthright. Among her "lessons learned" (the book is a tad didactic) is how it feels to be a stranger. She appreciates the hospitality that is central to Indian culture: "I promised myself that when new kids started at Berkeley High this fall, I'd do my best to make them feel at home. After all, I was half Indian, wasn't I?" (170).

With Dad's help, the girls make a business plan and secure a micro-loan for Danita. Perkins makes the subtle point that prosperity is changing how India cares for its children. Jazz studies the adoptive family photos lining the orphanage walls: "Some of the older parents' faces were white, but most of the newer photos were all of Indians—babies and adoptive parents" (158). Indians are adopting their orphans rather than sending them to white American families.

Mom never finds her birthfamily. When a young woman comes into the clinic to have her second baby and leaves it at the orphanage, Mom's grief for her own losses comes home to her and to Jazz. "The baby's mother stood up. Mom said something, but the girl shook her head. Slowly, carefully, she pulled her hand away from Mom's. Then she walked off without looking back, and my mother was left alone outside the orphanage." Jazz understands what to do. She hurries to her mother. "'I'm here, Mom,' I said, sitting beside her, in the place where the girl had been." Mom reaches out to her and asks, "'Why did she have to leave?'" Jazz doesn't know, but she holds onto her mother's hand and says, "'I'm glad she came.'" And Jazz realizes then that "neither of us was talking about the girl who had just left. We were remembering another day and another baby, long ago" (223–24).

One in fifty Americans is adopted. They are not only teens, but mothers and fathers, grandparents, cousins. This rare portrait of an adopted parent allows readers to see adoption and how it builds and affects families from a different angle than that of the adopted teen.

PRIVILEGED FAMILIES

Two of our adoptive families are exceptionally well off. The novels that describe them are both light and satirical in tone. Here, well-meaning adoptive parents and other adults want to define what being adopted means for the adopted children, instead of allowing them to do it for themselves. How they seize control of their identities is the source of humor and insight.

Like his wife Cynthia, Greg Leitich Smith finds humor in subjects more commonly treated as sad or serious, delivered with a heavy dose of didacticism. In *Ninjas, Piranhas, and Galileo* (2003), three seventh-graders—Elias, Honoria, and Shohei—at a prestigious private school in Chicago set out to win the science fair award. The coequal protagonists tell the story in alternating chapters; their friendship is the story's glue. Honoria has a crush on Shohei. Elias has a crush on Honoria. Blind to Honoria's crush on himself, Shohei tries to help Elias secure Honoria's affections. The adoption thread is a sideshow—but it is a pleasure to have adoption treated as just one among many defining traits. Japanese American Shohei O'Leary is the adopted child of Irish American parents. His family includes his younger brother, Tim, his parents' biological child. The adoptive parents, affluent, anxious, and high-achieving like all the characters here, lose no opportunity to expose Shohei to his birth heritage. Shohei has become adept at sidestepping the Japanese cultural offerings raining down upon him, such as the opportunity to attend a Kabuki version of *Titus Andronicus*. The novel is not about Shohei's journey as an adopted kid, so the absence of the birthparents from the story is acceptable.

When the boys eat lunch together at school, Shohei brings sushi. "Since the beginning of the school year, my mom had been getting up two and a half hours early every day to make and roll a fresh batch," Shohei says. "Don't get me wrong: I like sushi sometimes—and my mom's has gotten much better—but occasionally, like any red-blooded American, I crave something cooked, like a hot dog. Or baby-back ribs" (10–11).

When Elias arrives to work on their joint science project, he is taken aback at the sight of Shohei's room, recently re-envisioned by his mother. "I turned around and spread my arms. 'Welcome,' I said, 'to the Land of the Rising Sun'" (28). Mom has replaced his bed with tatami mats and removed Shohei's sports posters and replaced them with Japanese prints. While Shohei stoically endures his mother's attempt to marinate him in his birth culture, Tim embraces it. He calls his older brother *sensei,* and bows to him. Tim's attitude of devotion and familial respect is useful. Shohei puts him to work watering plants for his science project.

After another adoptive family moves into their building, Mom's Japanization efforts come to a head. The Eichbaums have two daughters adopted from China. Mom invites them to dinner. "Normally, I might've wanted to meet them," Shohei says. "But I knew the only reason they'd been invited was because my parents wanted me to bond on an adopted-Asian-American-kid level with Megan and Mallory" (85). To top this off, Shohei discovers his parents have signed him up for bonsai classes.

Shohei feels pressured. It doesn't help that he has screwed up the science fair project and Elias has stopped speaking to him. The adoptive-family get-together and bonsai classes are looming. "I was supposed to be celebrating, or whatever, my Japanese heritage. But my parents had never let *me* decide what that meant," he fumes. "When they'd remodeled my room, I'd wanted to put up a couple of samurai swords." Mom says no "because they were 'not going to glorify a sordid military tradition.'" They rejected Shohei's Godzilla film festival and *anime* ideas as too violent. They ruled out celebrating motor vehicles and consumer electronics despite *their* strong Japanese heritage. Shohei feels he ought to be in charge of what to honor and what to ignore—after all, isn't that one of the pluses of being adopted? He *is* studying Japanese, unlike his parents, who speak only English. "Dad's totally Irish American, and Mom probably is, too, but also maybe part Lithuanian and Polish, depending on who her real grandfather is. They're only a couple generations off the boat, but they've never had any interest in learning more about where they came from" (107–8). This train of thought gives Shohei an idea. When the Eichbaums arrive, Shohei greets them with his hair dyed "chemical neon green" and shamrocks on his cheeks, attired in a Notre Dame football team T-shirt and green soccer shorts. He leaps into the living room, shouting, "'Top o' the evening to you!'" Everyone is stunned. "'I think you have to get in touch with your Irish heritage,'" he tells his parents. "'I want to be as supportive as possible. You need to buy lots of tam-o'-shanters, shamrocks, and potatoes. You should also remodel Tim's room like a mud hut, or stone cottage, or whatever'" (114). To drive home the message, he starts to sing "It's a Long Way to Tipperary."

A few days later, Shohei's parents sit him down for a talk. He gets in first, asking them to tone down the culture immersion. They don't want him to lose out on what he needs, they say. His Japanese heritage is part of him. "'Yeah,' I said. 'But lots of things are part of me. Japan. America. Chicago. Ireland . . . sort of.'" The list includes being adopted, too. "'You guys have picked how much Irish you want to be,'" he says. "'Why can't I?'" (159–60). But when Shohei's parents float the possibility of visiting Japan next summer, he jumps at the chance.

In their fiction both Leitich Smiths draw attention to the fact that real and vivid ethnicities are hidden behind the mask of generic whitebread culture. Told with humor, their stories go down easily. Perhaps one day the serious message behind them will be heard as well.

First Daughter: Extreme American Makeover (2007), by Mitali Perkins, is the first volume in a lighthearted YA series about an adoptee whose white father is running for president of the United States. Perkins has chosen her subject well; there is more than enough content here to fill as many volumes as she cares to produce.

Adopted from a Pakistani orphanage at age three by white parents, Sameera Righton, sixteen, is the only child of a diplomat and politician father and human-rights advocate mother, and has just finished her sophomore year of high school in Europe. Sameera conforms to the breezy, independent, self-confident protagonist profile so beloved by YA authors, but here, for once, the character's biography supports that profile. Sameera has spent most of her life in the public eye and as a child is comfortable around adults. But as her father sews up the Republican nomination, the attention on her family kicks up several notches. None of the Rightons is prepared for what follows.

Perkins juggles multiple plot threads, characters, settings, ethnicities, and cultures with finesse and humor. The supporting cast of *First Daughter* includes a driven, thirty-something public relations blogmeister; a midwestern farm family; members of a South Asian college student club; a Muslim immigrant family; and assorted anti-immigrant bigots.

A central theme of the novel is the struggle between Sameera and her father's handlers over how to define her to the American public. Sameera stays in touch with a circle of trusted friends by blogging, but when she joins her parents for the last stage of the nomination battle, she discovers that Tara, the consultant hired to manage her dad's media image, has hired a web guru to create her "official" website. It is supposedly written by Sameera, but she has had nothing to do with it. Its purpose is to erase as much as possible of Sameera's ethnicity and downplay her difference from the white-bread culture they are convinced Americans expect their first family to embody. They rename her "Sammy." Tara tells her: "'You're not quite the all-American type, are you? And a name like 'Sameera' just underlines that'" (34). Sameera submits reluctantly; she wants to support her dad. The makeover goes beyond changing her name. Sameera is shocked the first time she sees SammySez.com. "A cartoon that looked like an anime girl was forming on the screen, accompanied by background music. The red-lipped, big-eyed manga creature was wearing a VOTE FOR RIGHTON button on her shirt" (39). A bubble of words appears: "Welcome to Sammy-Sez.com, the online journal written by the gurl who knows our next president better than anybody on the planet. I'm Sammy, and this is my virtual crib" (39). The content includes product placements and thinly disguised political electioneering.

Sameera has faith that Americans can relate to her as she is. Tara disagrees. "'Values in America don't change as fast as they do in Europe'" (34), she insists. Sameera won't look like an American to some voters. This sounds the theme: can Sameera be herself in modern America?

Sameera's busy life is chick-lit candy, but secretly laced with protein and vitamins. Sameera hates the online makeover but loves the real-world version. She shops for clothes, gets her hair and makeup done by professionals. From a small brown kid, she is transformed into a glamorous young woman. Beyond a little glitz, Perkins never strays far from the real world. A man at a country club fundraiser tells Semeera, "'Bring another platter of that shrimp by here, will you?'" (56). She realizes he's taken her for one of the waitresses. Sameera knows no makeover will ever make her look like a member of the dominant caste, and Perkins makes sure readers don't forget it either. This fact grounds her, keeping her often-regal treatment in perspective.[21]

Sameera finds ways to wiggle out of or around the restrictions placed on her. To stay sane, she sneaks out, disguised in Muslim attire, to a meeting of South Indian college students. She trusts them with her identity. Relieved to learn that she is not responsible for the idiotic SammySez.com site, the students, including handsome Bengali-speaking Bobby from South Carolina, urge her to take her blog public, so she can talk about the issues that matter to her. Bobby says, "'My guess is that the REAL Sameera has the gift of gathering circles of people around her. You might not even realize it yet, but the people around you do. Like us'" (212).

The nomination secured, the Rightons move on to what has to be the most positive general election campaign (we can only dream) in U.S. history. Sameera wants to share her experience, the people she's met, and start a wider conversation about what it means. On a weekly blog, she invites questions and puts out questions for discussion. Her first question is "How long does it take people to drop that ethnic adjective we put before the word 'American'?" She points out that "white kids get to do it after they lose their parents' accents" (242) and from then on they don't have to be Irish or Polish Americans, just Americans. But for people of color, it seems no matter how many generations they've been in the country, they have to keep that Asian or African descriptor. What makes it go away?

The blog is a success. SammySez.com is retired, along with the name "Sammy," with which the campaign PR people downplayed her origins. Sameera finds that being herself in public, rather than perky Sammy, isn't always easy. Asked about her adoption online, Sameera has to figure out how to deal with painful realities, such as the fact that when she was in the orphanage, she was the last child to find parents, and although other children were claimed by relatives, no one claimed *her.*

Volume one ends as Dad wins the White House. Sameera is almost, but not quite, too good to be true. She is a compassionate leader who up till now has felt plain and invisible. Her gleeful pleasure at her popularity is believable and endearing. What we have here is a role model.

ADOPTION AS METAPHOR

To tackle as big a subject as genocide in fiction presents almost insuperable difficulties for writers. How does one convey the scale of destruction, the systematic attempt by one human group to destroy another? Most approach the subject obliquely, telling an individual story in detail to suggest the larger one.

But sometimes writers want to convey the sheer scope and breadth of genocide directly, not in cameo. In Sherman Alexie's *Indian Killer* (1996) the Spokane Indian novelist and poet takes on the American Indian genocide. Published when the author was in his early thirties, it radiates the audacity of youth and the confidence of a writer who has mastered his tools. But the problem remains: how to do justice to events so horrific, violent, cruel, and senseless. Latin American writers invented magical realism for just such a purpose; Alexie borrows it but adapts it to his ends. *Indian Killer* is magical realism without the magic, but its use of metaphor stamps it as a member of the club. The metaphor Alexie chooses is adoption.

The novel opens with the delivery by a white doctor of a baby born to a teenage Indian mother of an unnamed tribe on an unnamed reservation. Immediately a helicopter flies the baby to a wealthy Seattle suburb and lands on the manicured lawn of a mansion with a swimming pool. Someone hands the baby to a white couple, Daniel and Olivia Smith. Olivia cradles baby John in her arms and holds him up to her empty breast.

The fact that this is magical realism seems to have escaped many reviewers, including American Indian critics. Most critics recognized

Indian Killer as an important literary work, praising it for its hard-edged, contemporary portrait of the urban Indian. Louis Owens, who hated it, felt it showed Alexie to be "a perhaps unwitting product of the dominant culture he abjures in his writing," and that he was "telling horror stories to titillate white readers."[22] Owens felt that Alexie was giving white readers what they wanted: a picture of Indians as pathetic victims of alcoholism and self-destructiveness.

Why is it magical realism and not just plain realism? Alexie knows adoptions are not negotiated in this way,[23] that helicopters do not actually land on adoptive parents' lawns to hand newborn infants over to them. While not fantastic, this event is absurd, the watermark of magical realism. What it represents is the stripping of culture and community from American Indians. It signals the book's theme that will be sounded in many different ways by a large cast of characters. In the context of a cultural genocide that has been by and large a resounding success, how do we determine what is authentic and what is fake among what has not been destroyed? What does it mean to be a "real Indian"? Whose birthright is it? If you were born on the reservation, as John is, and immediately removed from everything that relates to Indian culture—family, community, identity—are you still an Indian?

Indian Killer is considered crossover YA; most major characters are young adults. Despite its grim subject, the novel is quite funny. Serving in part as Alexie's alter ego is Marie Polatkin, a Spokane Indian student at the University of Washington. Like Alexie, Marie is infuriated at the appropriation of Indian identity by wanna-bes, liars, and opportunists. She herself has an authenticity problem; raised on the Spokane reservation, she was precocious and smart. Forced to choose between Spokane Indian culture and school, she chose school, skipping powwows and traditional events to study. Her fellow students may not be headed to university, but they have fully assimilated Spokane identities. "They had chosen their life, and Marie both resented and envied them. Because she could not dance or sing traditionally, and because she could not speak Spokane, Marie was often thought of as being less than Indian." Her parents are partly responsible; they refused to teach her the language because they didn't think it would be of use to her off the reservation, where they wanted her to go. "Instead of teaching her about Spokane culture, they bought her books by the pound at pawn shops, secondhand stores, and garage sales" (34).

Marie has to fight not just white cultural racism and bias, but bullying and taunting from her fellow Indians. Her story is interwoven with John's. They meet, and though they briefly connect a few times, their worlds don't really intersect much. Marie, isolated, troubled, and angry much of the time, is a fighter. She is a "real Indian." John is not.

Owens accuses Alexie of didacticism, and it's a fair comment in Marie's case. She enrolls in a class on Native American literature with mixed motives. She's heard Professor Mather gives Indians good grades, and she wants to do well. She is surprised by the reading list—it is a Who's Who of works by fake Indians. From here on, she wages war against Mather, questioning every fatuous assumption. Alexie assigns Marie the task of filling in readers on the many literary appropriations of Indian identity in fiction and nonfiction, especially "autobiographies" of Indians written partly or wholly by whites. These scenes are didactic but very funny. Mather lectures the class on "the long tradition of European-Americans who were adopted into Indian tribes. A red-headed, green-eyed Irish and British mix, Mather proudly revealed that he'd been adopted into a Lakota Sioux family, an example of the modern extension of that long tradition" (61). Later, when Marie asks why an Indian is not teaching the class, Mather is hurt; he reminds her he was adopted into a Lakota Sioux family. "'That just proves some Indians have no taste'" (313), Marie says.

Marie is at war with the fake Indianness represented by Mather and by one of the novelists whose work he assigns to his class, Jack Wilson. A rather sweet soul, Wilson, white, was orphaned by age ten and raised in a series of eleven foster families. "Dreaming of being Indian, he'd read every book he could find about the First Americans and had been delighted to learn that they raised their children communally. An Indian child moved freely between tepees, between families. A child could be loved and disciplined by any adult in the tribe. During the long, cold nights, every campfire was a welcome sight for a lonely child" (159). Over time, Wilson persuades not only others but himself that he is a Shilshomish Indian. This identity is cleverly chosen. Shilshomish tribal membership records are scanty, so his claim can't be easily verified or disputed. As a mystery writer of Indian characters, Wilson is reasonably successful. His assumed identity is a blanket that keeps him warm, but it's a stolen blanket.

John is both central and empty. His loving white parents have tried to raise him to appreciate his Indian heritage. His looks are not ambiguous; he definitely appears Indian. Now that he is an adult, a construction worker, they continue to check up on him and worry about him. When he was an infant they sought out an Indian priest to baptize him (the priest soon after disappears). They took him to pow-wows as a child. In high school, Daniel took him to an all-Indian basketball tournament. At the game he sees "Indians with brown hair and paler skin. Green-eyed Indians. Indians with black blood. Indians with Mexican blood. Indians with white blood. Indians with Asian blood. All of them laughing and carrying on." The laughter is amazing to John. "John wanted to own that laughter, never realizing that their laughter was a ceremony used to drive away personal and collective demons" (21). John is mentally ill, adrift in dreams. He fantasizes his birth and how life might have gone differently. The distance between John and his birthright is unbridgeable.

The thread connecting the central characters—John, Marie, and Jack—is a series of murders and scalpings of white men. Marie, embattled but secure in her Spokane identity, and Jack, armored in his comforting delusions, are able to survive. John, from whom all traces of heritage have been permanently eviscerated, does not survive. The book ends with his suicide.

Alexie doesn't give away the identity of the killer, who is still at large at the end of the novel. He lets us wonder if it's John or Jack or even Marie, but Alexie isn't much interested in the mystery of the killer's identity. The brutal killings—as Alexie makes crystal clear on the final page—are a collective, perhaps magical, response to half a millennium of genocide—intentional, incidental, and accidental. The chickens (here, they are owls) are coming home to roost.

The novel explores extinction obliquely, arriving at its meaning indirectly, just as a distant star can be seen more clearly using averted vision. Adoption has been used to extinguish the cultures of indigenous people around the world.[24] The adopter has the power. The adopted infant is powerless. Birth certificates are rewritten to extinguish the birthparents, replacing them with the adoptive parents. A fiction has made them disappear. As a metaphor for the cultural genocide of aboriginal peoples, we could do worse.

MOTHER-DAUGHTER JOURNEYS

The discovery of birthparents by writers of YA fiction is late, but welcome. Their presence enriches adoption narratives, deepens characters, and enlightens readers on how adoption comes about and affects the three parties involved. There is no way to appreciate the losses and gifts of adoption without including the birthparents. Although we say "birthparents," more often than not, that means "birthmothers." Birthfathers are rarely mentioned. But that too is changing. As we see in the final three books examined in this chapter, when we get to know the mothers well, the fathers come into focus.

However, the relationship of mother to child is unique, and in adoption, paramount. After carrying a child inside her body for nine months, feeling it move, the birthmother gives it up forever. Studies of birthmothers overwhelmingly show that this loss never completely heals.[25] For some it becomes the central, defining experience of their lives. For their children—especially their daughters when they come to give birth themselves—it is an emotionally unfathomable choice. Questions that only the birthmother can answer remain: "Plenty of impoverished mothers keep and raise their children; why didn't mine?" "What was wrong with me?" Here, three authors answer those questions through stories of adopted daughters and their birthmothers.

A Brief Chapter in My Impossible Life is among the very few fictional considerations of religious ethnicity in the context of adoption. In Dana Reinhardt's 2006 novel, Simone, a high school junior, is the older of two children in a white family. Mom is a lawyer for the American Civil Liberties Union. Dad, a political cartoonist, works from home. Simone's younger brother, Jake, is her parents' biological child. Simone, unlike her blonde family, is dark. The novel opens as Dad tells Simone that her birthmother Rivka has called and wants to get in touch with her.

Before going any further, let us stop and heave a sigh of relief that children's fiction has at last caught up to what has been the norm in domestic adoption for more than thirty years: contact among birth and adoptive families.

Simone is upset. A high school junior, she has found a place in her psyche to stow the fact of her adoption. "It's not like I haven't spent hours or days or weeks or even years thinking about the fact that I'm adopted" (6), she says. But, "you might be surprised to know that I've never wanted to learn anything about my real family tree" (7). She has persuaded herself to accept the fiction that Rivka, her birthmother, is just a name. Unlike Simone, her friend Minh, adopted from Vietnam, was told by his parents that his adoption was God's plan for their family. But Simone's parents don't believe in God, although they are nominally Christian. "We don't go to church or pray or do any of those things. And even though whenever someone asks me what I am, I say, 'Nothing,' my parents come from the Christian tradition: Catholic in my dad's case, Episcopalian in my mom's." While this rings true, Reinhardt goes on to put words in Simone's mouth that, to those whose forebears were Christian but who don't believe in or practice Christianity themselves, do not make sense. "As far as I know they didn't go through any kind of ritual to erase their Christian pasts and become something else. Doesn't this mean that to the rest of the world we're Christians, no matter how we define ourselves?" (28). The answer to whether the rest of the world defines Christianity as an inherited culture or ethnicity is "that depends." There is no single view on the issue. But to Christians, if we concede them the right to define themselves, the answer is unequivocally "no."[26]

Simone says firmly that she is not interested in contact with Rivka. Her best friend Cleo can't understand why. Isn't she curious? "How can I be curious?" Simone thinks. "I've spent all my life fighting off that curiosity" (22). For her part, Simone can't understand why her parents are so invested in having her call Rivka. It doesn't help that Minh is openly envious of her opportunity. "'You pick up the phone and you call her. What an incredible opportunity. I would kill for a chance like this. Damn. Give me her number. I'll call her!'" (61). Minh's orphanage in Vietnam burned down and his parents know only that he seemed well fed and didn't cry much.

Once again, let us stand back and admire Reinhardt for giving Simone a friend who is adopted. The extreme isolation in which so many YA adoptees find themselves is not the norm. Not only are they likely to find other adoptees at school or among relatives, but adoption agencies and adoptive parent organizations by the hundreds have been putting adoptees of all ages and backgrounds in touch with one another for decades.

A coincidence breaks the emotional logjam. Simone interviews Mom about her first civil liberties case for her school paper, and this leads Simone to the story of her own birth. While defending a Hasidic rebbe who ran afoul of his neighbors, Mom formed a friendship with his wife and family. The rebbe was cold and misogynistic, so when his sixteen-year-old daughter, Rivka, got pregnant, she and her mother did not tell him. Instead, they worked out an arrangement with Simone's mom and dad, who got married in order to adopt Rivka's baby.[27]

Simone gives in to her parents' suggestion that she invite Rivka to their home for Thanksgiving. To her secret delight, Rivka is young and beautiful, a professional photographer who lives alone on Cape Cod. After dinner they steal away to talk. Simone asks about her birthfather. We get only the sketchiest picture of him, but it's more than most authors provide. Joe was an attractive Lubavitcher and Rivka thought they were in love, but when she told him she was pregnant, he disappeared. Although hurt, Rivka realized she didn't want to get married anyway. She does not regret her decision. She tells Simone, "'God sent me your mother'" (107). When a birthmother tells us this, it sounds not like denial, but a prayer of gratitude.

Rivka invites Simone to her home for the weekend where they celebrate Simone's first Shabbat. Wary at first, Simone realizes that Rivka is not proselytizing, but sharing something deeply meaningful to her. Simone finds the experience moving. She is not sure what role religion plays in Rivka's life.

Even more than she wants to know the details of her mother's life, Simone wants to know about her religion. If Rivka is agnostic, as she has described herself, why does she pray? Here is where she discovers the ethnic tapestry of Judaism. Unlike her parents' Christianity, Judaism is a cultural identity broader and deeper and more ancient. "'Saying those blessings is more about tradition to me than religion. I do it because it's what Jews do. It's part of the Jewish tradition. And tradition gives me a sense of my place in the world. It defines me. Whether or not God exists doesn't matter that much to me in the end, I guess'" (128).

Simone discovers that Rivka is terminally ill with ovarian cancer and that this is why her parents pushed her so hard to call. At first Simone is angry, but those feelings soon give way to her desire to get to know her mother in the time they have left. Rivka passes on the torch of her Jewish ethnicity and all it means to her to Simone, who has read that the child of a Jewish mother is "automatically Jewish." Simone asks

Rivka if she herself is Jewish. Yes, Rivka says, technically she is. But she knew that Simone's parents would not raise her as a Jew, and Rivka was fine with that. "'We knew that they would be wonderful, loving parents, and that was more important than anything else.'" She also tells Simone that she could move to Israel and automatically get citizenship (impossible if her Jewish parent had been her father) and that in Nazi Germany she would have been sent to a concentration camp. But ultimately that's not what being Jewish is about, she says. "'I think being Jewish is about your personal relationship to the history, the rituals, the tradition, and the culture of Judaism'" (150).

A separate thread concerns Simone's deepening relationship with an observant Jewish classmate, Zack. As she struggles to come to terms with her birthmother's looming death, she decides to host a seder for Rivka. But how will she go about it? Zack takes her to his rabbi, a kind person who gives her advice, instructions, and comfort. When Rivka dies not long after, her ethnic identity survives. It has found a home in Simone. Now it is up to her to decide what to do with it.

This fine novel conveys what is lost and gained both in adoption and in reunion. For most infant adoptions in the United States today, the birthmother—like Rivka—chooses or at least approves the adoptive mother. Adoption facilitators and agencies negotiate the process. Would-be parents advertise for birthmothers and the process can be a lot less personal and loving than the one shown here. However, a Jewish or Mormon or Roman Catholic mother can ensure her child is adopted by someone who shares her faith. In international adoption, the birthfamily rarely has any say in how the child is raised. Adoption agencies that place children from abroad in American homes are often religiously affiliated. The first wide-scale international adoptions by Americans were facilitated by individuals and agencies with an evangelical, Protestant agenda. The goal was not just to provide homes to orphans, but to save their souls for Christ. Religious organizations of many faiths continue to play a prominent role in all forms of adoption.

Marie Myung-Ok Lee's adult/crossover YA novel *Somebody's Daughter* (2005) shuttles between the events of 1972 leading to Sarah Thorson's birth in Korea, and 1993, when she returns to search for her birthmother. Raised in a white Minnesota family, Sarah has a sister, Amanda, her parents' biological child. Sarah calls her parents Christine and Ken. Christine is one of our only fictional moms described as infertile. "Her thirties brought years of painful fertility treatments and bloody miscarriages before she gave up and decided to adopt. Then she got pregnant just months after I arrived" (38).[28]

Ken and Christine have told Sarah that her birthparents died in a car accident. They even brought in their Lutheran minister to explain: "'God called your Korean parents home so that you could become the daughter of your mother and father.'" Sarah's adoption is part of God's plan. As Sarah grows up she wants details on the car crash, on her birthmother. Christine tells her, "'We really knew nothing about her. I'm your mommy. Let's not talk about this anymore, it makes me sad.' She made little crying motions, pretending to wipe away tears, the same thing she did when I was bad, to show how I had disappointed her" (1). Sarah's parents carry rejection of difference to pathological extremes. "I had grown up in a house in which Korea had always been the oddly charged word, never to be mentioned in connection to me, the same way we never said 'Uncle Henry' and 'alcoholic' in the same sentence. It was almost as if Ken and Christine thought I needed to be protected from it" (2).

Lee's presentation of adoption, of the treatment of Korean American adoptees by other Korean Americans, and of adoptive parents are much more negative than in *If It Hadn't Been for Yoon Jun*. We meet no other adoptive families with children from Korea, so there is no one with whom to compare this family. Although attitudes toward adoption issues were fairly primitive in the 1970s, by 1993 parents who continued to raise their adopted child in this much isolation and denial would be exceptional. Open adoption, in which some contact exists between birthparents and adoptive parents, accounted for most domestic infant adoptions by the late 1980s. Birthparents, rather than agencies, were choosing the adoptive parents, usually meeting them in person or through an intermediary. Contested adoption custody cases and the pros and cons of surrogacy were major news stories across the United States. Romanian adoptions, highly publicized, started in 1989. The attitudes and isolation of Sarah's adoptive family, their minister, and all the U.S. settings are more typical of 1973 than 1993.

Sarah herself, her alienation, and need to search out her birthmother, are perfectly believable, however. Sarah drops out during her first year of college and asks her parents to send her to Korea as a belated high school graduation present to attend a Korean "Motherland" program for people of Korean heritage from other countries, held at a large university in Seoul. None of the Korean Americans in Sarah's class is adopted except her—again, the adoptee is presented as a very rare species.

The Korean American students in *Somebody's Daughter* are nosy, rude, and abusive to Sarah and Doug; the only one who does not reject Sarah, Doug is the son of a white American GI and Korean prostitute. While historically Korean Americans have been slow to welcome Korean adoptees and their families, Bernie Lee, a Princeton student, is in a class by himself. "'Hey Twinkie, do you even know your Korean family name?'" he asks Sarah. Why is she even taking the class? he wonders. "'It's not like you're going to go home and start talking to your *pahrents*'" (19). Except for Doug, the students exclude her from all their activities. The teachers never intervene or discourage the abuse.

Bernie's brutality and cruelty, and that of the students who follow his lead, are never explained. Comments like "'You know your mother must have been a whore or something—those are the kids that get put up for adoption. Normal kids are taken care of by the family'" (76) are par for the course. (This kind of taunting behavior would be more believable in younger children.) Sarah's teacher arranges for Jun-Ho, a kind, sympathetic young man in the military, to help Sarah practice speaking Korean, and reluctantly, he agrees to help her contact the orphanage from which she was adopted. There, Sarah discovers that she arrived at the orphanage as a newborn, covered in feces. Christine had manufactured the car accident story. Sarah and Doug begin an affair that brings comfort to each. Out of options for finding her birthmother, Sarah goes on a popular Korean reality TV show that reunites estranged families and tells her story. But although the program is widely seen, no one calls to claim her.

Sarah's story is interwoven with that of her birthmother, Kyung-Sook, living in an impoverished mountain village. Most of her narrative is set in 1972, leading up to and following Sarah's birth. Lee's portrayal of Kyunk-Sook and her world is vivid and convincing. Kyung-Sook's family has distinguished roots, but is now struggling. She plays the traditional Korean flute, dreaming of a future as a professional musician, and moves to Seoul to attend university.

Kyung-Sook's story parallels Sarah's. Both women drop out of college. Kyung-Sook discovers that traditional Korean music is out of vogue. She meets a white man, David, whom at first she finds repulsive.

But he woos her with restaurant meals and music, and glowing pictures of life in America, and soon she moves in with him. Kyung-Sook has few illusions about David, who renames her Karen. He is condescending and ignorant about Korea. He tells her about women's lib, but when all Kyung-Sook can say is "'women's u-rib,'" he says, "'We're going to have to work on your pronunciation.'" She speaks reasonably good English; his Korean is hopeless. She doesn't argue but reflects, "This man, in all his time here, knew little Korean other than *give me this* and *I know*" (165). David abandons her after she becomes pregnant, so Kyung-Sook returns home about to give birth. Horrified, her mother throws her out, so Kyung-Sook delivers her baby in the outhouse. Her mother spirits it away. Kyung-Sook stays in her village, eventually marrying a kind Christian convert, who starts a church there. They have no children. Kyung-Sook has seen Sarah on TV and makes her way to Seoul to look for her, but although the two brush past one another on a railway platform, they never meet. Kyung-Sook returns to her village, and Sarah returns to Minnesota. On her flight Sarah notices two women escorting Korean babies to join their new adoptive families in America. Sarah's own family comes to meet her at the airport. We last see her running toward them. Sarah's search has made her stronger and given her courage. But how or if the lessons she has learned will affect her family's dysfunctional dynamic is left unresolved.

Somebody's Daughter is sad, emotionally compelling, a rare effort to probe the reality behind the bland euphemisms and untested assumptions about the unmitigated joys of international adoption. As a novel, it is not entirely successful. Questions remain: How did Sarah, still covered in feces, get from her mountain village to a fire station in Seoul? Why are the Korean American students so uniformly vicious to her and Doug?

The biggest issue is that no one recognizes Sarah is biracial. One might argue that this could go unnoticed in the United States among whites who are notoriously unobservant in these matters. But no one in Korea recognizes her either, or even wonders if she is biracial. Yet Korea is a monoracial country in which being biracial has long been stigmatized. One would expect Bernie and his fellow students to have at least wondered. (They notice her eyelids, but no one draws any inference from that.) After months of intimacy with Sarah, Doug, biracial himself, fails to recognize she is biracial, too. When she goes on national TV, not a soul in Korea picks up on it. Lee's decision to make Sarah's father a chauvinistic American taking advantage of a naïve country girl, rather than a Korean man, is perfectly valid. However, Lee goes on to protect Sarah from the consequences of being mixed in a country that values monoraciality even more than the United States does. Making her multiraciality invisible also separates Sarah from those whose status is not invisible. Too often, transracially adopted characters seem to live in a world without any other form of multiraciality. Here, at least Lee gives us Doug.

Lee has simplified a complex story by stacking the deck: Sarah's family is ignorant and out of touch with what constitutes good adoptive parenting. Like her birthmother, Sarah is a victim, treated with contempt first in her Minnesota hometown—she has no close friendships, is shunned in high school—then by other Korean Americans in Seoul. Her victimization explains her alienation, but undermines the point Lee is making: that adoption itself has profound, life-changing, sometimes tragic effects. Lee did not need to make Christine the monster she is in order to explain Sarah's struggle with self-esteem and her need to search for her heritage. Even in adoptive families with more awareness, this can happen. Had Lee given Sarah better parents, a more supportive upbringing, and made her welcome in Seoul, her point would have been made much more effectively.

Despite these reservations, the book deserves a wide readership. It carries profound emotional truth. Although there are hints that Sarah has found, if not closure, then a kind of peace, the world and family she returns to at the end of the novel have been so negatively portrayed that it is difficult for readers to feel optimistic for Sarah's future.

The best portrayal to date of international adoption in YA fiction is *Throwaway Daughter* (2003), by Ting-Xing Ye with William Bell. Ye was raised in China and immigrated to Canada as an adult. This extraordinary novel, like *Somebody's Daughter,* tells the adoption story through multiple voices, past and present. Here they belong to Grace or Dong-Mei, the adoptee; Jane, her Canadian adoptive mother; Old Revolutionary Chen, her birth grandfather in China; Loyal, her birthfather; Mrs. Xia, the orphanage employee who took Grace in as an infant; and Chun-mei, Grace's birthmother. Among Ye's achievements is her compassion for all who played a role in the adoption and her understanding of the choices they had to make, or believed they did.

Grace is raised by white adoptive parents in a mostly white Ontario town. Her mother was unable to bear more children after Grace's older sister, Megan. Grace's parents, unlike Sarah's, help their daughter connect with her birth heritage. At first, she resists; Grace detests anything that makes her feel different. She refuses to come when her mother uses her Chinese name, Dong-mei. Mom, an elementary school teacher, is patient. "'It's not just a name, Grace,'" she tells her. "'It means much more.'" A Chinese Canadian friend, Frank Wu, mentors the family. He translates the words on a scrap of paper tucked in with Grace when she was found: "Chun-mei" and "Dong-mei," Spring Plum Blossom and Winter Plum Blossom. Grace thinks, "Why didn't this Chun-mei keep the baby and throw away the note? As far as I was concerned, the note as well as my Chinese roots could wither in hell" (4). Grace remains in denial until she is given the dreaded heritage assignment in school. She doesn't do it, because it asks for her birthday and the only birthday Grace has to celebrate is the date of her arrival in Canada from China.

The novel cuts to 1981 and "Old Revolutionary Chen," a peasant whose devotion to the Communist Party has earned him the position of Party secretary; he has even named his son Loyal as a show of respect. Chen is tormented by memories. His wife gave birth to five daughters before Loyal. Mao, Chen's hero, said it was wrong to value boys over girls, and Chen tries to believe this as daughter after daughter is born. "What I couldn't admit openly was that we farmers needed boys: not only were they the ones to carry on our family names but their muscles and power were essential to keep our stomachs filled." Girls are not as useful as boys. They aren't as strong. Boys are regarded as "feeding hands" and girls as "mouths." It costs more to raise girls than they are worth. Parents feed and clothe them only to have them leave home to look after their husband's parents and give birth to children who bear his name.

The continuation of his name is what Chen cares about most. During the years of famine, he starved his two youngest daughters so that he would have enough food for his son. "For a long time I have tried to shut out the memory of my lost girls. Each time their deaths surface in my mind, making me see them wasted to skin and bone, I close my eyes tight as if to squeeze the images out" (38). It doesn't work. Chen's tragedy is that he is not a monster. What might play out as vanity in a wealthy society has stark life-and-death consequences in a marginal one.

Now, with Loyal grown and married and expecting his first child, the stakes are even higher. The "one child per family" rule, imposed to bring China's population under control, is in force, and penalties for flouting it are severe. If Chun-mei doesn't have a boy, Chen's name will die out and the deaths of his little daughters that still torment him will have been in vain.

Mao is gone and Deng Xiao Ping has inaugurated a new era of economic reform. Loyal is energized by the prospect of getting rich. When an ill-advised business venture fails, he is driven back to the life of subsistence farming and dependence on his father. Material circumstances improve, but very slowly. Loyal knows why and how he survived the famine of his childhood, and it burdens him as it does his father. "As I got older I came to understand that sometimes in life sacrifice is necessary. My parents did their part so our family tree wouldn't cease to grow, and I was their hope, the seed." With Chun-mei pregnant, Loyal finds himself remembering his dead sisters. "I can't bear to let their death mean nothing, and I won't" (54). Chun-mei's well-to-do family had their land confiscated in 1950 and redistributed to farmers. Chen chose her as a bride for Loyal and the marriage has been reasonably happy. But with her pregnancy, the family is tense. So much is riding on it. Loyal takes Chun-mei to a fortuneteller who tells them she is going to have a boy.

Back in 1990s Canada, Grace is shocked by the sight on TV of demonstrators being gunned down in Tiananmen Square in Beijing. For the first time, she feels a connection to that faraway place. Ye skillfully shows how Grace's understanding of race and adoption evolves and how everything she experiences relates back to her identity as adopted. During a family discussion of genetics and heredity, Grace reminds them that she has no one to look at to see how she'll turn out as an adult. "'I'm going to be ugly, then,'" she says bitterly. "'Only ugly people would abandon their own baby'" (88).

Grace takes tentative steps toward accepting, if not embracing, her racial identity. She realizes that white people throw her into an Asian Canadian category and make no effort to distinguish beyond it. A grade-school teacher teaching a lesson on multiculturalism asks her how long her parents have lived in Canada. She tells him they were born in Canada. Well, he asks, where did *their* parents come from?

This novel is one of the few that portrays the differences between how minority and transracially adopted children are treated. Grace's experience more closely resembles that of mixed-heritage kids in biological families than that of minority monoracial families. Like multiracial individuals, the transracially adopted person is often invisible. "I was fed up with people who needed to label me in some way before they felt comfortable. I hated the Chinese-Canadian tag and resented being lumped in with kids like Amy Diep, whose family were Vietnamese 'boat people.'" People assume she is Korean like the gas station–milk store owner. "Once, I told Bobby McKay to piss off when he asked me to help him with his 'Flags of the World' geography project. He was doing Japan" (100). But she envies those kids because they are all of a piece with their families. They look like their parents and siblings; they visit Korea or Japan for holidays and come back with photos of their smiling extended families. Grace does not fit in her family. "I was a Parker but I wasn't."

Grace is occasionally targeted with racial epithets, but they don't get to her as deeply as the adoption issue. Oddly, writers of transracially adopted characters often make their characters more sensitive to their racial profile than to their adopted status. Yet adoption is a far more fundamental and important piece of identity. Again, Ye "gets it." Grace continues to resent her mother's unflagging commitment to keeping Grace in touch with her roots, the use of her name, anything that forces her to think about her adoption. Her loving family has done everything by the book. She is learning Mandarin, and the family has Chinese Canadian friends. And it is not enough. Labeled as having low self-esteem, Grace is sent to counseling, which doesn't help. She wonders how high the counselor's self-esteem would be if she knew her mother didn't want her and had gotten rid of her after she was born. Grace begins to fantasize about going to China, finding and confronting her birthparents with herself. "'Thanks for the baggage,' I'd say" (103).

Like Sarah, Grace asks her parents to send her to her birth country as a high school graduation gift. Mom is upset, confessing in tears that she wants Grace to have the chance to know her birthmother, "'but now that maybe you'll meet her, I feel jealous. I don't want to share you with anyone'" (106). Grace reassures her.[29] In China, Grace's course goes well. She opts out of the tour afterward, in order to search for her parents. She tracks down Mrs. Xia from the orphanage and finds her way to Chun-mei's village where, finally, we learn what happened back in 1981.

Chen and Loyal had been horrified when Chun-mei had a girl, but all was not lost—if they claimed the child died, Loyal and Chun-mei could try again for a boy. Aware that both men are desperate enough to kill her child, Chun-mei offers them a deal: she will make her daughter disappear and they can tell the village authorities the baby was stillborn. Chun-mei leaves with the baby and returns alone. Soon after, she divorces Loyal, who remarries. His new wife bears him a son.

Grace finds her way to the village and her mother. Although their reunion is short and bittersweet, mother and daughter fill one another's emptiness in the few days they have together. Chun-mei shows Grace a wedding present from her father, a watercolor of a black branch heavy with blossoms. "'But where are the leaves?'" Grace asks. "'That is what makes winter blossoms unique,'" Chun-Mei tells her. "'They bloom while surrounded by ice and snow'" (219).

The great irony of the story is that Ah-miao, Grace's half-brother, is marrying a woman whose wealthy family has no son. Loyal's son is dropping the Chen name and taking on his wife's name. "The boy child the Chens had done so much to get was going to leave them and join his in-laws in another village" (225–26). The Chen name will die when Loyal does. Chen has lost everything, even his faith in his Communist Party heroes. He has learned that what they preached about family and children and what they did privately were vastly different. As Grace leaves for Canada, old Chen tells her he has been a fool. He gives her an old copy of Mao's *Little Red Book*. On the plane, Grace throws the book by her grandfather's hero into the trash. "I have met one hero in my life," Grace thinks. "Her name is Chun-mei, and she is my mother" (227).

What or who is responsible for the tragedy that led Chun-mei to give up her daughter? Ye offers no easy answers. The failure of rich nations to share their wealth and make life bearable for millions of people who lead desperately marginal lives; harsh poverty unrelieved by either communist or capitalist policies; the need to give meaning to a hard life; guilt for past actions all play a role. There is more than enough blame to go around, but Ye gives us only one hero.

Adoption is built on tragedy. Even the happiest adoption story rests on a foundation of loss. Reframing this bitter truth, saying "God meant this child to be adopted by this family" or "your mother loved you so much she gave you away so you could have a better life," does not return what has been lost. *Throwaway Daughter,* like all the best writing on adoption, acknowledges that truth. To assimilate and transcend the loss, all members of the triad must face it with courage and honesty. Accepting that it will always be part of them, they discover loss is also a source of strength and a foundation strong enough to support them on their life's journey.

NOTES

1. Adoption History Project, "Timeline of Adoption History," University of Oregon, www.uoregon.edu/~adoption/topics/birthparents.htm (1 May 2008). This project based at the University of Oregon has placed primary and secondary source documents on the history of adoption in the United States online. Archival photos include an infamous incident in 1904 when a Mexican American family in Arizona was selected to adopt white children from New York City, part of the orphan train movement. Parents and children were Roman Catholics and the adoption was facilitated by the Catholic Church. However, white vigilantes abducted the children from their adoptive parents at gunpoint and redistributed them to white Protestant families.

2. Rose Kreider, "Adopted Children and Stepchildren: 2000," U.S. Census Bureau, *Census 2000 Special Reports*, Series CENSR-6RV (Washington, D.C.: U.S. Government Printing Office, 2003). Statistics on adoption are also drawn from the "Timeline of Adoption History."

3. "Timeline of Adoption History."

4. Jane Jeong Trenka, Julia Chinyere Oparah, and Sun Yung Shin, eds., *Outsiders Within: Writing on Transracial Adoption* (Cambridge, Mass.: South End Press, 2006).

5. "Timeline of Adoption History."

6. For example, one of the least diverse states in the United States is Iowa. According to the U.S. census, in 1970 the total Asian and Pacific Islander population for Iowa was 3,420. By 2000, it was 37,644. In thirty years, this population increased tenfold. Meanwhile, during the same period, the overall population of the state increased from 2,824,376 to 2,926,324, less than 4 percent.

7. The "Position Statement on Trans-Racial Adoption" of the National Association of Black Social Workers, published in 1972, reaffirmed in 1994, and never withdrawn, reflects the bitterness of the dispute over transracial adoption. It reads, in part, "We fully recognize the phenomenon of transracial adoption as an expedient for white folk, not as an altruistic humane concern for black children. The supply of white children for adoption has all but vanished and adoption agencies, having always catered to middle class whites, developed an answer to their desire for parenthood by motivating them to consider black children. This has brought about a re-definition of some black children. Those born of black-white alliances are no longer black as decreed by immutable law and

social custom for centuries. They are now black-white, inter-racial, bi-racial, emphasizing the whiteness as the adoptable quality; a further subtle, but vicious design to further diminish black and accentuate white. We resent this high-handed arrogance and are insulted by this further assignment of chattel status to black people." "Timeline of Adoption History."

8. "Timeline of Adoption History."

9. David Kirk, *Shared Fate: A Theory and Method of Adoptive Relationships*, 2nd ed. (Port Angeles, Wash.: Ben-Simon, 1984).

10. Kirk, *Shared Fate,* 61.

11. Kirk, *Shared Fate,* 61.

12. Kirk, *Shared Fate,* 62.

13. "Timeline of Adoption History."

14. "Timeline of Adoption History."

15. The names of T.J. and the black therapist Georgia Brown are a wink to readers, without broader significance. Names that draw attention to themselves can be a powerful literary tool when integrated with elements such as theme and mood (as in Sherman Alexie's *Indian Killer*). Here, the names merely pull the reader out of the fictitious dream.

16. For answers to the argument for adoption as a cure for poverty and poor birthparenting, see Trenka, Oparah, and Shin, *Outsiders Within*.

17. *Publishers Weekly* said of *Something Terrible Happened:* "The reader will burrow into this story and relish its nuggets of insight" (241, no. 41, 10 Oct. 1994). In its starred review of *Whale Talk, Publishers Weekly* said, "Crutcher's gripping tale of small-town prejudice delivers a frank, powerful message about social issues and ills" (248, no. 11, 12 March 2001). *Kirkus Reviews* called it "a compulsively readable story that rings true with genuine feeling" (1 March 2001). It was a featured title in *Booklist* (97, no. 11, 1 April 2001: 1462), and *Horn Book* (77, no. 3, May 2001: 320) gave it a rave review as well.

18. Determining that the two authors are one and the same involves a process on the lines of "six degrees of separation." For reasons of her own, Marie Myung-Ok Lee does not broadcast having authored *If It Hadn't Been for Yoon Jun*. The book is not listed on her website or online bios among her other works. The point of view is much more pro-adoption than in *Somebody's Daughter* but is not effusive or blind to adoption issues.

19. Adoption educators have long tried to foster the use of positive adoption language that does not denigrate any member of the adoption triad. "Real" and "natural" as applied to biological parents imply that adoptive parents are unreal and unnatural. Likewise, the adopted child is "biological," not "natural" or "real." "Biological parent" is not used to describe a birthparent per se, only to clarify a biological connection. Like the attempt by overly fervent adoption advocates to generate enthusiasm for the term "the woman in whose tummy you grew," using "biological" suggests that birthparents are merely a kind of organic

test tube for incubating the adoptive parents' child. The term widely accepted is "birthparents." "Placed for adoption" is preferred by adopters over "given up for adoption." But here there is disagreement. The verb "to place" is nicely neutral, conveying no emotional subtext. "To give up" has overtones of loss that make some adopters uncomfortable. However, as loss is indeed a part of adoption, many feel "giving up" is a perfectly accurate term. In my view, both are acceptable.

20. Giving their characters heritage assignments is useful to novelists, but whether they should be assigned in real life is another matter. Beginning in elementary school, children are assigned family-tree, genealogy projects. For adopted or foster children and those in troubled families, these assignments can be traumatic. Some educators are aware of this and redraw projects so as not to force children to share deeply personal information that reflects sadness and loss. However, many teachers remain insensitive to the ramifications of what they are asking. My own daughter, by the time she was in eighth grade, had been given three such school assignments.

21. The America Perkins gives us is several steps to the left of the one we currently inhabit. The Republican first lady to be is a passionate supporter of human rights around the world. The Democratic nominee is not only a woman, but a single mother whose son, now twenty-two, was born out of wedlock.

22. Louis Owens, *Mixedblood Messages: Literature, Film, Family, Place* (Norman: University of Oklahoma Press, 1998), 77–78.

23. The Indian Child Welfare Act (ICWA) of 1978 ended the practice of removing Indian children from their extended families and communities via adoption. To find adoptive parents for American Indian children, authorities must give priority first to extended family, second to the child's tribe, and third to another American Indian tribe. (Note that children covered by ICWA must be tribally enrolled themselves or eligible for tribal membership, which leaves out mixed-blood children who don't meet those qualifications.) Alexie's John Smith, however, would have been born before ICWA came into effect. Barbara Kingsolver's *Pigs in Heaven* (1993), the sequel to *The Bean Trees* (1988), offers a fictional treatment of how ICWA applies to adoption. Although both books qualify as crossover adult/YA, they are not discussed here because Kingsolver deftly removes the factor of transracial placement from the equation. Taylor, who seeks custody of Turtle, the American Indian child she has been raising, and Taylor's mother, Alice, learn they are sufficiently Cherokee to qualify for tribal enrollment themselves. And if that is not enough, Alice and Cash, Turtle's grandfather, who also wants custody of Turtle, fall in love. Because of these factors, ICWA can be satisfied as well as critics of American Indian transracial adoption.

24. The word "adopt" has other associations, too. What we consciously choose to be part of us, we adopt: ideas, religion, political opinions.

25. Adoption research spurred by the formation of birthparent advocacy organizations, such as Concerned United Birthparents, overwhelmingly supports this conclusion. Multiple surveys of birthmothers find that between 95 and 100 percent would like to be reunited with their birthchildren. A study of seventy-nine birthmothers found that "the relinquishment experience was a traumatic life event for 99% of the participants; 97% reported being misled or misinformed of the effects of relinquishment; and 94% of the participants reported that they did not receive adequate counseling at the time of the relinquishment." Judy Kelly, "The Trauma of Relinquishment: The Long-Term Impact of Relinquishment on Birthmothers Who Lost Their Infants to Adoption During the Years 1965–72" (M.A. thesis in Psychology and Counseling, Goddard College, 1999), www.adopting.org/uni/frame.php?url=http://home.att.net/~judy.kelly/thesis.htm (8 May 2008). Disturbingly, 41 percent also reported having received hysterectomies. Throughout the twentieth century, birthmothers were routinely segregated from the rest of society in homes, awaiting the births of their "illegitimate" children. Victims of discredited pseudoscientific eugenics theories and disproven social science beliefs, many out-of-wedlock birthmothers were subjected to horrific treatment, including sterilization. Also see "Timeline of Adoption History."

26. Reinhardt appears to equate Christianity with ethnicity, perhaps not recognizing that for the biography she has given to Simone's parents, such an equation is nonexistent. A nonobservant Jew is a Jew who is nonobservant. A nonobservant, atheist Episcopalian is not a Christian. The reason is that Christianity, like any other religion that perpetuates itself through evangelism—inviting others to join its community, seeking converts—severs ties to a particular ethnicity.

27. Interestingly, although this is a very unusual set-up in real life, it is similar to the one featured in *First Daughter.* There, Sameera's parents met while visiting her in an orphanage and married in part to be able to adopt her. This allows the author to dispense with messy fertility issues.

28. Given the book's audience, the author may feel comfortable providing such details. (The fiction of the spontaneous post-adoption pregnancy still refuses to die.) But for YA or even middle-grade readers, authors' reluctance to portray adoptive parents as infertile is puzzling. After all, Billy could say, "Mom and Dad tried everything to have a baby, but it didn't work, so they adopted me." One wonders if authors themselves suffer from a vicarious "role handicap" and fear readers will look down on or pity their adoptive parents as lacking in some way unless they are shown to be capable of biological reproduction.

29. Grace has grown up feeling rejected by her birthmother. Now her adoptive mother feels rejected by her. Their shared loss brings them together. This moment is right out of David Kirk's *Shared Fate.*

FICTIONAL WORKS CITED OR CRITIQUED

Note: An asterisk denotes works critiqued as well as cited in the chapter.

Sherman Alexie, *Indian Killer* (New York: Warner, 1996).*

Julia Alvarez, *Finding Miracles* (New York: Laurel Leaf, 2004).*

Chris Crutcher, *Whale Talk* (New York: Laurel Leaf, 2001).*

Rose Kent, *Kimchi & Calamari* (New York: HarperCollins, 2007).*

Barbara Kingsolver, *The Bean Trees* (New York: HarperPerennial, 1988).

———, *Pigs in Heaven* (New York: HarperPerennial, 1993).

Marie G. Lee, *If It Hadn't Been for Yoon Jun* (New York: Avon, 1993).*

Marie Myung-Ok Lee, *Somebody's Daughter* (Boston: Beacon, 2005).*

Lee McClain, *My Alternate Life* (New York: Smooch-Dorchester, 2004).*

Mitali Perkins, *First Daughter: Extreme American Makeover* (New York: Dutton, 2007).*

———, *Monsoon Summer* (New York: Delacorte, 2004).*

Barbara Ann Porte, *Something Terrible Happened* (New York: Orchard, 1994).*

Dana Reinhardt, *A Brief Chapter in My Impossible Life* (New York: Wendy Lamb–Random House, 2006).*

Greg Leitich Smith, *Ninjas, Piranhas, and Galileo* (New York: Little, Brown, 2003).*

Ting-Xing Ye, *Throwaway Daughter* (London, U.K.: Faber and Faber, 2003).*

Pat Costa Viglucci, *Cassandra Robbins, Esq.* (Madison, Wisc.: Square One, 1987).*

· 6 ·

Mixed Heritage in Nonfiction for Young Adults

Nonfiction books for young adults about mixed-heritage identity are scarce and heavily weighted toward self-help offerings. Adding to a smattering of historical studies and presentations of hot-button social issues are subjective accounts—memoirs, collections of interviews, and personal essays—of mixed-heritage people. This chapter surveys current offerings in print categories. In recent years, web-based, interactive groups have formed that provide, through blogs and forums, opportunities for young adults worldwide to meet online and share issues that concern them. A selection of websites for mixed-heritage youth is included in the bibliography.

HISTORIES OF RACE

Two YA books offer histories of race, only one of which addresses multiraciality. Although adoptive parenting has existed in human societies from the earliest known civilizations, to date no history of adoption exists for young adults. One is needed.

Among the "What were they thinking?" packaging decisions in books about youth of mixed heritage, winner in the nonfiction category is Gary B. Nash's otherwise excellent *Forbidden Love: The Secret History of Mixed-Race America* (1999), a straightforward, fascinating, and comprehensive, if rather academic, history of how the United States has treated interracial unions over the years. Nash covers colonial history, hypodescent and slavery, and antimiscegenation laws. The book features close-up looks at historical unions of interest among all races, from the well-known—Pocahontas and John Rolfe—to the lesser-known—Sam Houston and his mixed-blood Cherokee wife. But, as Brent Staples noted in his *New York Times* review, "the title 'Forbidden Love' is misleading, especially for adolescent readers, for a book that dwells more on broad social themes than on the intimate details of individual lives."[1] The lurid title is problematic for another reason as well. How many teenagers care to be overheard asking, "Do you have *Forbidden Love?*" at the library or bookstore, much less be seen by their peers carrying it around? As Staples points out, the book is a historical survey, not a *People Magazine* look at mixed-race celebrities. Young adults brave enough to ask for it by name may find themselves sadly disappointed.

The book is well written and illustrated with well-chosen art, photos, and memorabilia. Nash is especially enlightening on the two hundred years of interracial unions among American Indians and Europeans up through the Revolutionary War. Among the remarkable and rarely told stories is that of Mary Musgrove, daughter of a Scots-Irish trader and Creek woman, who became an important powerbroker in eighteenth-century South Carolina. Through several marriages, she acquired land and worked as an interpreter between Indians and whites, eventually mediating major political disputes. "White colonists were learning to sneer at what they called 'half-breeds.' But in many places and through many decades they relied on such mixed-race people as Mary Musgrove to link Indian and English societies together," Nash says. "In reality, Mary Musgrove was a 'double-breed,' extraordinarily important for two societies precisely because, rather than a half-person, she was fully English and fully Creek" (45).

Nash does a good job covering the 1967 *Loving* case that ended all bans on interracial marriage. He demonstrates familiarity with the scientific research on multiraciality and provides a wide-reaching bibliography. He shows how the ban on interracial unions was an essential component of institutionalized racism, from slavery to Jim Crow legislation. The couples he showcases are drawn from all walks of life, from government to the arts. Staples points out that Nash glosses over less-than-upbeat biographical details; for example, in his discussion of the NAACP's executive director in the 1940s, Walter White, Nash fails to mention that White's father, struck by a car in Atlanta, was "mistakenly delivered to the section of a hospital that was reserved for whites only.

When a brown-skinned relative showed up, the attendants pulled White's father from the examination table and dragged him to the filthy, crowded colored ward, where he later died." And White's own interracial heritage, Staples adds, was "a source of trauma and confusion."[2] Nash does indeed place interracial unions in a rosy light. However, given the vastly greater body of literature that has presented these unions as unnatural and vile, not to mention centuries of antimiscegenation laws, Nash may be forgiven for looking on the bright side. In any event, this is a minor quibble about a comprehensive survey of an important subject rarely explored.

Marc Aronson, winner of the Robert F. Sibert Medal for *Sir Walter Raleigh and the Quest for El Dorado* and author of *Witch Hunt: Mysteries of the Salem Witch Trials,* presents key historical events in his nonfiction books for young adults. His agenda is twofold: to inform readers about the events he describes and to teach them to think about the nature of history itself—what it is, who writes it, who interprets it, and how it is used and misused. In *Race: A History Beyond Black and White* (2007), he takes on a huge topic, racial prejudice in the Western world. (Although anti-Chinese and anti-Japanese racism are briefly covered in chapters on racism in the United States, Aronson gives most attention to anti-black racism and anti-Semitism.)

Aronson's hypothesis is that all definitions of race, regardless of who is doing the defining, rest on the assumption that human beings can be classified in separate categories according to inherited and immutable physical differences that can be ranked hierarchically relative to one another. With examples drawn from European and American history, he traces the idea of race over roughly five thousand years. Like Nash's book, *Race* features first-rate illustrations. Many chapters begin with sketches of contemporary teen life that are then connected to the historical events unfolding in that chapter. For example, the ancient Persian attack on Greece is compared to the Super Bowl.

The strength of *Race* is its scale and the presentation of numerous historical events large and small in the context of racial prejudice. Aronson explores how the idea of race has evolved through historical events, how individual ideas—benign in themselves—are distorted and applied to achieve ends they were never intended to address. He weaves science, technology, and popular culture into the discussion, making connections that shed light on each. In a discussion of stereotyping, Aronson observes that "the very word 'stereotype' comes from printing—it refers to the process that allows the same cluster of words to be printed over and over. The press that could spread reading also made it much easier to share hate-filled and damaging ideas and images" (106). The final chapter, "Black Is a Way of Acting," is a snapshot of our world today, of the choices we can make about how we treat race.

Aronson does not address or discuss the role of multiraciality in defining race and policing its boundaries. This is a serious omission. Antimiscegenation laws were one of the principal tools upholding the fiction of biologically distinct races in the United States for nearly three centuries. The words "muiltiracial," "biracial," "mixed race," "miscegenation," and "antimiscegenation" do not appear in the index. There is a "racial mixing" entry, but the issue is mentioned only in passing. The bibliography does not include multiracial resources, such as Nash's *Forbidden Love,* and no mixed-race websites are listed. While providing a definition of who is a Jew—"Jewish law says only the child of a Jewish mother is Jewish" (86)—Aronson does not examine the consequences, historical and contemporary, of its application. Mixed-heritage young adults, including interfaith Jews whose mothers are not Jewish, will not see themselves or the bias directed at them *because* of their mixed status in this book.

As our society becomes ever more mixed, all races, cultures, and ethnicities, including Jews, are deeply engaged in and worried about how to maintain and control their identities—languages, religions, customs, traditions—from the inside. The same racial and ethnic definitions that led to the horrific events Aronson chronicles so well have also allowed groups, including Jews, to sustain and transmit their cultures down the years, often during times of great oppression. This boon has come at the expense of mixed-heritage people who straddle the line, who blur the cultural boundaries by outmarriage. To keep the group "unadulterated," they must be cast out. We won't be able to understand race and racism fully, much less transcend and overcome them, until we can see and acknowledge those, past and present and in every culture, who straddle the boundaries the rest of us have worked so hard to sustain.

Reservations aside, *Race* is an important book, a step toward a social conversation that not just young adults, but all of us desperately need to have. Aronson is the first to suggest that many ideas he puts forward in this book are evolving, have changed, and may change again. He does not present himself and his views as unconnected to the historical "facts" he lays out. In the first chapter he admits to knee-jerk racial prejudice, and in his deeply felt remarks on the Holocaust and how it colors his views of Germans today, he demonstrates the kind of honesty needed to begin a genuine dialogue on race.

In *The Half-Jewish Book: A Celebration*, Daniel Klein, a Jew, and his non-Jewish wife, Freke Vuijst, set out to cover the ground Aronson omits in relation to Judaism. The book straddles the line between popular history and self-help and, although written for adults, its youth-oriented focus puts it squarely within crossover YA territory. Photos and bios of half-Jewish celebrities and young pop-culture icons, though dated, make the point that there are a lot of half-Jews out there who, no matter what anyone else says, happily assert their Jewish identity.

After cheerfully acknowledging that their own child fails to meet the definition of a Jew that many Jews adhere to, the authors set out to assert the contrary in as many ways as they can find. Despite its upbeat, pop-culture focus (most of the text celebrates half-Jews in every walk of life, especially the arts), the authors don't slide over tough issues. The last chapter, "Half-Jews and the Holocaust: The Ultimate Reference Point," addresses how Nazi Germany categorized people of part-Jewish descent, how the Nuremberg Laws were first applied to define the *mischlinge* (literally "mixed"), and how the laws eroded over time. In 1933, 44 percent of German Jews were in interfaith marriages; many of interfaith ancestry had been raised as Christians. Those categorized by law as mischlinge occupied a racial limbo. Those with one Jewish parent were "first degree," those with a Jewish grandparent, "second degree." Which parent was Jewish, the family's gentile connections, and their attitude toward the Reich also had a bearing on how mischlinge were categorized. Overall, their prospects for escaping the death camps were better than for "full" Jews. The reason for making the legal distinction, the authors assert, was to avoid having the gentile relatives of half-Jews protest their treatment, but also that the second-degree mischlinge might be absorbed into the Aryan population. "There is no ambiguity about the long-range plan for half-Jewish Mischlinge at this point; the Nuremberg Laws stated unequivocally that the aim of a legal solution to the Mischling question must be the disappearance of the Mischling race" (289), the authors say. "Most historians agree that if the war had continued, the half-Jews would have ultimately been murdered along with the full Jews, that in the end, it was not 'Hitler's caution' that saved the half-Jews but the collapse of Hitler's regime" (295). Trauma and bitterness over the different treatment accorded the two categories has colored the discussion among Jews about half-Jewish identity.

The authors say they "thought long and hard about whether or not to include a section about half-Jews in the Holocaust in this book. On the one hand, it did not seem in keeping with the celebratory spirit of the rest of this volume" (282). But they decided to include this discussion because the Holocaust is central to the self-definition of half-Jews as much as it is to full Jews. "Again and again we were told, 'Even though I am only half-Jewish, when push comes to shove, I am a Jew, because if I had been in Europe during World War Two, I would have been a victim of the Final Solution'" (282). This argument, that they are Jews because they would have been treated as Jews had they lived in Nazi Germany, can be turned on its head, however. One can point to the different treatment of mischlinge as evidence that they are *not* full Jews. "If I would have been spared by the Nazis, not required to wear a yellow star, not sent to a death camp, because of my half-Jewish status, can I now call myself a Jew?" This definition has the danger of allowing someone outside the group to determine qualification for membership in it. In addition to its glimpse of a little-known (outside Jewish culture) facet of the Holocaust, the treatment of mixed-heritage Jews, this episode demonstrates how historical events shape and change group identity.

The book demonstrates how the experience of being told one is culturally inauthentic transcends all races and cultures. Interviewees recount their experience and how they've come to terms with it. A kibbutz volunteer of Protestant-Jewish heritage describes his stint as an "equal-opportunity victim" on the kibbutz. "The Jews didn't accept me completely—I had the wrong Jewish parent, don't you know? And the Palestinians I worked with didn't completely trust me. But when I got over feeling sorry for myself, I found my status rather liberating. In this land of lines drawn in blood, I could slip from one group to the other much more easily than most people could—I was sort of an equal-opportunity schmoozer, too" (178).

SELF-HELP FOR MIXED-HERITAGE YOUTH

Nonfiction series for teens that focus on social issues and problems associated with growing up are legion. Most of the books are brief and formulaic, with a short shelf life. The formula includes a little historical context, rarely sourced; advice from a few "experts"; interviews with sketchily described teens on the subject; descriptions of celebrities who face or have faced the issue; and an appendix of resources: books, websites, helping organizations. Despite manifestly good intentions, many seem hastily written by authors who know little of the subject, although that is hard to determine since the formula does not allow for depth.

The biggest problem with adding mixed heritage to these kinds of series is context: invariably the series focus is on serious behavioral and societal ills. This issue does not arise only with racial identity. Any teens whose identities are not white, heterosexual, able-bodied, American-born, or who don't live in an intact nuclear family may see their own identity category prominently displayed next to the books on date rape, child molestation, and teen pregnancy. In addition to *Coping as a Biracial/Biethnic Teen* (1995) and *Coping in an Interfaith Family* (1993), other issues to be coped with in the series include physical challenges, eating disorders, parents with AIDS, gay parents, chronic illness, illiterate parents, immigrant parents, special needs classmates, date rape, being a foster child, suicide, grief, drug abuse, and depression.

Enslow's "Hot Issue" series prompts the same concern; in addition to *Multiethnic Teens and Cultural Identity: A Hot Issue* (2001), the series includes books on hate and racism, and cult awareness. Besides *Adoption: Social Issues Firsthand* (2006), Greenhaven's Social Issues Firsthand series titles include: *Homosexuality, Poverty, Suicide,* and *Terrorism.* Greenhaven's Opposing Viewpoints bundles identity topics (adoption, homosexuality) with child abuse, racism, and homelessness. One wonders if anyone anywhere in the publishing process gave a thought to the significance of bundling books about identity with those on desperate social problems. All get filed in the bookstore's "self-help" section, further adding to the conflation of mixed or "nontraditional" heritage with social ills requiring help and healing.

Even when they are well written, as some are, these books suffer from another deficit common to the self-help genre: compartmentalization. They zero in on "the" problem topic in isolation from other elements of identity and experience. What about the gay teen whose dad is black and whose mom is a Thai immigrant? He'll need at least three books. Or the amputee adopted as a "special needs" child from Guatemala at the age of eight? The fact is, we experience life all at once, not in neat series categories, and one must question how useful these so-lutions in search of problems actually are for young readers. Their shelf life is shortened by the tendency of most to include lists of pop celebri-ties with the "problem": sitcom stars whose TV series have entered re-run twilight; musicians whose groups are history; athletes long retired.

While they are hot off the press, these books offer a few genuine pluses: they are good for reluctant and less-than-proficient readers and provide adjunct resources—self-help groups, websites, and books. How-ever, much of this is available today in a more up-to-date format online. Websites for mixed-heritage teens also provide forums to discuss issues. Arguably, the availability of these resources online has rendered the by-the-numbers, self-help book for teens obsolete. There is a great need for good nonfiction resources in print, however, that pursue topics in more depth, in a fuller social and historical context than web-based resources can provide. An endeavor far better suited to a book format, discussed below, is the interview book.

The YA series titles on adoption are not usually written for teen adoptees (a smaller demographic). Rather, these books seem aimed at general readers. Some are excellent, but most try to address all the forms of adoption together, although they are quite different—a stepparent adoption raises issues of blended families and coping with two fathers or mothers; an international adoption may involve issues of racism, ethnic-ity, searching for birthparents, and maintaining birth heritage. Domestic adoptions raise a third set of issues. These books, with their short page counts, could hardly cover one kind, much less all.

Adoption represents a choice—although not the adoptee's choice—and can be quite controversial. Several series present some of these de-bates to young adults. Enslow's Hot Issues and Greenhaven's Opposing Viewpoints series lay out important issues for a broad YA audience. Among series that address teens who are adopted is Scarecrow's Ultimate Teen Guides. *Where Are My Birth Parents? A Guide for Teenage Adoptees* (1993), by Karen Gravelle and Susan Fischer, is out of date and disap-pointingly superficial. Despite the title, it contains little specific infor-mation on how to search.

Straddling two genres—self-help and memoir—Sundee Tucker Frazier's *Check All that Apply: Finding Wholeness as a Multiracial Person* (2002) offers a multiracial person's take on managing mixed heritage. Written from a Christian perspective for a Christian publisher, some of the content is relevant only to those who share the author's faith or who at least see the world through a religious perspective. The author relies on up-to-date science and has no evangelical agenda, so readers who don't share her faith won't feel targeted. Rather than concentrate on finding "solutions" to problems, Frazier does something very rare: she focuses on forgiveness and healing: "Metaphorically, multiracial people display the life that flows from racial reconciliation" (135). The first third of the book focuses on identity. What is most useful is that she writes from her personal experience, not only sharing it in memoir form—useful as that is—but conveying what has worked for her in her struggle to manage her own multiracial identity: "My yearning for reconciliation between hostile racial groups predates my entrance into this world. Black and white are written together on my DNA," she says. "Sometimes I feel it is an issue of survival for me that they get together (it's not true, but it can feel that way). How can I, permanently, a mixture of both, exist in a world where blacks and whites are forever separated?" (137–38). She asks readers to use their experience to reach out to others: "Paradoxically, being in the middle often means being on the margins. This experience can increase our compassion for those who are marginalized for *any* reason" (142). This perspective is echoed in Rebecca Walker's memoir, discussed later in this chapter. Forgiving racism in family members without letting it define us, exercising compassion for those who are stuck in old racial paradigms, are not topics usually covered in self-help series, with their emphasis on "solutions."

Frazier embraces both black and white identities, while affirming the right of others to make a different choice. "I can't say I'm only black or only white and not be contributing to my own demise. I must live the truth of who I am, regardless of societal costs" (162). Frazier chose her book's title for the same reason: to embrace more than one identity, rather than simply reject the monoracial choices held out to her. "We can find belonging with our various peoples, maybe not with all of them, but with those who share the same desire for truthfulness, for sanity. We will belong with those who are secure enough in their identity to accept us with our identities. We need to get with others who share our *heart,* not our exact ethnic makeup" (163). Because of its focus on the emotional consequences of living with mixed heritage in a monoracial world, *Check All that Apply* is an important and useful book, but one that requires readers to be comfortable with the author's Christian mindset. The book includes a comprehensive bibliography and an extensive annotated resource list.

HOW IT FEELS

Becoming an adult involves discovering those who've gone before us, learning that others have stood where we are standing now, and listening to what they have to tell us about it. Adolescence is at times lonely and scary, as we prepare to leave the shelter of family and familiarity, facing the rapidly approaching time when we must take full responsibility for ourselves and our choices. Finding a group that will accept us as entitled to membership is one way we gain the courage and strength to make the transition from dependence to independence. "I am a Jew and therefore I belong here; I am the biological child of this family and therefore I belong here; I am gay and therefore I belong here; I am black, a Latin American immigrant, Tlingit," and so forth. As we have seen in this book, mixed heritage undermines and reduces the availability to us of such groups. Not only that, but our very existence may be seen as a threat to the sanctity of identity categories among people whose right to belong is unquestioned. We may cause them to question whether these categories are real or right in the first place.

Seeing themselves reflected in photos, stories, memoirs, and interviews can help to reduce loneliness and alienation for mixed-heritage youth. The hunger for visibility among this population can't be overestimated, yet their cultural invisibility continues, as has been shown throughout this book. Because they share only the "multi" with their peers who may combine any number of races and ethnicities, there is no group to go to where they are guaranteed to meet others just like them. As long as we believe that our racial and ethnic differences are biologically based and important, as well as visible to the naked eye, multiracial and multiethnic people are going to be excluded from membership in those categories or, at the very least, will have to prove again and again their right to belong.

Among the most valuable books for young adults on mixed heritage are those that contain the experiences and opinions of other young adults, similarly situated. Pearl Fuyo Gaskins's *What Are You?* (1999) includes statements by and photographs of multiracial youth growing up mixed, as Gaskins herself did. The interviews suggest that not much has changed since Gaskins was a teen. Chela Delgado, daughter of a white mother and black father recalls that in middle school, "people always wanted to know—what was I? In seventh grade, when I was twelve and thirteen, I was sort of still trying to figure it out." Years later, she is still trying: In a room full of white people, she will think, "Gosh, I'm the only black person in here." And in a room full of black people, she thinks, "Gosh, I'm the only white person in here" (15).

Mixed people are more often recognized and therefore validated by people of color than by whites. "Other minorities—especially Hispanics and blacks—notice it much more. They may not know what I am, but they'll ask me about it. They're just more sensitive to that kind of stuff, I guess. They look for it because it is more of an issue in their lives than it is in most white people's lives" (35), says Jennifer Ho, twenty-four, daughter of a white mother and Chinese father.

Whites have told her that being able to pass for white is an advantage. "I've even had people say that I'm lucky I can pass for white—that I should be grateful." This angers her, "because they're very condescending about it. It's like, 'Shut up and pass for white,' as if it's a gift that they do this for me, like a privilege I have" (34).

Regardless of the intended audience, most adoption books include transracial and intercountry adoptees with same-heritage adoptees. Not only is much of their experience vastly different, it can be painful to see the chapter on how to search for birthparents when you have been adopted from an anonymous orphanage. If you are a mixed-race teen adopted from Ecuador by a white family, the chapter on whether, when, and how to tell friends you're adopted isn't much use. Same-race and transracial adoption are so dissimilar and their impact on adoptees' and adoptive families' lives so dissimilar that they do not belong in the same book together. Combining them simply reminds transracial adoptee readers of their status as a minority within a minority.

Among the few YA books to zero in on a specific group of transracial adoptees is *After the Morning Calm: Reflections of Korean Adoptees* (2002). These twenty-six personal accounts, including photos, of growing up in white families offer eloquent testimony to the commonalities among these adoptees. Korea was the first country to send large numbers of young children to Western countries for adoption. The editors, Sook Wilkinson and Nancy Fox, celebrate the successes of international adoption but also highlight the serious issues confronting adoptees. Adoption professionals themselves, they "have observed that many adoption-related questions and issues surface as the children enter into adolescence and young adulthood along with their increased cognitive and emotional capacities. Often, many wrestle with them silently and alone" (14). Reaching out to other adoptees, some contributors include their personal contact information.

Because these adoptees were sent to largely white communities in the Midwest, many grew up starved for the sight of others who looked like them. Some describe trips to Korea to seek out birthparents or simply to reconnect with their first culture. Not all these experiences were happy or emotionally satisfying, yet they were felt to be valuable anyway. One hard lesson these adoptees learn is that their home country is still monocultural and monoracial. Korean American adoptees—some multiracial offspring of American GIs, black and white, and Korean women—would visit Korea, eager to find themselves reflected at last, only to be told firmly that they are not Korean at all. Valuing diversity and multiculturalism is something Americans at least pay lip service to and for many it is a deeply held belief. Monocultural societies around the world feel little impetus to value diversity, however. The experience of having this door shut in one's face can be devastating. Kate Hers, twenty-six, says, "Korean people feel that being Korean is unique in nature, something to be proud of, this sameness that runs throughout the blood of 'my people.'" Hers says she knows now that she will "never entirely fit the code" (74–75). She weighs the relative values of monocultural versus multicultural values. "In Korea, being Korean is just one thing. There is no distinction between race, culture, and nationality. People do not have to explain themselves because everyone's background is similar, or at least they pretend to be." Americans take it for granted that just because one's face appears Asian, that does not mean one is not an American. "Being an American means many different things. When Korean people assume that an American is white and only speaks English, I see their limitations in thinking," she says. "I am not sure they will ever understand that being Korean can mean many different things to different people" (76).

Sunny Jo, twenty-six, adopted by a Norwegian family, went from one monocultural country to another. She found that in Norway, the only culturally acceptable identity was Norwegian. "Norway took my Asian name and culture, told me I should be ashamed of it, and that Norwegian names and habits were better," she says. "But I was never good enough and I could never reach the inner circle of Norway" (168). As an adult, she immigrated to a diverse country, Canada, where she found a place for herself.

Peter Kearly, thirty, adopted by an Irish American family, was reminded of his status whenever his family traveled between Detroit and Windsor, Ontario, and he was scrutinized narrowly by border officials. In high school he tried to cut and paste an Asian identity for himself from among all the stereotypes, good and bad. "I didn't want to be like the Asian geeks I saw in movies like 'Sixteen Candles' and 'Revenge of the Nerds,'" he says. On the other hand, "I did not want to be another typical Asian overachiever, both praised as a model minority that other people of color should follow and denigrated as an emasculated sex-starved wallflower. I tried to stay away from the other Asian guys at school" (64). Similar issues came up around dating. Were white girls dating him or his exotic ancestry? He noticed the Asian girls were dating white boys. As often happens, life got easier in college. Now a college English instructor, Kearly has come to accept that "I am valued because I know English well *and* because I am not white." He appreciates that his success can be encouraging for students of color in search of role models. "However, I am also aware that my colleagues may see in me a source of ethnic diversity that I myself would not claim" (65).

Many experiences Korean adoptees share in this book are of a piece, reflecting their unique experiences of intercountry adoption. For adoptees from Latin America, China, Vietnam, and Eastern Europe, different conditions pertained. Books crafted along the lines of *After the Morning Calm* and *What Are You?* would be equally valuable for them and many times more useful than yet another self-help book on "coping" with being adopted.

MEMOIRS

For a memoir to interest us as readers, we need to connect with the author, just as we do with a fictional protagonist. And also like fiction, the memoirist must be intriguing enough to engage our interest. For a memoir to interest a publisher, the story told needs to stand out as unusual, exceptional. What gets memoirs published, as often as not, is the author's unusual provenance—she is famous or the child or close relative of someone famous—or the startling, sensational events of the author's life. Most memoirs of mixed-heritage individuals fall into these categories—some with a vengeance. Consequently, while young adults may see some of their experience reflected in these memoirs, much of it is unique to the memoirist. For this reason, interview books may be more valuable tools for young adults. However, memoirs offer the important advantage of depth.

Lisa Jones, author of *Bulletproof Diva: Tales of Race, Sex, and Hair* (1994), is the daughter of black poet Amiri Baraka and Jewish author Hettie Jones, who was disenfranchised by her family for marrying a black man. The marriage did not last, and Lisa and her sister were raised by their mother. This book is drawn from a collection of columns on style, culture, music, and trends, written in the early 1990s. Jones identifies herself as multiracial technically, while firmly choosing a black identity. She makes a good case for her choice, but fails to give serious consideration to why others might make a different one. Jones assumes that the only reason the child of one white and one black parent would call herself multiracial is to seek special advantage or edge herself closer to whiteness. To be fair, most of the columns from which the book was drawn were written before Root's *Racially Mixed People in America*[3] appeared in 1992, which began to change how multiraciality was understood.

Affirming only black identity without disrespecting her mother requires some complicated conceptual maneuvering: "My pride in being a black woman actually brings me closer to my (white) mom. This identity gives me a stronger sense of history and self, and I can come to my mother as what the New Age folks might call a 'fully realized person.' If I called myself 'interracial' (in my mind, and I know others see this differently), I would need her presence, her 'whiteness,' to somehow validate my 'half-whiteness'" (33).

Regardless of how she identifies personally, Jones's respect for her mother comes through loud and clear: "My mother, more than anyone I know, has taught me difference as pleasure. Not as something feared or exotic, but difference as one of the rich facts of one's life, a truism that gives you more data, more power, and more flavor" (33). Jones's mother shared her own love of black culture with her daughters: "Motherhood has been more than a domestic chore or emotional bond for my mother. It's a political location—one she's taken seriously enough to go up against the world for. She always stands ready to testify about how her children and blackness have broadened her own life. In the music—jazz, blues, the language—she found her own" (34).

Jones makes it clear that however she defines herself racially, part of that definition will always include unconditional affirmation of her mother as she is: "There's no place that I'm ever gonna go (by way of geography or ideology) where I can't bring my mother, and where I can't bring myself, which she has in large part made possible" (35).

Like several of our memoirists, Jones is the child of parents whose generation included idealistic civil rights activists, leading-edge baby boomers, black-white couples who met registering black voters or demonstrating against the Vietnam War or listening to Janis Joplin and Jimi Hendrix. Maintaining that commitment to fundamental social change—a belief that not only could the walls separating castes and cultures be torn down, but that they ought to be—grew harder in the 1980s in an increasingly conservative, inward-turning cultural climate.

The award for Hardest Family to Grow Up In has to go to Gregory Howard Williams, author of the memoir *Life on the Color Line: The True Story of a White Boy Who Discovered He Was Black* (1995). The older of two sons of a light-skinned black father and white mother, Williams assumed as a child that his family was white. When he was ten, his parents split up; the boys were left with their charming but alcoholic father, who told them they were black. He took them to his hometown, Muncie, Indiana, and deposited them with his alcoholic mother, with whom they lived in sordid squalor. The hero of Williams's remarkable story is an extraordinary middle-aged black woman, Dora Terry, who rescued the boys from a very uncertain future, took them into her home, and raised them herself.[4] Williams's biography is at least as dramatic and angst-filled as the fake memoirs described in chapter 3, but this story is supported by photos, documentary evidence, and his public career as dean of Ohio State University's College of Law.

Any notion that being light-skinned and therefore able to "pass for white" is any kind of benefit is laid to rest here. Merely by appearing in his own skin, Williams was assumed to be trying to pass. Being raised on the color line was like being forced to drive down the yellow line separating two directions of traffic. Early on, he was singled out by his father as the "white" son, his brother as "black," a distinction that did neither any favors. Williams describes what happened when, in middle school, he asked Mayme, a dark-skinned classmate, to a Boy's Club party—his first date. Walking to the party, he noticed cars were slowing down and drivers gawking at them on the busy street. "Were we laughing too loud?

Then I realized—they were shocked to see a 'white' boy on South Madison Street with a black girl." Things went downhill. "Though neither of us said a word, Mayme too sensed the surrounding hostility. The hardness returned to her face, and we began to walk faster and speak in monosyllables. A teenager leaned out a car window and shrieked, 'Nigger lover!' Other drivers honked their horns." At the party, "even among our classmates, unfriendly faces followed our every move. Soon their antagonism engulfed us, but we struggled to maintain our smiles as we doggedly went from game to game. It was hard to keep up the façade, and I was relieved when it was time to leave" (166).

This tightrope walk continued in high school. The tension of trying to assess where to go, where he would be welcome, is almost palpable. He describes entering the auditorium on his first day of high school. "Black students huddled together on the south side. Whites filled the north. The middle section flowed between them like a deep unnavigable river." His hope that the school's large size would give him anonymity was quickly dashed. Now what? "Goose bumps popped out on my arms as I realized that, on the very first day, I had to make a fateful choice. If I sat with the white students on the north side of the auditorium, the blacks would believe I didn't want to associate with them. Yet, if I joined the black students, I would be an all-too-conspicuous 'white' face in a sea of the multiple hues of brown." Williams stood, frozen and uncertain. "Finally, aware I had no real decision to make, I slowly moved down the aisle to join the black students." He spotted a popular brown-skinned cousin, who hailed him, but "I had an aching fear that even though I had made my choice, they might not accept me." As he found a place to sit, "feeling the burning stares of white students from across the room, Jemima rose from her seat. Every muscle in my body relaxed as she sat down beside me" (191). The issue did not go away. Black students asked why Williams didn't pass, since he could. Every time, he had to justify himself, his choice—or make clear that there was, in fact, no choice. He could never make the dangerous mistake of assuming there was a place at the table for him. The memoir concludes with Williams's high school graduation.

A more peaceful memoir, *The Color of Water: A Black Man's Tribute to His White Mother* (1996), presents James McBride's life story. His white mother raised him and his eleven siblings as black, in a black community. After his father died, she remarried; his black stepfather was the only father James knew. Both marriages were happy. A devout Christian, she valued education highly, and eventually all twelve children would receive college degrees, and most graduate degrees. When her children asked about her race, she said she was "light-skinned." In fact, she was white. Her rabbi father and his family emigrated from Poland. McBride weaves her story into his own. Although McBride's appearance was dark enough that he did not have to deal with the "passing" issue that haunted Williams, being multiracial was not easy. As a student at Oberlin College, he found that the white students "seemed free in ways I could not be." He eventually made lifelong white friends there, but it was easier to relate to black students. "During the rare, inopportune social moments when I found myself squeezed between black and white, I fled to the black side, just as my mother had done, and did not emerge unless driven out by smoke and fire." Multiraciality is not yet laid to rest. "Being mixed is like that tingling feeling you have in your nose just before you sneeze—you're waiting for it to happen but it never does. Given my black face and upbringing it was easy for me to flee into the anonymity of blackness, yet I felt frustrated to live in a world that considers the color of your face an immediate political statement whether you like it or not" (261–62).

McBride pursued a successful career as a journalist, but racial identity issues haunted him. "The color boundary in my mind was and still is the greatest hurdle. In order to clear it, my solution was to stay away from it and fly solo" (262). He got and quit jobs at *The Boston Globe, The Washington Post,* and other journals. "Being caught between black and white as a working adult was far more unpleasant than when I was a college student. I watched as the worlds of blacks and whites smashed together in newsrooms and threw off chunks of human carnage that landed at my feet," McBride says. "I'd hear black reporters speaking angrily about a sympathetic white editor and I'd disagree in silence. White men ruled the kingdom, sometimes ruthlessly, finding clever ways to gut the careers of fine black reporters who came into the business full of piss and vinegar, yet other white men were mere pawns like myself" (263). Writing this memoir was McBride's self-prescribed therapy.

Rebecca Walker, daughter of black novelist Alice Walker and Jewish attorney Mel Leventhal, records her unique childhood in *Black, White and Jewish: Autobiography of a Shifting Self* (2002). Her parents' custody arrangement, by which she would live with one parent for two years, then switch to the other, kept her from putting down roots anywhere. As her father's life became increasingly white, with a second marriage to a white Jewish woman, Rebecca felt the distance grow between them. There was also distance between her and her mother's black relatives in Georgia, who read whiteness into her behavior and let her know about it. Readers accompany her through a bewildering hall of mirrors, as she tries to make friends and nail down verities of identity and selfhood most of us take for granted. Where was home, metaphorical and actual? Who claimed her as theirs and whom did she claim? Walker's parents took a very hands-off approach to raising their daughter; she was free to find her own path, by no means always a blessing. The memoir cuts between past and present. Still unanchored and floating, "I am more comfortable in airports than I am in either of the houses I call, with undeserved nostalgia, Home. I am more comfortable in airports than I was in any of the eight different schools where I learned all of the things I now cannot remember. Airports are limbo spaces—blank, undemanding, neutral. Expectations are clear" (3).

Most of the memoir covers Walker's adolescence and teen years. She was a wild child by some measures, though as contemporary memoirs go, her experience was tame. Walker recognizes that she was the product of her parents' hopes for and belief in a multiracial future. They met as civil rights activists and married in 1967: "My parents tell me I can do anything I put my mind to, that I can be anything I want. They buy me Erector sets and building blocks, Tinkertoys and books, more and more books." She was loved and cherished, not "tragic" (24). But there is tragedy here nonetheless. It lies in the distance between the worlds she moves through. Asked as an adult what it feels like "to have white inside of you," Walker says, "The only time I 'feel white' is when black folks point out something in me they don't want to own in themselves and so label 'white.'" Among the items labeled, she includes her tendency to psychoanalyze, tolerance for cold, and "hard earned sense of entitlement" (305). Her light phenotype makes her feel less black.

Asked "when someone black starts talking about 'my people' have been oppressed for so long, do you identify with those people?" she can't slide into yes without thinking, because "I was never granted the luxury by being claimed unequivocally by any people or 'race' and so when someone starts talking about 'my people' I know that if we look hard enough or scratch at the surface long enough, they would have some problem with some part of my background, the part that's not included in the 'my people' construction." And there is also "the question of how I can feel fully identified with 'my people' when I have other people, too, who are not included in that grouping. And this feeling I have, of having other people too, is in effect even when the other people under consideration do not claim me" (306). What Walker, like Sundee Tucker Frazier, concludes is that this legacy is related to her sense of solidarity with those suffering from legacies of oppression and exclusion because of their identities: slaves, Jews, interned Japanese Americans, American Indians. Walker's divided identity itself allows her to identify with more than one group at a time, including groups she does not personally belong to and that may be in conflict with one another. Her struggle to find commonality with the different racial and ethnic identities that are her personal legacy has educated her heart to see beyond difference to what we all share as human beings.

Angela Nissel, a producer and writer for the TV sitcom *Scrubs,* is the daughter of a white father and black mother. In her memoir *Mixed: My Life in Black and White* (2006), she describes growing up with her younger brother and single mother in a diverse Philadelphia neighborhood in the late 1970s. Humor is Nissel's chosen vehicle for conveying the absurdity, contradictions, hypocrisy, and blind prejudice that know no racial boundaries. Funny as *Mixed* is, much of Nissel's story is difficult, including her spell as a patient in a psychiatric facility as a college student. The memoir is a relief not just for its humor, but because Nissel is not the child of someone famous and because the events she describes took place within the context of a relatively normal urban, working-class childhood.

Trying to fit in with the black kids and the white kids, "I convinced myself that the teasing had to stop one day, and after that I would be welcomed into the fold as an honorary white person. As bad as the ridicule got at times, watching the three blacks on the block who were never invited to play with the white kids helped keep me from crying or running home and telling my parents every time someone started teasing me" (37).

When she brought out a black Barbie to play with the white girls, "they treated her like dirt, like she was Scurvy Barbie," Nissel reports. "'Ewww! That's not Barbie,' Michelle said, backing her Western Barbie away." Nissel had come to the same conclusion, "and not just because she was the queen of the pack. Anyone who watched television could tell Black Barbie wasn't as important as White Barbie," Nissel knew. "White Barbie dominated the commercials: she was the one cruising the coast in a Corvette; she was the one taking the elevator to the second floor of the Dream House. Black Barbie appeared only in a still shot behind White Barbie for about two seconds before the commercial faded to black" (37). Nissel never *is* welcomed into that fold. In the end, it is the black kids who include her, the white kids who tell her she can't play with *them* anymore if she plays with the black kids. But at age ten, when she and her mother move into a black community, Nissel is bullied by black girls at school.

Pam, the teenage after-school caregiver her mother hired, tries to eliminate Nissel's residual whiteness. Pam's Real Black Person Rules mandate that she wear clean clothes and name-brand sneakers. "If your sneakers get scuffed, you should throw them out." Nissel duly covers up the generic brand name on her new sneakers (her mother refuses to shell out big bucks for a name brand as Pam mandated) and creatively stencils "Reebok" on them instead. The ruse works briefly, until Nissel hears kids laughing at her. "Handy as Wite-Out is, it isn't made for large-scale projects like sneaker copyright infringement. When I looked down to see what they were laughing at, I saw that I now had BALLBOKS instead of REEBOKS" (94–95).

ESSAY ANTHOLOGIES

Anthologies of personal essays have become popular in recent years. *Half and Half: Writers on Growing Up Biracial and Bicultural,* edited by Claudine O'Hearn, contains eighteen essays on biracial and bicultural identity. Despite the subtitle, not all of the essays concern growing up. Some read like essays for a creative writing MFA program, more literary tours de force than deeply felt. Entries from stars—among them Julia Alvarez, Malcolm Gladwell, Gish Jen, Bharati Mukherjee, Lisa See, and Danzy Senna—are mostly recycled writings, cannibalized from work intended for a different purpose with only the most tenuous connection to the topic. This kind of quick-and-dirty anthology project adds little if anything to the cultural discourse.

At the other end of the personal essay spectrum is the fine collection, cited in chapter 4, *Half/Life: Jewish Tales from Interfaith Homes,* edited by Laurel Snyder. The contributors' reputations are less stellar than in *Half and Half,* but the essays are far superior in quality and depth. They are also emotionally powerful and insightful. The authors are mostly young, children of leading-edge baby boomers (Joyce Maynard is an exception). Usually, the father is the Jewish parent. Consequently, many Jews do not recognize them as Jewish. The pain expressed by those who are told their Jewish identity is illusory, is reminiscent of that expressed by Louis Owens in *Mixedblood Messages.*

Dena Seidel had a horrific childhood tossed between an alcoholic, drug-addicted Jewish father and mentally ill, evangelical Christian mother, interspersed with stints in New Age foster care. She has fought hard to achieve the stable life she now enjoys as an observant Jew. Her moving essay concludes with an incident that occurs while she prepares a Passover Seder for family and friends. Her Hasidic neighbor rings her doorbell and asks her to go push a button for him because, as it is the Sabbath, he cannot do it himself.[5] Seidel explains to him that they are about to have a seder and suggests he ask someone else. When the man does not accept her explanation, she says, "'We consider ourselves Jewish. This is going to be confusing for my children. Can't you ask another neighbor?'" After he lets her know that in his eyes she is not a Jew, Seidel says, "'I know you can't understand. But please respect our household.'" The neighbor shrugs and leaves, and thereafter avoids her. Incidents of such casual cruelties are scattered throughout the book. But for many essayists, like Seidel, finding a way to embrace their Jewish identity amid such persistent invalidation has given them a gift, a new understanding of identity. Georgiana Cohen says, "It feels like I've traveled in six different directions to get to the tentative place where I currently am—but no one way is right, nor is any incorrect." Although it was not a straight or a short path—Cohen compares herself to the "wandering Jew"—"I am more at peace with my Jewishness—and the responsibility it entails—now than ever before." Cohen is hanging onto her heritage with a firm grip. "My half-Jewish self is what was born into my blood, and is what part of me will always be self-conscious of in the eyes of discriminating rabbis." She will pass it on to her Christian husband and to her children, when they have them. "We don't plan to raise them as one thing or the other—right now, the plan is just to raise them, and raise them well. They won't be halves, just well-loved wholes" (148).

The main lesson from YA nonfiction on mixed heritage is that there is far too little of it and what does exist is too often substandard or dated or irrelevant. Cultural invisibility is still the norm for mixed-heritage people. "Why are so few courses taught in our colleges and universities on interracial issues and about interracial people?" diversity scholar David Schoem asks.[6] He points out that he, a white man, was asked to write the chapter on teaching interracial courses for a book largely written by multiracial people and wholly about multiraciality because he is the best qualified person to do so. "The challenge to my authorship, I believe, is not whether I should be the author, but why there aren't a great many more faculty to choose from to write this chapter, and where all my colleagues in the social sciences are who have yet to teach this course or others like it," Schoem says. "Why is the subject of interracial issues and interracial people still so often ignored, simply an add-on or a supplementary reading, or an unworthy topic for undergraduate, graduate or scholarly study?" (22). And, we add, for consideration by younger people, high school students in the Eriksonian stage of identity formation.

It is hoped that this book will help persuade readers that we cannot advance the conversation about race and ethnicity our society needs to have until we come to terms with mixed heritage in its myriad manifestations. With the election of Barack Obama as the first mixed-heritage president, the United States has taken an important step down this road.

NOTES

1. Brent Staples, "Children's Books," *New York Times,* 12 Sept. 1999 www.nytimes.com/books/99/09/12/reviews/990912.12childrt.html?_r=1&oref=slogin/ (24 Sept. 2007).

2. Staples, "Children's Books."

3. Maria P. P. Root, ed., *Racially Mixed People in America* (Newbury Park, Calif.: Sage, 1992).

4. This kind of informal, nonrelative adoption is not unusual within black communities, nor is the devotion and commitment Miss Dora manifested.

5. People who are not Jewish, *Shabbos Goyim,* may be asked to accomplish tasks that Jews of some sects are forbidden to carry out on the Sabbath.

6. David Schoem, "Teaching an Interracial Issues Course," in *Multiracial America: Resource Guide on the History and Literature of Interracial Issues,* ed. Karen

Downing, Darline Nichols, and Kelly Webster (Lanham, Md.: Scarecrow Press, 2005), 22.

NONFICTION WORKS CITED OR CRITIQUED

Note: An asterisk denotes works critiqued as well as cited in the chapter.

Marc Aronson, *Race: A History Beyond Black and White* (New York: Atheneum, 2007).*

Barbara C. Cruz, *Multiethnic Teens and Cultural Identity: A Hot Issue* (Berkeley Heights, N.J.: Enslow, 2001).

Sundee Tucker Frazier, *Check All that Apply: Finding Wholeness as a Multiracial Person* (Downers Grove, Ill.: InterVarsity Press, 2002).*

Pearl Fuyo Gaskins, *What Are You? Voices of Mixed-Race Young People* (New York: Henry Holt, 1999).*

Karen Gravelle and Susan Fischer, *Where Are My Birth Parents? A Guide for Teenage Adoptees* (New York: Walker, 1993).

David M. Haugen and Matthew J. Box, eds., *Adoption: Social Issues Firsthand* (Farmington Hills, Mich.: Greenhaven Press–Thomson-Gale, 2006).

Lisa Jones, *Bulletproof Diva: Tales of Race, Sex, and Hair* (New York: Doubleday, 1994).*

Daniel Klein and Freke Vuijst, *The Half-Jewish Book: A Celebration* (New York: Villard, 2000).*

James McBride, *The Color of Water: A Black Man's Tribute to His White Mother* (New York: Riverhead, 1996).*

Gary B. Nash, *Forbidden Love: The Secret History of Mixed-Race America* (New York: Henry Holt, 1999).*

Renea D. Nash, *Coping as a Biracial/Biethnic Teen* (New York: Rosen, 1995).

Angela Nissel, *Mixed: My Life in Black and White* (New York: Villard, 2006).*

Claudine O'Hearn, *Half and Half: Writers on Growing Up Biracial and Bicultural* (New York: Random House, 1998).

Gwen Packard, *Coping in an Interfaith Family* (New York: Rosen, 1993).

Laurel Snyder, ed., *Half/Life: Jewish Tales from Interfaith Homes* (New York: Soft Skull, 2006).*

Rebecca Walker, *Black, White and Jewish: Autobiography of a Shifting Self* (New York: Riverhead, 2002).*

Sook Wilkinson and Nancy Fox, eds., *After the Morning Calm: Reflections of Korean Adoptees* (Bloomfield Hills, Mich.: Sunrise Ventures, 2002).*

Gregory Howard Williams, *Life on the Color Line* (New York: Plume, 1995).*

Bibliography

PRINT AND ONLINE SOURCES

1990 Jewish Population Survey. Jewish Outreach Institute, www.joi.org/qa/stats/ (21 March 2008).

Adoption History Project. "Timeline of Adoption History," University of Oregon, www.uoregon.edu/~adoption/topics/birthparents.htm (1 May 2008).

Alexie, Sherman. "I Hated Tonto (Still Do)." *Los Angeles Times,* 28 June 1998.

Allen, James Paul, and Eugene James Turner. *We the People: An Atlas of America's Ethnic Diversity.* New York: Macmillan, 1988.

Aronson, Marc. *Beyond the Pale: New Essays for a New Era.* Lanham, Md.: Scarecrow Press, 2003.

Azoulay, Katya Gibel. *Black, Jewish, and Interracial: It's Not the Color of Your Skin, but the Race of Your Kin, and Other Myths of Identity.* Durham, N.C.: Duke University Press, 1997.

B. C. Teen Readers Choice Stellar Book Award. "Sylvia Olsen Interviews." 25 Feb 2007, www.stellaraward.ca/2008/interview.php?id=12/ (25 April 2008).

Belge, Kathy. "An Interview with Jacqueline Woodson: Author Jacqueline Woodson Talks to *Lesbian Life.*" *About.com: Lesbian Life,* lesbianlife.about.com/od/artistswriterset1/a/JWoodson.htm (29 Aug. 2007).

Berzon, J. R. *Neither White nor Black: The Mulatto Character in American Fiction.* New York: New York University Press, 1978.

Brunsma, David L. "The New Color Complex: Appearances and Biracial Identity." *Identity: An International Journal of Theory and Research* 1, no. 3 (2001): 225–46.

Cao, Lan, and Himilce Novas. *Everything You Need To Know About Asian-American History.* New York: Plume, 1996.

Cart, Michael, and Christine A. Jenkins. *The Heart Has Its Reasons: Young Adult Literature with Gay/Lesbian/Queer Content.* Lanham, Md.: Scarecrow Press, 2006.

Cauce, Ana Marie, Yumi Hiraga, Craig Mason, Tanya Aguilar, Nydia Ordonez, and Nancy Gonzales. "Between a Rock and a Hard Place: Social Adjustment of Biracial Youth." In *Racially Mixed People in America,* edited by Maria P. P. Root. Newbury Park, Calif.: Sage, 1992.

Child Welfare League of America. "International Adoption: Trends and Issues." National Data Analysis System (April 2007), www.childwelfare.gov/system wide/statistics/adoption.cfm/ (25 April 2008).

Christie, Agatha. *Murder After Hours.* 1946. Reprint, New York: Dell, 1977.

Craig, Amanda. "Black Is the New White." *TimesOnline* (UK), 31 Jan. 2004. entertainment.timesonline.co.uk/tol/arts_and_entertainment/books/article 1006827.ece (22 July 2008).

Cruz, Barbara C., and Michael J. Berson. "The American Melting Pot? Miscegenation Laws in the United States." *OAH Magazine of History* 15, no. 4 (Summer 2001).

Dalmage, Heather. *Tripping on the Color Line: Black-White Multiracial Families in a Racially Divided World.* New Brunswick, N.J.: Rutgers University Press, 2000.

Darby, Mary Ann, and Miki Pryne. *Hearing All the Voices: Multicultural Books for Adolescents.* Lanham, Md.: Scarecrow Press, 2002.

Desetta, Al, ed. *The Heart Knows Something Different: Teenage Voices from the Foster Care System.* New York: Persea, 1996.

Dickens, Charles. *Martin Chuzzlewit.* 1843. Reprint, London: Penguin Classics, 2002.

Downing, Karen, Darlene Nichols, and Kelly Webster. *Multiracial America: Resource Guide on the History and Literature of Interracial Issues.* Lanham, Md.: Scarecrow Press, 2005.

Edwardson, Debby Dahl. "Worldview in Contemporary Indigenous/Native American Literature: Language, Landscape and the Spiritual Geography of Story." MFA critical thesis, Vermont College, Union Institute and University, Fall 2004.

Fernández, Carlos A. "La Raza and the Melting Pot: A Comparative Look at Multiethnicity." In *Racially Mixed People in America,* edited by Maria P. P. Root. Newbury Park, Calif.: Sage, 1992.

Fiedler, Leslie. *The Collected Essays of Leslie Fiedler,* vol. 1. New York: Stein and Day, 1971.

———. *Love and Death in the American Novel.* New York: Dell, 1966.

Frazier, Sundee Tucker. *Check All that Apply: Finding Wholeness as a Multiracial Person.* Downers Grove, Ill.: InterVarsity Press, 2002.

Fredrickson, George M. *The Black Image in the White Mind: The Debate on Afro-American Character and Destiny, 1817–1914.* New York: Harper & Row, 1971.

Gaskins, Pearl Fuyo. *What* Are *You? Voices of Mixed-Race Young People.* New York: Henry Holt, 1999.

Gay, Kathlyn. *Cultural Diversity: Conflicts and Challenges.* Lanham, Md.: Scarecrow Press, 2003.

Goodman, Ellen. "Transcending Race and Identity." *The Boston Globe,* 25 January 2008.

Gowen, Kris, and Molly McKenna. *Image and Identity: Becoming the Person You Are.* Lanham, Md.: Scarecrow Press, 2005.

Hearne, Joanna. "'The Cross-Heart People': Race and Inheritance in the Silent Western." *Journal of Popular Film and Television* 30, no. 4 (Winter 2003): 182.

Henry, William A. "Beyond the Melting Pot." *Time,* 9 April 1990.

Herman, Melissa. "Forced to Choose: Some Determinants of Racial Identification in Multiracial Adolescents." *Child Development* 75, no. 3 (2004): 730–48.

Hollinger, David A. "Amalgamation and Hypodescent: The Question of Ethnoracial Mixture in the History of the United States." *The American Historical Review* 108, no. 5, www.historycooperative.org/journals/ahr/108.5/ hollinger/ (8 Oct. 2008).

Hughes, Barbara. "Double Belonging Families Affirmed at Virginia Beach." *The Catholic Virginian* 81, no. 21 (14 Aug. 2006). www.aifusa.org/Catholic_ Virginian_article_081406.html (22 July 2008).

Johnson, Georgia. "The Colonized Child on the Tundra." *Journal of Children's Literature* 21, no. 1 (1995): 24–30.

Jones, Lisa. *Bulletproof Diva: Tales of Race, Sex, and Hair.* New York: Doubleday, 1994.

Kashima, Tetsuden. *Judgment without Trial: Japanese American Imprisonment during World War II.* Seattle: University of Washington Press, 2003.

Kelly, Judy. "The Trauma of Relinquishment: The Long-Term Impact of Relinquishment on Birthmothers Who Lost Their Infants to Adoption During the Years 1965–72." M.A. Thesis in Psychology and Counseling, Goddard College, 1999.

Kirk, David. *Shared Fate: A Theory and Method of Adoptive Relationships,* 2nd ed. Port Angeles, Wash.: Ben-Simon, 1984.

Klein, Daniel, and Freke Vuijst. *The Half-Jewish Book: A Celebration.* New York: Villard, 2000.

Kreider, Rose. "Adopted Children and Stepchildren: 2000," U.S. Census Bureau, *Census 2000 Special Reports,* Series CENSR-6RV, U.S. Government Printing Office, 2003.

Lee, Sharon M., and Barry Edmonston. "New Marriages, New Families: U.S. Racial and Hispanic Intermarriage." *Population Bulletin* 60, no. 2 (June 2005): 12.

MacCann, Donnarae, and Gloria Woodard, eds. *The Black American in Books for Children: Readings in Racism,* 2nd ed. Lanham, Md.: Scarecrow Press, 1985.

Molin, Paulette F. *American Indian Themes in Young Adult Literature.* Lanham, Md.: Scarecrow Press, 2005.

Nakashima, Cynthia L. "An Invisible Monster: The Creation and Denial of Mixed-Race People in America." In *Racially Mixed People in America,* edited by Maria P. P. Root. Newbury Park, Calif.: Sage, 1992.

Nash, Gary B. *Forbidden Love: The Secret History of Mixed-Race America.* New York: Henry Holt, 1999.

National Association of Black Social Workers. "Position Statement on Trans-Racial Adoption." In "Timeline of Adoption History." Adoption History Project, University of Oregon, www.uoregon.edu/~adoption/topics/birth parents.htm (1 May 2008).

Nissel, Angela. *Mixed: My Life in Black and White.* New York: Villard, 2006.

Owens, Louis. *Mixedblood Messages: Literature, Film, Family, Place.* Norman: University of Oklahoma Press, 1998.

Pew Forum on Religion & Public Life. "The U.S. Religious Landscape Survey Reveals a Fluid and Diverse Pattern of Faith." 25 Feb. 2008, pewresearch.org/pubs/743/united-states-religion/ (27 March 2008).

Phoenix, Ann, and Barbara Tizard. *Black, White or Mixed Race? Race and Racism in the Lives of Young People of Mixed Parentage.* London: Routledge, 2002.

Pilgrim, David. "The Tragic Mulatto Myth." Jim Crow Museum of Racist Memorabilia, Ferris State University, Nov. 2000. www.ferris.edu/news/jimcrow/mulatto/ (13 Sep. 2007).

Price, Darby Li Po. "Multiracial Comedy as a Commodity in Hawaii." In *The Sum of Our Parts: Mixed-Heritage Asian Americans,* edited by Theresa Williams Léon and Cynthia L. Nakashima. Philadelphia, Pa.: Temple University Press, 2001.

"Review of *Send One Angel Down.*" *Publishers Weekly* 247, no. 18 (1 May 2000): 71.

"Review of *Something Terrible Happened.*" *Publishers Weekly* 241, no. 41 (10 Oct. 1994).

"Review of *Whale Talk.*" *Publishers Weekly* 248, no. 11 (12 March 2001).

Rich, Motoko. "Gang Memoir, Turning Page, Is Pure Fiction." *New York Times,* 4 March 2008.

Root, Maria, P. P., ed. *Multiracial Experience: Racial Borders as the New Frontier.* Thousand Oaks, Calif.: Sage, 1996.

———. *Racially Mixed People in America.* Newbury Park, Calif.: Sage, 1992.

Rosner, Shmuel. "The Passover Test: What the Passover Seder Reveals About Interfaith Couples." *Slate,* www.slate.com (17 April 2008).

Schoem, David. "Teachng an Interracial Issues Course." In *Multiracial America: Resource Guide on the History and Literature of Interracial Issues,* edited by Karen

Downing, Darline Nichols, and Kelly Webster. Lanham, Md.: Scarecrow Press, 2005.

Siegel, Jennifer. "Study of Interfaith Kids Upends Ideas of Identity." *Forward* (8 July 2005).

Smith, Cynthia Leitich. "Multicultural Humor, Seriously." *Cynsations*, 27 July 2004. cynthialeitichsmith.blogspot.com/2004/07/multicultural-humor-seriously .html (6 April 2008).

Snyder, Laurel, ed. *Half/Life: Jewish Tales from Interfaith Homes.* New York: Soft Skull, 2006.

Spickard, Paul. *Mixed Blood: Intermarriage and Ethnic Identity in Twentieth-Century America.* Madison: University of Wisconsin Press, 1989.

Staples, Brent. "Children's Books." *New York Times,* 12 Sept. 1999 (24 Sept. 2007).

Stephan, Cookie White. "Mixed-Heritage Individuals: Ethnic Identity and Trait Characteristics." In *Racially Mixed People in America,* edited by Maria P. P. Root. Newbury Park, Calif.: Sage, 1992.

Tarr, C. Anita. "An Unintentional System of Gaps: A Phenomenological Reading of Scott O'Dell's *Island of the Blue Dolphins.*" *Children's Literature in Education* 28, no. 2 (1997): 61–71.

Tatum, Beverly Daniel. *"Why Are All the Black Kids Sitting Together in the Cafeteria?" And Other Conversations About Race.* New York: Basic, 1997.

Taylor, Rhonda Harris, and Lotsee Patterson. "Getting the 'Indian' Out of the Cupboard: Using Information Literacy to Promote Critical Thinking." *Teacher Librarian* 28, no. 2 (Dec. 2000), www.teacherlibrarian.com/tlmag/ v_28_/v_ 28_2_feature/ (24 Sept. 2007).

Trenka, Jane Jeong, Julia Chinyere Oparah, and Sun Yung Shin, eds. *Outsiders Within: Writing on Transracial Adoption.* Cambridge, Mass.: South End Press, 2006.

Walker, Alice. "In Search of Zora Neale Hurston." *Ms. Magazine* (March 1975).

Williams, Mark, and John Kenneth White. "Barack Obama and the Politics of Race." www.mindstorminteractive.net/clients/idonline/index/ (9 April 2008).

Williams-Léon, Theresa, and Cynthia L. Nakashima, eds. *The Sum of Our Parts: Mixed-Heritage Asian Americans.* Philadelphia, Pa.: Temple University Press, 2001.

Wilson, Terry P. "Blood Quantum: Native American Mixed Bloods." In *Racially Mixed People in America,* edited by Maria P. P. Root. Newbury Park, Calif.: Sage, 1992.

Young, Abe Louise, and The Youth Board of Next Generation Press, eds. *Hip Deep: Opinions, Essays and Visions from America's Teenagers.* Providence, R.I.: Next Generation Press, 2006.

WEBSITES

americanindiansinchildrensliterature.blogspot.com: Debbie Reese's blog critiquing literature by and about American Indians.

www.asian-nation.org: Comprehensive website devoted to all things Asian American, with extensive historical and cultural information, including pages on transracial adoption and Asian multiraciality.

www.discourses.org/Bib/Identity.htm: Teun A. van Dijk's 2004 Bibliography of Books on Identity. A comprehensive selection of books and printed resources on issues related to identity.

www.uoregon.edu/~adoption/: The Adoption History Project, based at the University of Oregon, with a timeline of adoption history, archived primary-source materials, and a host of related resources.

Interfaith Issues

www.dovetailinstitute.org: Serves all kinds of interfaith families, but especially Christian and Jewish families. Resources include the organization's journal as well as books and links.

www.interfaithfamily.com: Primary focus on supporting Jewish interfaith families in maintaining their Jewish culture ("Encouraging Jewish Choices and a Welcoming Jewish Community"). However, site contains numerous articles in a searchable database by members of interfaith families who are honoring more than one religious and cultural tradition. Diverse viewpoints are encouraged. Forums and extensive resources are provided.

www.interfaithstudies.org: Offers comprehensive interfaith resources, including some for young adults.

www.religioustolerance.org: Devoted to encouraging religious tolerance, with information, articles, and a forum on all world religions as well as interfaith marriages and families.

Multiraciality

www.ameasite.org: The Association of Multiethnic Americans with resources on multiraciality, including historical timeline, books, and other information about medical, political, and cultural issues of concern to multiracial people.

www.drmariaroot.com: Maria P. P. Root's personal website contains extensive academic resources on multiraciality.

www.eurasiannation.com: Dedicated to people of mixed European and Asian descent and contains articles and forums on current issues.

www.intermix.org.uk: Based in the United Kingdom, addresses all kinds of multiracial experience, including adoption, and includes articles, forums, cultural and political resources.

magazine.interracialweb.com/index.php: Online magazine and clearinghouse with multiracial resources, blogs, and forums.

www.mixedasians.com: Primarily an online community of people sharing part-Asian descent.

www.mixedfolks.com: Comprehensive website that contains forums and numerous resources with an emphasis on mixed-heritage celebrities.

multiracial.com/site/: The Multiracial Activist with extensive resources on multiracial advocacy as well as extensive bibliographies including books for children and young adults. Includes a blog and forum.

www.projectrace.com: Project Race, an advocacy organization, seeking the inclusion of a multiracial category of racial identity on forms, and addressing healthcare issues of concern to mixed individuals; Teen Project Race reaches out to multiracial young adults.

www.realhapas.com: An attempt to restore the original meaning of "hapa" to its Hawaiian roots and focuses on issues related to people of part-Hawaiian descent. Site includes blogs, forums, and links.

Youth-Oriented Mixed Heritage

www.metisse.com: Online magazine for girls and women who are multiracial. Strong on health, beauty, celebrity info.; includes forums.

www.mixedheritagecenter.org: Youth-oriented clearinghouse for articles, books, film, podcasts, blogs, and other resources on all kinds of mixed heritage, including adoption. School-based mixed-heritage groups are included.

www.racialicious.com: Devoted to discussion of race in the context of pop culture. Articles and forums.

Index

1990 Jewish Population Survey, xxiiin4

abolitionists, 2, 7, 44, 63n15
"acknowledging difference," 157. *See also* David Kirk
Adoff, Arnold, 73
adopted characters in YA fiction: analyzed, 151–97; family demographics, 154–55; as parents, 170–72; as siblings, 154, 158
adoption, xviii; of American children by foreigners, 152; of black children by white parents, 153, 193n7; heritage projects, 165–67, 189, 195n20; influence of children's books on, 153; informal, 152, 213, 220n4; losses, 156–57, 172, 181, 184, 192, 196n29; as metaphor, 151, 177–80, 195n24; myths, xx, 156–57; open, 162, 181, 185; personal accounts, 209–11; as secondary identity, 139–41; statistics, xiii, 151, 152, 172, 193n6, 196n25; terminology, 194–95n19; YA fiction, 151–97; YA self-help, 206. *See also* birthparents; adopted characters

adoption, transethnic domestic, 181–84
adoption, transracial domestic, xviii, 151, 153, 206; as metaphor, 151, 177–80; in YA fiction, 26–27, 155–56, 158–63, 172–80
Adoption History Project, 193n1
adoption, mixed-heritage international: losses, 169, 170, 192–93; in YA fiction, 151, 152, 163–72, 174–77, 181–93
Adoption: Social Issues Firsthand, 205
adoptive parents: and birthparents, 161, 162, 180, 181; cultural competence of, 153, 172–73; in YA fiction, 154–63, 185, 188–89, 196n28; of mixed-heritage children, xviii, 152, 168; "passing for biological," 156–57; as "real" parents, 147n3, 155–56, 194–95n19
African American. *See* black
After the Morning Calm (Wilkinson and Fox, eds.), 209–11
ALA. *See* American Library Association
Aleutian Sparrow (Hesse), 85–86
Alex award, 59

231

About the Author

Nancy Thalia Reynolds is the author of four books, including *Adopting Your Child* (1993), and holds a BA from Sarah Lawrence College and an MFA in writing for children and young adults from Vermont College of Fine Arts. As a child she lived in a small town in Brazil, then lived as a young adult in Canada, where she received a law degree from Osgoode Hall, York University, in Toronto. Her articles on family life and education have appeared in parenting and adoption periodicals over two decades. She reviews children's books for *Kirkus Reviews* and resides in a multiracial neighborhood north of Seattle. Her family includes a biological son and a daughter adopted from northeastern Brazil. Three races, three nationalities, and ten (known) ethnicities are represented in her family. Reynolds, her husband, and their son are white; their daughter is multiracial.